RESTITUTION

AND

BANKING LAW

Also available

The Restitution Law Review

The Restitution Research Resource, 2nd ed
Peter Birks and Robert Chambers

Restitution and the Conflict of Laws
edited by Francis Rose

Restitution and Contract
Andrew Skelton

The Company Financial and Insolvency Law Review

Forthcoming

Lessons from the Swaps Litigation
edited by Peter Birks

Resulting Trusts: Practical Issues
edited by Peter Birks

RESTITUTION

AND

BANKING LAW

Edited by

FRANCIS D ROSE

informa law
from Routledge

First published 1998 by Mansfield Press

Published 2013
by Informa Law from Routledge
2 Park Square, Milton Park, Abingdon, Oxon OX14 4RN

and by Informa Law from Routledge
711 Third Avenue, New York, NY, 10017, USA

Informa Law is an imprint of the Taylor & Francis Group, an informa business

British Library Cataloguing in Publication Data
Data Available

ISBN 13: 978-0-9526499-1-5 (hbk)

Typeset in 10pt Times New Roman by

Preface

Free and informed debate is a vital element in the advance of society and commerce. It helps to expose matters of which we may be ignorant or insufficiently conscious, allows for them to be critically assessed, and better equips us for the future. Just over three decades ago, most lawyers were unaware of the operation within our law of principles of restitution of unjust enrichment, let alone the possibility that Restitution might form a major, independent division of the law. The structure and content of the Law of Restitution remain subject to continuing rigorous reassessment; but this takes place against a familiar framework of restitution's availability where (i) there has been an enrichment of the defendant (ii) at the expense of the plaintiff (iii) for which justice requires restitution, though (iv) subject to defences, (v) the measure of restitution being either the value received by the defendant or the value surviving.

The publication of two highly influential books on Restitution and the teaching of the subject within the universities to students of whom many have gone on to become leading practitioners and academics has caused an explosion in the literature on the subject – including a dedicated journal, the *Restitution Law Review* – and a massive overhaul of the law and practice. The Restitution Section of the Society of Public Teachers of Law was founded to encourage discussion of the subject and to re-examine the relationship between Restitution and other legal categories. It has provided an international forum for discussion for academics, practitioners and judges; and their published deliberations have made a significant contribution to the way in which we perceive this area of law, stimulating new lines of thought and exerting a powerful influence on litigation and practice.

To a large extent, this has depended on recognising the place of, and according independent status to, restitutionary principles operating within more familiar areas of law, particularly areas traditionally defined by areas of commercial activity rather than by legal theory. There is nothing wrong with such definitions. Law is a practical subject and theory must be reconciled with what people do in real life. The other side of the coin is that specialist areas of practice benefit from a better understanding of the legal principles which affect them. Nowhere is this more true than in banking and finance. The vast majority of Restitution cases are concerned with money. Many of the leading cases are banking cases. It is therefore more than timely not just to look to Banking Law for the lessons it provides for the general law of Restitution, but to consider the implications for Banking Law of recent learning on Restitution.

This book does not attempt to survey all those areas where Banking Law and the Law of Restitution connect. That would require a much larger book covering all aspects of the two subjects – a job already ably discharged by existing texts – and would have placed undue emphasis on the relation between them. It considers a number of important matters of current interest which were discussed at the SPTL Restitution Seminar in September 1997.

The collection begins by casting new light on a familiar theme, a bank's unauthorised payment in respect of a cheque to a third party, whether the obligation of its customer in respect of which the cheque is drawn is discharged and whether the bank can recover the unauthorised payment. The difficulty in this area lies in the inscrutability of the old decision in *Price v Neal* (1762). The general restitutionary issues cannot be properly understood without taking into account the practical environment in which they occur. The bank, though in one sense an intermediary with the power to affect the position of its customer, acts by virtue of the mandate agreement with him rather than as his agent. And there are commercial considerations, namely the security of transactions and integrity of negotiable instruments. Justice Deon van Zyl examines these issues from a comparative perspective, taking into account not only Commonwealth and American decisions but the approach of civil law jurisdictions. This is not simply of academic interest. All lawyers learn more about their own law by observing developments in other jurisdictions. In modern Banking Law it is essential. Within the United Kingdom alone, there are two major international financial centres, in London and Edinburgh, each with a different legal tradition and each part of a larger continental economic community, let alone an integral part of the global financial market.

The multipartite nature of financial arrangements is a continuing theme. Charles Mitchell re-examines an area commonly described as concerning the compulsory discharge of another's liability, with particular reference to banking cases, and presents a new analysis of the area. He argues that, to decide whether an injured party should be allowed to accumulate recoveries from two others liable for her loss and, if not, whether one or both of them should bear the burden of paying her, the courts should consider three issues in turn: whether the parties are co-extensively liable for the loss; whether they are alternatively liable; and whether the burden of paying for the loss should be borne by one of them alone or should be shared. The subject has been the subject of extensive litigation in the USA and is at the heart of a spate of recent litigation concerning building societies, solicitors and mortgage indemnity guarantee insurers. It provides important lessons for our commercial law generally.

Possibly the liveliest issue of the moment is the effect of the House of Lords' recent judgment in *Barclays Bank Plc v O'Brien* (1993). Business involves risks, the deterrent effect of which can be reduced by the provision of security – which, however, needs to live up to its name. Where the law is in doubt, ultimately it can be reviewed by the highest court of appeal; but landmark decisions can also provoke uncertainty, requiring more detailed resolution. This is particularly so where the interests of a commercial lender have to be reconciled with an individual providing surety in the form of her or his home and sole substantial asset. Three discussions of this thorny area are included in this book. Janet O'Sullivan provides a general survey of the issues presented by *O'Brien* on which Graham Virgo has added his comments. Subsequently, an independent analysis of one of the post-*O'Brien* cases, *Barclays Bank Plc v Boulter* (1997), has been contributed by Kit Barker.

The effects of *O'Brien* in making the surety's relief dependent on the lender's notice of undue influence operating on the surety and the requirement of manifest disadvantage to raise a presumption of undue influence are generally regarded as satisfactory. However, though it is no doubt a relief for lenders, the willingness of the courts to accept that the opportunity for the surety to be properly advised of the wisdom of her action is subject to criticism; as is the House of Lords' decision in *Smith v Bank of Scotland* (1997) to assimilate the Scottish law on constructive notice of misrepresentation with the law in *O'Brien*. Having established an entitlement to relief, it is at the end of the day essential that relief is properly given, and to recognise the distinction, in talking of rescission on terms, between: balancing the surety's entitlement to rescission with the making of counter-restitution; and whether undue influence affects only part of the transaction, and so whether partial rescission should be available.

Attempts to work out the detailed ramifications of *O'Brien* are unfortunately apt to be accompanied by further difficulties, as *Barclays Bank v Boulter* demonstrates. In general terms the case may appear to be an exercise in judicial indulgence towards a weaker party facing the threat of an unfavourable decision on costs, not in itself an insignificant consideration in litigation. Unfortunately, the decisions of the higher courts carry wider implications for the law and the legal process. One interpretation of *Boulter* is that the *O'Brien* notice principle is part of a defence of bona fide purchase, the place of which in restitutionary claims is controversial. In the present context, this needs to be considered in light of the general issue of locating the burden of proof. The law is demonstrably unclear, but identification of the uncertainties is a vital step on the path towards clarification.

Just as the decision in *O'Brien* has created ripples throughout domestic banking law, so has the collapse of Robert Maxwell's empire created havoc on a larger scale. In particular, *Macmillan Inc v Bishopsgate Investment Trust Plc (No 3)* (1995) has raised a number of issues about the cross-border enforcement of rights in securities. To step into the international arena, with different jurisdictions containing different rules of law, is to add the complication of the conflict of laws to determination of the law governing priority for claims to shares. The discussion by Gabriel Moss and Felicity Toube makes clear how unclear it may be how to resolve such issues, given the range of distinguishable topics which have to be considered and the fact that they will not necessarily all be resolved in identical fashion, the Court of Appeal coming down in favour of characterising "the issue" in question. However, the more recent decision in *Re Harvard Securities Ltd* (1997) shews that *Macmillan* is not the last word on this aspect of the Maxwell saga.

The determination of claims to shares and the proceeds of their sale in *Macmillan* brings to centre stage the relationship between the law of Restitution and the law of Property. Two of the Court of Appeal judges were prepared to go along with Millett J's interestingly phrased assertion that the claim was one "lying in restitution", without finding that this settled the matter. Nick Segal's account considers the practical importance of this debate, *eg* in deciding the applicability and extent of the defences of change of position and bona fide purchase, together with the circumstances in which the holder of a subsequent equitable interest can secure priority over a prior equitable interest by acquiring or dealing with the legal estate.

The relationship between unjust enrichment and property also informs Lionel Smith's consideration of whether tracing is necessary in a case involving payment by electronic funds transfer. New developments pose new problems but, as with so many problems identified within a particular practical context, resolution requires going back to principles applying throughout the law generally. A distinction can be drawn between: claims against a direct recipient based on an enrichment received directly from the plaintiff, which does not require tracing; and claims against a direct recipient for a substituted asset or against remote recipients, which do. This has implications both for electronic funds transfers and commercial law generally.

Another recent growth activity is money-laundering. Inevitably this involves participation by parties other than those from whom money is diverted and the ultimate recipients, raising not only restitutionary issues but others closely connected with them. A wealth of case law on equitable remedies has culminated in the recent decision of the Privy Council in *Royal Brunei Airlines Sdn Bhd v Tan* (1995), imposing liability on accessories dishonestly assisting a breach of fiduciary obligation and providing the basis for further developments in this area. Michael Tugendhat's extension of the debate to common law remedies, and consideration of liability for negligence, is therefore more than timely. Greater awareness of potential common law liability is of course likely to encourage tort claims, and eventually to require reassessment of equitable liability and its relationship with legal liability in this and other areas.

Accessory liability for dishonest assistance is commonly considered together with liability for knowing receipt, another currently controversial area and one of the subjects of Michael Bryan's review of banks' liability for receiving misdirected payments. Again the role of the banking cases cannot be properly appreciated without taking account of the particular relationship between a bank and its customer, *ie* that of debtor-creditor, so that a bank is entitled to use money deposited with it for its own purposes. This means that a bank receiving a misdirected payment should make restitution to the party at whose expense the payment is made and may debit its customer's account when doing so. A bank may, however, plead the defence of ministerial receipt if, in good faith and without notice of the payor's claim, it received the money as agent of its customer and paid it over accordingly. This analysis exposes an inconsistent approach in equity if a bank is held liable to account as a receipt-based constructive trustee for money received in breach of a fiduciary obligation, an inconsistency which needs to be recognised and clearly resolved by the courts.

Banks are not alone in being apprehensive about the direction which legal developments might take. In particular, such apprehension is likely to be accompanied by fear of increased exposure to liability. But banks are as likely to be plaintiffs as defendants; and, whatever capacity they have, they are prone to suffer from the time and expense consumed by uncertainty about the current state of the law and the ways in which it may develop. The broader implications of the papers presented at the conference are the subject of Peter Birks' additional paper drawing their themes together. As he observes, the traditional concern of commercial law to strike a balance between giving effect to commercial transactions and safeguarding the interests of those affected by them is reflected in the balance struck in the law of restitution between reversing unjust enrichment and providing defences to those who would be unfairly subject to liability. In general, defendants should only be liable if they have received that which they should not have received or if they have been dishonest, and they will have a defence if they have honestly changed their position so that it would be unreasonable to require them to make restitution. The honest and efficient bank should not end up being worse off than it should have been. And all banks will prima facie be entitled to recover when their wealth has come into the hands of others who should return it.

This collection of papers demonstrates not only the advantage but the necessity of bringing together leading academics and practitioners to consider major areas of difficulty at the interface between general divisions of the law such as the Law of Restitution and contextual areas such as Banking. Only by the identification and thorough analysis of such difficulties can conduct be properly planned and the law developed. Following on *Restitution and the Conflict of Laws* (1995), this collection of papers is one of a series of books from the Mansfield Press in which these issues are being examined. Further volumes currently in preparation include *Restitution and Contract*, *Lessons from the Swaps Litigation* and *Resulting Trusts: Practical Issues*. Other titles are also in the pipeline.

Thanks are due to the British Academy for financial support for the conference and to John Stevens for his assistance in producing this volume. I am also grateful not only to the authors of the papers but also to those who chaired the sessions at which they were originally presented, those who delivered comments on the papers at those sessions and everyone else who joined in the ensuing debates. In their different ways, all of them have contributed to this book, which we hope will be as useful in practice as it was interesting to compile.

Francis Rose
4 Essex Court
Temple
London EC4Y 9AJ
22 February 1998

Contents

List of Contributors

Editor

Francis Rose
Professor of Commercial and Common Law, University of Buckingham

Assistant Editor

John Stevens
Lecturer in Law, University of Birmingham

Contributors

Deon van Zyl
Dr Jur, LLD, Judge of the Cape High Court

Charles Mitchell
Lecturer in Law, King's College London

Janet O'Sullivan
Fellow of Selwyn College, Cambridge

Graham Virgo
Fellow of Downing College, Cambridge

Kit Barker
Lecturer in Law, University of Southampton

Gabriel Moss
QC, 3/4 South Square, Gray's Inn

Felicity Toube
Barrister, 3/4 South Square, Gray's Inn

Nick Segal
Solicitor, Partner, Allen & Overy

Lionel D Smith
Fellow of St Hugh's College, Oxford

Michael Tugendhat
QC, 5 Raymond Buildings, Gray's Inn

Michael Bryan
Senior Lecturer in Law, University of Melbourne

Peter Birks
QC DCL FBA, Regius Professor of Civil Law, University of Oxford and Fellow of All Souls College, Oxford

Table of Cases

Table of Statutes

Table of Codes and Conventions

1

Unauthorised Payment and Unjust Enrichment in Banking Law

DH VAN ZYL*

A. INTRODUCTION

The title of this paper was initially intended to be "Indirect or Third-Party Enrichment in Banking Law". During the course of my research on and preparation of the subject matter, however, it became clear to me that such title might be misleading in the context of establishing whether or not a bank, which has made an unauthorised payment in respect of a cheque drawn on it by a customer or client, should have an enrichment claim against the payee or recipient of the payment.[1] The more so is this the case when the unauthorised payment in issue is that which arises from the honouring by a bank of a forged cheque or of a cheque which has been countermanded. In such cases the payee or recipient is usually described as the third party (C) in the "triangular situation" in which the other two role players are the customer (A), as ostensible drawer of the cheque, and the bank (B), as drawee thereof.[2]

* Dr Jur (Leyden), Ph.D, LLD (Cape Town), D Litt (Free State); Judge of the Cape High Court.

The abbreviations used include the following: ASSAL (*Annual Survey of South African Law*); CILSA (*Comparative and International Law Journal of Southern Africa*); MBL (*Modern Business Law*); SALJ (*South African Law Journal*); THRHR (*Tydskrif vir Hedendaagse Romeins-Hollandse Reg*); TRW (*Tydskrif vir Regswetenskap*); TSAR (*Tydskrif vir die Suid-Afrikaanse Reg*).

[1] In this paper I shall refer to a "customer" rather than a "client" and to a "recipient" rather than a "payee", although the terms are at times used interchangeably. This is the terminology preferred by H Luntz, "The Bank's Right to Recover on Cheques Paid by Mistake" (1968) 6 Melb ULR 308. At 309 n 4 the learned author explains that the term "payee" may cause confusion between the designated payee on a cheque or bill of exchange and the person who actually receives payment.

[2] The image of a "triangular situation" involving three parties is reflected in an article by FR Malan, "The Rule in *Price v Neal*" (1978) 11 CILSA 276, 276, where he describes the issues arising from a bank's right of recovery under these circumstances as "problems of enrichment equalisation in intricate triangular situations". See *infra*, text to n 79.

The possible enrichment of the third party in this situation is far removed from the "third party enrichment" which arises when transactions between A and B, on the one hand, and B and C (a third party), on the other, have the result that C is enriched at the expense of A. Enrichment of this nature is frequently referred to as "indirect enrichment", which, under certain circumstances, may give rise to an action by A against C.[3]

In the civil law (in the sense of the Roman law based European *ius commune*) the enrichment action in such cases has sometimes been described as the "extended" *actio negotiorum gestorum* arising from the unauthorised administration (*negotiorum gestio*) of the affairs of another.[4] As will be pointed out later, this action may have some relevance in South African law as an alternative to an enrichment action by a bank against a third party where the bank has made an unauthorised payment to such third party. The difference is, however, that the alternative action may be available against the customer (A) rather than against the third party (C). This is an illustration of how the wonderful world of the "mixed" or "hybrid" legal system, such as that of Scotland and South Africa, can function in practice: by its very nature it can extract the best from both common and civil law sources and, in this way, resolve issues in a creative and innovative way.[5]

Although I have used the term "unauthorised payment" in the title of this paper, it must be pointed out that, in almost all the sources to which I have had recourse, the term "mistaken payment", or a variation thereof, is used. This is the case, it would seem, in at least those legal systems to which I have referred for purposes of this paper. In this regard, however, it must be remembered that "unjust enrichment" and "restitution" are not synonymous. These

[3] See AM Honoré, "Third Party Enrichment" [1960] *Acta Juridica* 236 and JP Dawson, "Indirect Enrichment" in *Ius Privatum Gentium: Festchrift für Max Rheinstein* 2 (1969) 789. The latter deals more specifically with German law, as do C-W Canaris, "Der Bereicherungsausgleich im Dreipersonenverhältnis" in *Festschrift für Karl Larenz* (1973) 799 and U Meyer, *Der Bereicherungsausgleich in Dreiecksverhältnissen* (1979). On indirect or third party enrichment in "mixed" legal systems such as those of Scotland and South Africa see the recent contributions of NR Whitty, "Indirect Enrichment in Scots Law" in [1994] JR 200 and 239 and JC Sonnekus, "Ongeregverdigde Verryking en Ongeregverdigde Verarming vir Kondikering in Drie-Party Verhoudings" in [1996] TSAR 1. On the somewhat different approach in English law see LD Smith, "Three Party Restitution: A Critique of Birks's Theory of Interceptive Subtraction" (1991) 11 OJLS 481 and K Bärker "Restitution and Third Parties" in [1994] LMCLQ 305. These and other authorities are dealt with in my judgment in *Absa Bank Ltd v Stander* 1998 (1) SA 939(C).

[4] See DH van Zyl, *Negotiorum Gestio in South African Law* (1985), 113-118, with historical foundations in DH van Zyl, *Die Saakwaarnemingsaksie as Verrykingsaksie in die Suid-Afrikaanse Reg* (diss Leyden 1970), 60-61, 80-81, 87-88, 95-96.

[5] See on the interaction of civil and common law in South Africa RW Lee, "The Roman-Dutch Law in South Africa: The Influence of English Law" in (1969) 1 *Colombo LR* 1; DP Visser, "Daedalus in the Supreme Court: The Common Law Today" in (1986) 49 THRHR 127; R Zimmermann, "Synthesis in South African Private Law: Civil Law, Common Law and *Usus Hodiernus Pandectarum*" in (1986) 103 SALJ 259; D van der Merwe, "Judicial Institutions in the Civil Law: Towards a Theory for Common-Law Adjudication" in [1993] TSAR 580.

concepts have, indeed, been the source of endless confusion because of the different meanings they bear in common and civil law.[6]

B. THE RELATIONSHIP BETWEEN BANKER AND CUSTOMER

It is generally accepted that the relationship between banker and customer is one of mandate rather than agency. The customer is the mandator and the bank the mandatory. In the case of a current account, there is a general mandate which provides that the bank will accept and pay cheques drawn upon it, subject thereto that the customer has sufficient funds in, or overdraft facilities attaching to, his current account.[7] A further provision is that the cheque must be valid and payment thereof authorised. This means that the bank must act within the terms of its mandate from the customer by not, for example, paying out a cheque bearing the forged signature of the customer and likewise not honouring a cheque on presentation when it has been countermanded or "stopped" by the customer. If a forged or countermanded cheque is indeed paid out, the bank acts without a mandate or authority and cannot debit the customer's account with the amount of the cheque.[8]

It is of singular importance to note that the underlying agreement between the customer and the person in whose favour a cheque is drawn is irrelevant for purposes of determining the rights and obligations arising from the mandate agreement between the bank and customer. A bank which effects payment of a cheque in accordance with its mandate and within its authority has no interest in the underlying agreement or in the reason for the payment by cheque. It is, for all practical purposes, no more than a conduit or "neutral functionary" whose payment of the cheque facilitates performance by the customer, as debtor in terms of the underlying agreement, to the third party payee, as creditor in terms thereof. By paying the cheque the bank does not effect performance of the customer's obligation to the third party. It is the

[6] See E Schrage, B Nicholas, "Unjust Enrichment and the Law of Restitution: A Comparison", in E Schrage (ed), *Unjust Enrichment: The Comparative Legal History of the Law of Restitution* (1995) 9-30; DH van Zyl, "Unjustified Enrichment and Restitution: An Awakening Giant Creates Confusion" in (1996) 21 TRW 1.

[7] *Barclays Bank Ltd v WJ Simms Son & Cooke (Southern) Ltd* [1980] QB 677, 699C, per Robert Goff J: "It is a basic obligation owed by a bank to its customer that it will honour on presentation cheques drawn by the customer on the bank, provided that there are sufficient funds in the customer's account to meet the cheque, or the bank has agreed to provide the customer with overdraft facilities sufficient to meet the cheque." JC Stassen, "Die Regsaard van die Verhouding tussen Bank en Kliënt" in (1980) 2 MBL 77, 80, suggests that there is also an agreement of loan for consumption (*mutuum*) between bank and client in the sense that ownership of the money deposited by the customer passes to the bank, which in turn undertakes to pay out on behalf of or return to the customer the same amount of money, when required.

[8] *Barclays Bank v Simms* [1980] QB 677, 699G-H.

customer who performs with the assistance or through the mediation of the bank. The customer remains the *solvens* (payor) and the third party the *accipiens* (payee or acceptor) in terms of the underlying agreement.[9]

Two teasing questions arise from these principles, namely, in the first place, whether or not payment by a bank without mandate or authority has the effect of discharging the customer's obligation or debt in terms of the underlying agreement and, secondly, whether or not the bank has a remedy to recover the unauthorised payment.

C. THE DOCTRINE IN *PRICE v NEAL*

The starting point of the debate relating to the recoverability of the unauthorised payment of a cheque by a bank is the judgment of Lord Mansfield in the famous case of *Price v Neal*,[10] which dates back to 1762. One Lee (who was subsequently hanged for his trouble) forged the drawer's signature on two bills, which were both indorsed "for a valuable consideration" to the defendant and paid by the plaintiff as drawee. According to the brief report, the defendant "acted innocently and bona fide, without the least privity or suspicion of the said forgeries or of either of them; and paid the whole value of those bills". A jury found for the plaintiff. In a special case referred to Lord Mansfield for his opinion, the jury's verdict was set aside. The gist of the brief judgment was the following:[11]

> "It is an action upon the case, for money had and received to the plaintiff's use. In which action, the plaintiff can not recover the money, unless it be against conscience in the defendant, to retain it: and great liberality is always allowed, in this sort of action.
>
> But it can never be thought unconscientious in the defendant, to retain this money, when he has once received it upon a bill of exchange indorsed to him for a fair and valuable consideration, which he had bona fide paid, without the least privity or suspicion of any forgery.
>
> Here was no fraud: no wrong. It was incumbent upon the plaintiff, to be satisfied 'that the bill drawn upon him was the drawer's hand,' before he accepted or paid it: but it was not incumbent upon the defendant, to inquire into it. Here was notice given by the defendant to the plaintiff of a bill drawn upon him: and he

[9] Malan (1978) 11 CILSA 276, 283, points out that the same principle applies in German Law: "A bank effecting payment on its customer's instruction performs *vis-à-vis* its customer in terms of the bank/customer agreement. It has no interest in the reason for payment. It does not determine the purpose of the payment. Nor does it inform the payee of the 'cause' of the payment. The bank is a neutral functionary bringing about the physical prestation. It is not the *solvens.*"

[10] (1762) 3 Burr 1354; 97 ER 871.

[11] (1762) 3 Burr 1354, 1357.

sends his servant to pay it and take it up. The other bill, he actually accepts; after which acceptance, the defendant innocently and bona fide discounts it. The plaintiff lies by, for a considerable time after he has paid these bills; and then found out 'that they were forged': and the forger comes to be hanged. He made no objection to them, at the time of paying them. Whatever neglect there was, was on his side. The defendant had actual encouragement from the plaintiff himself, for negotiating the second bill, from the plaintiff's having without any scruple or hesitation paid the first: and paid the whole value bona fide. It is a misfortune which has happened without the defendant's fault or neglect. It there was no neglect in the plaintiff, yet there is no reason to throw off the loss from one innocent man upon another innocent man: but, in this case, if there was any fault or negligence in any one, it certainly was in the plaintiff, and not in the defendant."

To establish the ratio of this judgment is an exercise which has taxed many legal minds over a period of more than two centuries. The rule or doctrine emanating from it was succinctly described by Dean Ames of Harvard University on the basis "that a drawee pays (or accepts) at his peril a bill, on which the drawer's signature is forged".[12] The learned author conceded, however, that it was difficult to pin down the reason for the rule to defences such as negligence of the drawee or estoppel. His own suggestion was that it was a case of "equal equities", in which event the defendant, as holder, should have the "legal title".[13]

A different approach was advocated by Professor Ralph Aigler, who suggested that Lord Mansfield had subconsciously, without expressing it in so many words, relied on practical business considerations in laying down his rule, namely that there was a need to determine a point at which a business transaction should be regarded as closed.[14]

[12] JB Ames, "The Doctrine of *Price v Neal*" (1891) 4 HLR 297, 297.

[13] *Ibid*, 299: "The true principle, it is submitted, upon which cases like *Price v Neal* are to be supported, is that far-reaching principle of natural justice, that as between two persons having equal equities, one of whom must suffer, the legal title shall prevail. The holder of the bill of exchange paid away his money when he bought it; the drawee parted with his money when he took up the bill. Each paid in the belief that the bill was genuine. In point of natural justice they are equally meritorious. But the holder has the legal title to the money. A court of equity (and the action of assumpsit for money had and received is, in substance, a bill in equity) cannot properly interfere to compel the holder to surrender his legal advantage." This accords with the judgment of Cowen J in *Canal Bank v Bank of Albany* (1841) 1 Hill 287 (NYSC).

[14] RW Aigler, "The Doctrine of Price v Neal" (1926) *Michigan LR* 809, 811: "It is now generally considered that back of Lord Mansfield's conclusion was a perhaps subconscious, at least unformulated, appreciation that in the conduct of such business affairs it is desirable that a point be fixed at which the parties might be warranted in considering the transaction closed. This is the ground, it is generally agreed, upon which the doctrine must rest. A contrary decision would have meant that for a period of time, indefinite in extent, the one to whom the money has been paid would have to be prepared to meet a demand to refund. It is not suprising that such suspense with the inevitable tendency to slow up commercial transactions should have been deemed undesirable."

Opinions such as these had the effect that the doctrine enunciated in *Price v Neal* was, in general, accepted with acclamation in the United States of America, where it was recognised as an exception to the general principle that money paid by mistake may be recovered.[15]

In Canada a similar position prevailed. *Price v Neal* was followed in a number of important decisions on the basis, it would seem, that the drawee bank should be regarded as having relied on its knowledge of the customer's signature rather than on a representation or warranty of the cheque's genuiness. A right of recovery was thus denied in the early cases of *Rex v Bank of Montreal*[16] and *Bank of Montreal v The King*.[17] Professor Nicholas Rafferty observes that the latter case is unsatisfactory in that differing interpretations of *Price v Neal* were adopted by the various judges.[18] This is bound to cause confusion, yet there is no indication that Canadian courts are leaning towards a more flexible approach, as appears from the fairly recent case of *Arrow Transfer Co Ltd v Royal Bank of Canada.*[19]

[15] Malan (1978) 11 CILSA 276, 277. The principle of "finality of payment or acceptance" appears in the *Uniform Commercial Code* (1978) ("UCC"), §3-418, where it is stated that "payment or acceptance of any instrument is final in favor of a holder in due course, or a person who has in good faith changed his position in reliance on the payment". In comment 1 on this paragraph sound business sense is raised to justify the exception on the basis that "it is highly desirable to end the transaction on an instrument when it is paid rather than reopen and upset a series of commercial transactions at a later date when the forgery is discovered". See also the *Restatement of the Law of Restitution* (1937), §30: "The holder of a bill of exchange or promissory note who has received payment thereof from one whose name was forged thereon as a party of from a drawee on a bill on which the drawer's name was forged, is not thereby under a duty of restitution if he paid value and received payment without reason to know that the signature was forged." In comment *a* on this paragraph, Seavey and Scott observe that it is "in accord with mercantile convenience, supporting the finality of transactions with mercantile instruments in situations where ordinarily it is reasonably possible for the payor to ascertain the fraud". See further WE Britton, *Handbook on the Law of Bills and Notes*, 2nd ed (1961), 375-388; A Barak, "The Uniform Commercial Code - Commercial Paper: An Outsider's View" in (1968) 3 *Israel LR* 7 and 184; RW West, "Easy Come, Easy Go; UCC. Section 3-418 and the Restitutionary Rights of Banks: *National Savings and Trust Co v Park Corp*" in [1985] *Detroit College of Law Review* 681; WD Kloss, "Mistaken Payment and Restitutionary Principles under the Uniform Commercial Code" in (1987-88) 56 *U of Cincinnati LR* 1075 (discussion of *Morgan Guaranty Trust Co v American Savings and Loan Association* (1986) 804 F 2d 1487 (9th Cir); L Kalevitch, "Luck of the Drawee: The Finality of Bank Payments to Holders in Due Course" (1988) 105 *Banking LJ* 416 (likewise a discussion of the *Morgan Guaranty Trust* case); SB Dow, NS Ellis, "The Payor Bank's Right to Recover Mistaken Payments: Survival of Common Law Restitution under Proposed Revisions to Uniform Commercial Code Articles 3 and 4" in (1990) 65 *Indiana LJ* 779. A useful overview of United States law on the subject is that of Luntz (1968) 6 Melb ULR 308, at 333–335.

[16] (1906) 11 OR 595.

[17] (1907) 38 SCR 258.

[18] N Rafferty, "Forged Cheques: A Consideration of the Rights and Obligations of Banks and their Customers" in (1979-80) 4 *Can Bus LJ* 208, 221–224.

[19] [1972] SCR 845; (1972) 27 DLR (3d) 81. A right to recover is, however, granted if the body of the cheque is forged: *Dominion Bank v Union Bank of Canada* (1908) 40 SCR 366. Forged or unauthorised endorsements are covered by the provisions of the *Bills of Exchange Act* (RSC 1970), §50. See further AW Rogers (ed), *Falconbridge on Banking and Bills of Exchange*, 7th ed

The most recent attempt to analyse Lord Mansfield's decision in *Price v Neal* is that of Professor Steven B Dow,[20] who suggests that the doctrine contained therein may be traced to the still earlier case, decided in 1733, of *Jenys v Fawler*.[21] In that case Lord Raymond CJ refused to admit evidence that the drawer's signature was forged. According to the succinct report, he was "strongly inclined, that even actual proof of forgery would not excuse the defendants against their own acceptance", since it would create a "danger to negotiable notes" if an acceptor could avoid liability by raising forgery as a defence. According to Dow,[22] this "presumably meant that the transferability of negotiable instruments and their function as a medium of exchange would be impaired if potential purchasers of accepted bills had to be concerned with the validity of the drawer's signature".

Dow does not see *Price v Neal* as being in conflict with the *locus classicus* on restitution, *Moses v Macferlan*,[23] decided by Lord Mansfield two years earlier. In both cases equity lies at the root of the action of assumpsit for the recovery of mistaken payments ("money had and received").[24] Lord Mansfield retained his flexible approach to the extended application of this action, as appears from his observation in the above quoted portion of the judgment, that "great liberality is always allowed in this sort of action".

The denial of the right to recover money paid by mistake was based on equitable considerations and, it would appear, public policy in the form of, as Dow puts it, "commercial policy".[25] Yet it is none too remarkable that courts have, over the past two centuries, suggested any number of explanations of the *ratio* underlying the judgment, which is not a model of clarity by any means.[26] As Dow points out,[27] Lord Mansfield relied initially on the fact that the defendant had in good faith paid "fair and valuable consideration"

(1969) 569 and 572-574; IGF Baxter, *The Law of Banking*, 3rd ed (1981), 13–19; PD Maddaugh, JD McCamus, *The Law of Restitution* (1990), 244–249.

[20] SB Dow, "Restitution of Payments on Cheques with Forged Drawers' Signatures: Loss Allocation under English Law" in [1996] *Restitution Law Review* 27, 29–32.

[21] (1733) 2 Strange 946; 93 ER 959.

[22] [1996] RLR 27, 30.

[23] (1760) 2 Burr 1005; 97 ER 676.

[24] See the discussion of the early history of this action for restitution by JH Baker, *An Introduction to English Legal History*, 3rd ed (1990), 409–426 and the authorities cited by Dow [1996] RLR 27, 29 n 6. In *Moses v Macferlan* (1760) 2 Burr 1005, 1012, Lord Mansfield is reported as saying that "the gist of this kind of action is, that the defendant, upon the circumstances of the case, is obliged by the ties of natural justice and equity to refund the money".

[25] [1996] RLR 27, 30, where he describes the basic issue framed by Lord Mansfield as "one of conscience rather than commercial policy and the transferability of negotiable instruments".

[26] Scrutton LJ cannot be taken to task for saying, in *Holt v Markham* [1923] 1 KB 504, 514, that the history of the action for money had and received is a "history of well-meaning sloppiness of thought". It is not unlikely that *dicta* such as that of Lord Mansfield in *Price v Neal* prompted him to say this.

[27] [1996] RLR 27, 30–31.

without having any knowledge of the forgery. Later in the judgment, however, he raised aspects such as: the existence of a duty to ascertain the genuineness of the drawer's signature before accepting or paying a bill; the absence of a corresponding duty on the defendant to do so; the prejudice which the defendant might suffer because of the plaintiff's delay in discovering the forgery; estoppel; possible negligence of the plaintiff and the absence of negligence on the part of the defendant; and an unwillingness to shift the loss from one innocent person to another. What adds to the confusion is that Lord Mansfield does not mention the importance of commercial or business considerations relating to the use of negotiable instruments. Dow makes it clear that Lord Mansfield was well aware of commercial policy in this regard. He explains it thus:[28]

> "His failure to mention the commercial policy implications involved in the case suggests that they did not play a significant role in his decision. One likely explanation for the omission was that for him the nature of the money action was one of conscience and equity. The equities of the case were to be determined with respect to only those parties involved in the case without concern for the larger business world. Moreover, in this case there was no need to resolve a clash between the equitable considerations of the action and the transferability of negotiable instruments. On the facts of the case, the result Lord Mansfield believed was dictated by conscience was, at the same time, consistent with promoting negotiability."

D. DEVELOPMENTS AFTER *PRICE v NEAL*

In later cases courts took note of what Lord Mansfield had said in *Price v Neal* but tended to focus on a single aspect of his multifaceted *ratio* for justifying reliance on his decision. This can be gleaned from cases such as *Jones v Ryde*,[29] *Smith v Mercer*[30] and *Wilkinson v Johnson*.[31]

An important development was introduced thereafter by *Cocks v Masterman*,[32] in which Bayley J expressed the opinion of the court "that the holder of a bill is entitled to know, on the day when it becomes due, whether it is an honoured or dishonoured bill, and that, if he receive the money and is suffered to retain it during the whole of that day, the parties who paid it can-

[28] [1996] RLR 27, 31.
[29] (1814) 5 Taunt 488; 128 ER 779.
[30] (1815) 6 Taunt 76.
[31] (1824) 3 B & C 428. In this case *Price v Neal* and *Smith v Mercer* were distinguished and a claim for recovery of the money in question was successful.
[32] (1829) 9 B & C 902; 109 ER 335.

not recover it back".[33] The learned judge then proceeded to confuse the issue somewhat by suggesting that "the parties who pay the bill ought not by their negligence to deprive the holder of any right or privilege".[34] Dow criticises this dictum as creating "a weakness in the rule that became significant as later courts adopted different views on what counted as negligence".[35]

An extension of the *ratio* in the *Cocks* case was effected by Mathew J in *London and River Plate Bank v Bank of Liverpool*[36] when he held that the *ratio* in *Price v Neal* was not negligence, but estoppel, and that the rule in *Cocks* was "indispensable for the conduct of business".[37]

A further important development was the decision by Parke B in *Kelly v Solari*[38] that negligence was irrelevant in assessing whether or not money paid under a mistake of fact could be recovered. He held that a recovery was competent "however careless the party paying may have been, in omitting to use due diligence to inquire into the fact".[39] Dow sees this as an undermining of the doctrine in *Price v Neal* which commenced during the second half of the nineteenth century and continued until well into the twentieth century.[40]

E. A NEW APPROACH IN MODERN LAW: *NATIONAL WESTMINSTER v BARCLAYS*

The case of *National Westminster Bank Ltd v Barclays Bank International Ltd*[41] constituted a turning point in the development of the common law after *Price v Neal*. The plaintiff bank paid out a cheque on which the signature of its customer, the drawer, was forged. An action was brought against both the collecting bank and the payee for recovery of the amount paid. The claim was successful.

[33] (1829) 9 B & C 902, 908-909.

[34] *Ibid.*

[35] [1996] RLR 27, 35. See also *Mather v Lord Maidstone* (1856) 18 CB 273; 139 ER 1374; *Hart v Frontino Gold Mining Co* (1870) LR 5 Ex 111 and *Simm v Anglo-American Telegraph Co* (1879) 5 QBD 188.

[36] [1896] 1 QB 7.

[37] *Ibid*, 10-11. To this he added (at 12): "[n]ow that clear rule is one that ought not to be tampered with. It is one of the few rules of business which is perfectly clear and distinct and ... unimpeachable".

[38] (1841) 9 M & W 54.

[39] *Ibid*, 59.

[40] [1996] RLR 27, 38-49, with special reference to *Imperial Bank v Bank of Hamilton* [1902] AC 49, the Canadian case of *Bank of Montreal v The King* (1907) 38 SCR 258 (see the text to nn 16 to 19 above) and the judgment of the Supreme Court of Ceylon in *Imperial Bank of India v Abeyesinghe* (1927) 29 Ceylon NLR 257.

[41] [1975] QB 654.

Kerr J commenced his judgment by describing the "main issue" to be decided in the following terms:[42]

> "The main issue raised in this action, which is of some general importance to bankers and apparently arises for the first time for decision in an English court, is whether a bank which has honoured an apparently genuine cheque on which the signature of its customer was in fact skilfully forged can recover the money from the payee of the cheque after he has acted to his detriment in direct reliance on the cheque having been honoured. For convenience I will refer to the document throughout as a cheque, although a forged cheque is of course in law not a cheque or negotiable instrument but a mere sham piece of paper."

The plaintiff claimed that its payment on the cheque had been under a mistake of fact on the basis of its genuine belief that the drawer's (their customer's) signature was genuine, whereas it was forged. The collecting bank pleaded no knowledge of either of these matters. The recipient pleaded estoppel by representation, alleging that the plaintiff had represented that the cheque was genuine and that he had acted thereon to his detriment. He also pleaded that the bank had been negligent by breaching its duty of care to payees in connection with the honouring of cheques.

The learned judge dismissed the negligence plea out of hand, holding[43] that, "in deciding whether or not to honour a customer's cheque, at any rate when it is in proper form and the customer's signature appears genuine, a bank owes no duty of care to a payee".

In dealing with the relevant authorities relating to the plea of estoppel, Kerr J stated at the outset:[44]

> "There is a line of cases relating to negotiable instruments proper, *ie* instruments which are not mere forgeries in toto but contain at least one genuine signature and which have been negotiated to at least one innocent holder . . ."

The learned judge proceeded to observe[45] that they "reveal a variety or amalgam of reasons underlying the decisions, from which it is difficult to extract any clear principle . . ." In this regard he was of the view that the

[42] [1975] QB 656–657. The reference to "a mere sham piece of paper" has prompted Dow [1996] RLR 27, 49 to discuss this case under the title "The Sham Doctrine in Late Twentieth Century Loss Allocation". He points out that, although Kerr J cited no authority for this view, it was consistent with the views expressed in treatises and in certain cases from common law jurisdictions dealing with the issue, *eg Koster's Premier Pottery v Bank of Adelaide* (1981) 28 SASR 355 (SA SC); *First Sport Ltd v Barclays Bank Plc* [1993] 1 WLR 1229, 1238 (*per* Kennedy LJ dissenting).

[43] [1975] QB 654, 662D.

[44] *Ibid*, 666B.

[45] *Ibid*, 666C.

dictum by Mathew J relating to estoppel in the case of *London and River Plate Bank v Bank of Liverpool*[46] was perhaps "the most satisfactory explanation of the ratio of the decision in *Price v Neal*", although it was questionable whether such *dictum* could be applied to either of the bills featuring in *Price v Neal*.[47]

The gravamen of Kerr J's decision in regard to the defence of estoppel was that the English cases dealing with this defence were not applicable to a totally forged or "sham" bill. Cognisance was taken of the Canadian decision of *Bank of Montreal v The King*[48] and approval was expressed in respect of the majority judgment in *Imperial Bank of India v Abeyesinge*,[49] in which it was held that the forged document in question was not a cheque at all so that cases dealing with negotiable instruments were not relevant.[50] This led the learned judge to hold, in regard to the defence of estoppel raised by the payee, one Ismail, as follows:[51]

> "It seems to me ... that Mr Ismail can in the present case only succeed in raising an estoppel against the plaintiffs if the mere fact of a banker honouring a cheque on which his customer's signature has been undetectably forged carries with it an implied representation that the signature is genuine. I can see no logical basis for this. At most, it seems to me, the paying banker is thereby representing no more than that he believes the signature to be genuine . . . Furthermore I think that the law should be slow to impose on an innocent party who has not acted negligently an estoppel merely by reason of having dealt with a forged document on the assumption that it was genuine."

Another finding by Kerr J was that the defence of "change of position", for example if the defendant has acted to his detriment by spending or paying away the money he has received, did not bar the plaintiff's right to recover it.[52] This finding has been criticised by Professor Geva as not being defensible or persuasive.[53] For present purposes it is not necessary to debate the issue.

46 [1896] 1 QB 7, 10-11: "It seems to me the principle underlying the decision is this: that, if the plaintiff in that case so conducted himself as to lead the holder of the bill to believe that he considered the signature genuine, he could not afterwards withdraw from that position . . ."

47 *National Westminster v Barclays* [1975] QB 654, 669G.

48 (1907) 38 SCR 258.

49 (1927) 29 Ceylon NLR 257.

50 These cases are dealt with by Kerr J at [1975] QB 654, 670–674. The said proposition is generally accepted. See Goff and Jones, *The Law of Restitution*, 4th ed (1993), 711; Dow [1996] RLR 27, 50. See also *infra*, text to n 71.

51 [1975] QB 654, 674C-D.

52 *Ibid*, 675G–676D. Reliance was placed in this regard on *Standish v Ross* (1849) 3 Exch 527, *Durrant v Ecclesiastical Commissioners* (1880) 6 QBD 234 and *Baylis v Bishop of London* [1913] 1 Ch 127.

53 B Geva, "Reflections on the Need to Revise the Bills of Exchange Act – Some Doctrinal Aspects" (1981-82) 6 Can Bus LJ 269 309–312. See also PD Maddaugh, JD McCamus, *The Law*

To return to Professor Dow, he evaluates[54] the so-called "sham doctrine" introduced by the *National Westminster* case and suggests that it is questionable and unnecessary in view of the "problematic consequences" which arise from it. In essence his argument is, first, that a totally forged instrument may indeed still be negotiable, secondly, that the "sham doctrine" is at odds with the statutory scheme of the *Bills of Exchange Act* and, thirdly, that it has created two distinct classifications of bills of exchange bearing forged signatures. This would mean that the doctrine evolved over many years since *Price v Neal* would not be applicable to "the very problem it was developed to govern". With reference to the recognition, in the law of restitution, of the unjust enrichment principle as set forth in *Lipkin Gorman v Karpnale*,[55] Dow suggests[56] that, ultimately, "the key factor may be the revival of justice and conscience as the basis of all restitutionary actions". The "sham doctrine" should be jettisoned, there should be a return to the principles set forth in *Moses v Macferlan*[57] and an expansion of the principles embodied in *Price v Neal* by making them applicable also to cases involving the mistaken payment of "sham items".

I cannot, with respect, fault the logic of this approach since it would appear that the *National Westminster* case might indeed have created a somewhat artificial distinction between totally and partially forged instruments. That certainly does not appear to be consonant with the intention of Lord Mansfield in *Price v Neal*, nor was it considered in this light by more than two centuries of legal learning constituting the legacy of *Price v Neal.*

F. COUNTERMANDED CHEQUES: *BARCLAYS v SIMMS*

Robert Goff J (now Lord Goff of Chieveley) took the novel approach of Kerr J in the *National Westminster* case[58] a step further in the case of *Barclays Bank Ltd v WJ Simms Son & Cooke (Southern) Ltd.*[59] The facts, briefly, were that a customer of the plaintiff bank drew a cheque in favour of the first defendant, a building company to which it was indebted for certain construction work. The first defendant's banker, to whom the first defendant owed

of Restitution (1990), 244–249. At 249 the learned authors suggest "that it is doubtful that the *National Westminster* cause of action will be recognized in Canada." *Cf* Dow [1996] RLR 27, 54–57.

[54] *Ibid*, 51.
[55] [1991] AC 548.
[56] [1996] RLR 27, 59.
[57] (1760) 2 Burr 1005.
[58] See above, §5.
[59] [1980] QB 677.

money, thereupon appointed the second defendant as receiver in terms of a mortgage debenture held by them. When the plaintiff's customer learned of this, he instructed the plaintiff to stop payment of the cheque. Unaware of this countermand, the second defendant paid the cheque into the first defendant's bank account, requesting special clearance thereof. The plaintiff, overlooking the countermand, mistakenly paid out the cheque. It later sought to recover the amount of the cheque from the defendants. The claim was successful.

The defendants relied on three main defences: first, that there had been no mistake of fact between the plaintiff or either of the defendants, alternatively it had been the plaintiff's unilateral mistake; secondly, that the money had been paid by the plaintiff and received by the first defendant in discharge of an obligation owed to it under the building contract, alternatively under the cheque; thirdly, that the plaintiff had failed to give notice of its claim on the day the cheque was paid, thereby depriving the defendants of the opportunity to give notice of dishonour on that day and hence changing their position to their detriment.

At the outset Robert Goff J defined the issue to be decided as follows:[60]

> "This case raises for decision the question whether a bank, which overlooks its customer's instructions to stop payment of a cheque and in consequence pays the cheque on presentation, can recover the money from the payee as having been paid under a mistake of fact. The point is one on which there is no decision in this country; and it is a point, I was told, of considerable importance to bankers, not only because it is an everyday hazard that customers' instructions may be overlooked, but because modern technology, rather than eliminating the risk, has if anything increased it."

The learned judge commenced by considering the principles on which money is recoverable on the ground that it has been paid under a mistake of fact. He reviewed the leading authorities on the law relating to mistaken payments[61] and then enunciated a number of principles which could be deduced from that "formidable line of authority":[62]

> "(1) If a person pays money to another under a mistake of fact which causes him to make the payment, he is prima facie entitled to recover it as money paid under a mistake of fact.

[60] *Ibid*, 682E–F.
[61] At 686–689 he referred to the early cases of *Kelly v Solari* (1841) 9 M & W 54, *Aiken v Short* (1856) 1 H & N 210 and *Chambers v Miller* (1862) 13 CB(NS) 125. He then, at 690–695, dealt with three major decisions of the House of Lords, namely *Kleinwort, Sons & Co v Dunlop Rubber Co* (1907) 97 LT 263, *Kerrison v Glyn, Mills, Currie & Co* (1911) 81 LJKB 465 and *RE Jones Ltd v Waring & Gillow Ltd* [1926] AC 670.
[62] [1980] QB 677, 695B–D.

(2) His claim may however fail if: (a) the payer intends that the payee shall have the money at all events, whether the fact be true or false, or is deemed in law so to intend; (b) the payment is made for good consideration, in particular if the money is paid to the discharge, and does discharge, a debt owed to the payee (or a principal on whose behalf he is authorised to receive the payment) by the payer or by a third party by whom he is authorised to discharge the debt; or (c) the payee has changed his position in good faith, or is deemed in law to have done so."

The next question to the considered was, in what circumstances a bank, which has paid a cheque drawn on it by one of its customers, may recover from the payee on the basis of a mistake of fact.[63] In this regard the learned judge made the following significant observations:[64]

"It is a basic obligation owed by a bank to its customer that it will honour on presentation cheques drawn by the customer on the bank, provided that there are sufficient funds in the customer's account to meet the cheque, or the bank has agreed to provide the customer with overdraft facilities sufficient to meet the cheque. Where the bank honours such a cheque, it acts within its mandate, with the result that the bank is entitled to debit the customer's account with the amount of the cheque, and further that the bank's payment is effective to discharge the obligation of the customer to the payee on the cheque, because the bank has paid the cheque with the authority of the customer . . .

In other cases, however, a bank which pays a cheque drawn or purported to be drawn by its customer pays without mandate. A bank does so if, for example, it overlooks or ignores notice of its customer's death, or if it pays a cheque bearing the forged signature of its customer as drawer; but, more important for present purposes, a bank will pay without mandate if it overlooks or ignores notice of countermand of the customer who has drawn the cheque. In such cases the bank, if it pays the cheque, pays without mandate from its customer; and, unless the customer is able to and does ratify the payment, the bank cannot debit the customer's account, nor will its payment be effective to discharge the obligation (if any) of the customer on the cheque, because the bank had no authority to discharge such obligation."

In this *dictum* the learned judge stresses the legal nature of the relationship between the banker and customer as being one of mandate with its concomitant rights and obligations.[65] If a bank pays out on a forged cheque or in conflict with a countermand, it acts in breach of obligations arising from the mandate and effects the payment without authority to do so. Such payment

[63] [1980] QB 699–700.
[64] *Ibid*, 699C–699H.
[65] See *supra*, §2.

has no legal or binding effect on the customer and deprives the bank of the right to debit the customer's account with the amount paid out.

A further logical consequence of the unauthorised payment is that it can never serve to discharge the customer's obligation to the payee in terms of any underlying agreement between them. When the bank makes a payment without the customer's authority it does so neither as a mandatary nor as an agent, so that the payment has no effect whatever on the rights or obligations arising from such underlying agreement. The customer/drawer remains obligated to the payee and the latter retains his right to claim performance from the customer/drawer. The bank, however, is out of pocket in the amount of the cheque which it has paid out. Does it have a claim to recover this amount from the payee?

In his judgment Robert Goff J had no doubt that the bank did, *prima facie*, have the right to recover the money from the payee unless the payee had, in good faith, changed his position or was deemed in law to have done so.[66]

The last question to be considered by the learned judge related to the circumstances in which the payee or recipients of a bank's payment under a mistake of fact should, on the principles in *Cocks v Masterman*,[67] have a good defence to the bank's claim to recover the money.[68] In this regard he adopted the analysis of the relevant authorities by Kerr J in the *National Westminster* case[69] and suggested[70] that the principle to be derived from the *Cocks* case was probably the following: if the plaintiff should fail to give notice of a forgery on the day of payment of the forged bill and indicate his intention to recover the amount paid on the basis of his ignorance of the forgery at the time of payment, he would deprive the defendant of the opportunity of giving notice of dishonour on the day the bill falls due and the defendant would hence be deemed to have changed his position to his detriment.

The learned judge understood from this that the defence of change of position was based on the need for the defendant to give notice of dishonour: it would have no application where notice of dishonour was not required. He found support for this proposition in *Imperial Bank of Canada v Bank of Hamilton*,[71] in which a totally forged cheque was regarded as not being a negotiable instrument at all.[72] In any event, in terms of section 50 (2)(c) of the

[66] [1980] QB 677, 700D.
[67] (1829) 9 B & C 902; 109 ER 335.
[68] [1980] QB 677, 700H–703C.
[69] See *supra*, §5.
[70] [1980] QB 677, 701F–H.
[71] [1903] AC 49.
[72] Reliance was likewise placed on the *National Westminster* case (see the text to n 50 above) and reference made to the criticism in *Paget's Law of Banking* 8th ed (1972), 377–378. This criticism was countered [1980] QB 677, 702F, on the following basis: "If the money is recovered, then the bill will not have been paid on the due date or at all, for the payment will not have discharged

Bills of Exchange Act 1882, notice of dishonour is dispensed with when a cheque is countermanded so that the payee cannot invoke the defence established in the *Cocks* case.

Applying the aforementioned principles to the facts of the case before him, Robert Goff J held that the plaintiff was entitled to succeed in its claim.

Professor Goode[73] has criticised the *Simms* judgment strongly, suggesting that the defendants should have succeeded on two grounds which were not argued nor dealt with by the learned judge. The first was that, while the countermand of payment terminated the plaintiff's *actual* authority to pay the cheque, the defendants were entitled to rely on the plaintiff's *apparent* authority to make payment. This would have the effect that the drawer's liability to the payee would be discharged. The second was that a payee who gives up a cheque on which he has a valid claim for payment "inevitably suffers a change of position" by losing the rights attaching to the cheque.

There is not the slightest merit in these submissions and it is not surprising that they were not argued. If the bank has no authority to pay out a cheque it certainly cannot have "apparent" authority to do so, unless the suggestion is that the bank misrepresented that it had authority. Furthermore, as pointed out above, payment without authority can under no circumstances discharge the underlying agreement between the drawer and payee or have any legal effect on it whatever. The second argument must likewise be rejected since it is based on the faulty premise that the unauthorised payment discharged the drawer's indebtedness to the payee.[74]

I have no hesitation in respectfully associating myself with the findings of Robert Goff J in the *Simms* case, for the reasons so lucidly set forth in his judgment. Unfortunately it has not met with the approval of the Appellate Division (now the Supreme Court of Appeal) in South Africa, as will be seen from the ensuing discussion.[75]

the debt due on the bill. It follows that, in such a case, the bill is in fact dishonoured on the day it falls due . . ." See the criticism of this statement by EM Grosskopf JA in *B & H Engineering v First National Bank of SA Ltd* 1995 (2) SA 279 (A) 289 H-290J. This case is dealt with in depth *infra*, §7. It should be noted that the latest edition of *Paget's Law of Banking* – M Hapgood (ed), 11th ed (1996) – is not critical at all of the *Simms* decision.

[73] RM Goode, "The Bank's Right to Recover Money Paid on a Stopped Cheque" in (1981) 97 LQR 254, 255–256.

[74] P Matthews, "Stopped Cheques and Restitution: Another View" [1982] JBL 281, 281, submits that Goode's suggestion "is misconceived, and could be productive of much confusion in the commercial world if relied on".

[75] See *B & H Engineering* 1995 (2) SA 279 (A), which will be dealt with *infra*, §7. In the United States §4-407 of the *Uniform Commercial Code* provides in cases such as these that the bank is subrogated to the rights of the recipient against the drawer, or those of the drawer against the recipient, so as to prevent unjust enrichment. See H Luntz (1968) 6 MULR 308, 325–329, who refers to conflicting Australian decisions on the subject. See also GA Weaver, CR Craigie, *The Law Relating to Banker and Customer in Australia* (1975), 447–453 and KG Nicholson, "Recovery of Money Paid Under a Mistake of Fact" (1986) 60 ALJ 459. From the Canadian

G. SOUTH AFRICAN LAW: FROM *PRICE v NEAL* TO *BARCLAYS v SIMMS* AND BACK AGAIN

The first in depth discussion of the rule or doctrine in *Price v Neal* in South African context was an article by Professor (now Judge) Frans Malan in 1978.[76] In it he propounded the view that *Price v Neal* was good law and should be followed. This was in contrast with the initial view of Professor Cowen that it should not be followed:[77]

> "It would certainly be unfortunate if an English rule whose rationale has never been clear, which has been condemned as harsh, and which moreover involves illogical distinctions, should be incorporated as part of South African law, unless the courts were compelled to adopt the rule in the light of clear principle or authority. And no such compulsion, it is submitted, exists."

In his aforesaid article Malan[78] described the rule in *Price v Neal* as posing "one of the most complex questions in the law of negotiable instruments" but continued by saying that it is not so much a matter pertaining to negotiable instruments as it is one relating to liability for unjust enrichment. The questions arising from the rule, he says, are "illustrations of problems of enrichment equalisation in intricate triangular situations".[79]

The earliest case to which reference is made in the context of the doctrine in *Price v Neal* is *Natal Bank Ltd v Roorda*.[80] In this case the plaintiff bank mistakenly paid out a cheque which had been stopped. The bank was not empowered to debit the account of the drawer, its customer, and consequently sought to recover the amount of the cheque from the defendant in his capacity as payee/recipient thereof. With reference to *Kelly v Solari*[81] Smith J

perspective Geva (1981–82) 6 Can Bus LJ 269, 304–307 is critical of *Simms* and finds support in *Shapera v Toronto Dominion Bank* (1970) 17 DLR (3d) 122, in which it was held that an unauthorised payment discharged the legal liability of the customer/drawer to the recipient/payee. A somewhat different approach is advocated by MH Ogilvie, "Recovery of Money Paid Under Mistake of Fact: When the Bank Loses" in (1986-1987) 1 *Banking and Finance LR* 413. More supportive of the *Simms* decision are Maddaugh and McCamus, *supra* n 53, at 236–243.

[76] FR Malan, "The Rule in *Price versus Neal*" in (1978) 11 CILSA 276.

[77] DV Vowen and L Gering (eds), *Cowen on The Law of Negotiable Instruments in South Africa*, 4th ed (1966), 393. Thereafter Cowen qualified his view somewhat in an article. See DV Cowen, "A Bank's Right to Recover Payments made by Mistake: *Price v Neal* Revisited" in (1983) 16 CILSA 1. See also the qualified acceptance of the rule by AN Oelofse, "Die Toepassing van die Reël in *Price v Neal* in Suid-Afrika" in (1981) 3 MBL 120.

[78] Malan (1978) 11 CILSA 276, 276.

[79] See also *supra*, text to n 2.

[80] 1903 TH 298.

[81] (1841) 9 M & W 54. According to the learned judge 1903 TH 298, 303, the principles set forth in this case were similar to those of Roman-Dutch law.

held[82] that it was clear law that money paid under a mistake of fact may, in general, be recovered. Even though there had been "some negligence" on the part of the plaintiff, it was not "such gross negligence" as would preclude it from succeeding its action. Nor was there, in the court's view, "any detriment ... sustained by the defendant".

The case of *Leal & Co v Williams*[83] related to a forged endorsement on a bank draft. In an *obiter* observation[84] Innes CJ suggested that, at common law, the bank which had made the mistaken payment could recover it from the payee. It was prevented from doing so, however, by the provisions of section 58 of the *Bills of Exchange Proclamation* 11 of 1902.

In *John Bell & Co Ltd v Esselen*[85] the secretary of the plaintiff company fraudulently used one of its cheques to pay a personal debt to the defendant as payee. The plaintiff's bank paid out the cheque to the defendant, who received the amount thereof in good faith. An action by the plaintiff against the defendant was unsuccessful at first instance. An appeal against this decision was likewise unsuccessful, the *ratio* of the judgment[86] being that the plaintiff had not knowingly made a payment in the mistaken belief of fact that the payment was due, in which event it was not entitled to institute a *condictio indebiti* for recovery of the payment. This decision has, not unexpectedly, been severely criticised, the plaintiff's mistaken belief that the payment is due being totally irrelevant for purposes of the *condictio indebiti.*[87]

In his aforesaid article Malan suggests that the relevant action of the drawee bank against the payee or recipient of the cheque should be the *condictio sine causa specialis* rather than the *condictio indebiti*, since it is not the bank itself which is making performance to the payee.[88]

Another reason suggested for using the *condictio sine causa* rather than the *condictio indebiti* appears from the judgment in *Govender v Standard Bank of*

82 *Ibid*, 302–303.
83 1906 TS 554.
84 *Ibid*, 559.
85 1954 (1) SA 147 (A).
86 *Ibid*, 151C–G, *per* Centlivres CJ.
87 See AM Honoré, "Condictio and Payment" [1958] *Acta Juridica* 135, 139; JE Scholtens, "Elusive Payments and the Condictio Indebiti" in (1959) 76 *SALJ* 119, 121–122. The latter also discusses the judgment in *Commissioner for Inland Revenue v Visser* 1959 (1) SA 452 (A), in which a *condictio indebiti* was denied because the payment in question was not mistaken. Although the *ratio* of the judgment has been criticised, the result may be justified on the basis of estoppel. See Malan (1978) 11 CILSA 276, 279, where *King v Cohen Benjamin & Co* 1953 (4) SA 641 (W) is also discussed.
88 Malan (1978) 11 CILSA 276, 287–288. Malan also suggests (*ibid*) that both the payment by the bank and the acquisition by the recipient ("holder") should be without legal ground (*sine causa*) to found an enrichment action. There is no authority for this point of view and it is neither necessary nor justified. See also the criticism of JC Stassen, AM Oelofse, "Terugvordering van Foutiewe Wisselbetalings: Geen Verrykingsaanspreeklikheid sonder Verryking nie" in (1983) 5 MBL 137, 144.

South Africa Ltd.[89] In this case the plaintiff bank erroneously effected payment on a cheque after it had been stopped by the drawer. It was argued that the mistake by the bank was negligent and unreasonable so that a *condictio indebiti* could not succeed. Reasonableness was not, however, a prerequisite for the *condictio sine causa* so that a plaintiff in the bank's position would be well advised to make use of the latter action rather than the former. In this regard Rose-Innes J stated:[90]

> "It may be an open question whether the action in this case falls to be decided according to the principles governing the *condictio indebiti*, in which event negligence of the plaintiff may preclude the *condictio*, or whether the claim is a *condictio sine causa*, in which event negligence of the plaintiff may be irrelevant. A formalistic approach, of course, should be avoided where possible. In some cases it is necessary to classify the cause of action. In others, where no issue turns upon classification of the cause of action, a plaintiff need not place a label upon this case. If he is able to show that the law entitles him to relief it is not necessary for him to commit himself in advance in his pleadings to one form of action to the exclusion of another. It may, however, in this case be of importance in the issue of negligence to bear in mind that the *condictio indebiti* and the *condictio sine causa* have different requisites, and to determine which is the appropriate action and consequently what are the appropriate requirements which plaintiff must establish in order to succeed.
>
> In the case of the *condictio indebiti*, a person who makes a payment of money (or delivers a thing) to another due to a reasonable error of fact in the belief that the payment is owing, whereas it is not, may claim repayment to the extent that the person who received the payment has been enriched at his expense."

It is quite correct that, at the present time, it is a requirement of the *condictio indebiti* in South African law that the error of the plaintiff should be reasonable or excusable. In his thesis on the subject Professor Daniel Visser has spoken out strongly against the retention of this prerequisite.[91] The Appellate Division, however, although holding that the distinction between error of law and fact was no longer justifiable, retained the prerequisite of excusability.[92] I must agree with Professor Visser that there is no justification for the retention of this prerequisite in modern South African law. It has had the effect,

[89] 1984 (4) SA 392 (C).

[90] *Ibid*, 396C-F.

[91] DP Visser, *Die Rol van Dwaling by die Condictio Indebiti* (diss Leyden 1985), 253-255; 288-298. See also Visser, "Error of Law and Mistaken Payments: A Milestone" in (1992) 109 *SALJ* 177.

[92] *Willis Faber Enthoven (Pty) Ltd v Receiver of Revenue and Another* 1992 (4) SA 202 (A). But see *Bowman, De Wet and Du Plessis NNO v Fidelity Bank Ltd* 1997 (2) SA 35 (A), 45A-C, where Harms JA suggests that excusability of the error might not have been a requirement of the "extended" *condictio indebiti*.

indeed, of creating artificial distinctions between various kinds of enrichment actions and causing would-be plaintiffs to have to make a choice of the most convenient action for his purposes.

A more serious problem in the *Govender* case arises from the finding of the learned judge[93] that a *condictio indebiti* was not the proper action because there was no debt owed by the bank to the payee. This creates the impression that there has to be some or other causal link between the bank's payment and the recipient's acceptance thereof. The essence of the *condictio indebiti* is that it provides relief when a payment has been made which is not due (*indebitum*). The mere fact of a payment being made by mistake and without being owed, created, in Roman law already, a quasi-contractual bond between payer and payee.[94] That is when a causal link comes into existence and creates a cause of action.

Certainly the most controversial and, in my respectful view, incorrect finding of the learned judge in the *Govender* case is that payment of the countermanded cheque discharges the debt or obligation of the payee in terms of his underlying agreement with the drawer. The basis of this finding was that even an unauthorised payment may effect discharge of a debt.[95] The learned judge referred in this regard to a passage from Pothier cited in *Commissioner for Inland Revenue v Visser.*[96] The passage has clearly been misinterpreted, since it stipulates that the payment must be made in the name of the debtor and for purposes of discharging him from his obligation.[97] It is clear that the bank is not effecting any payment in the name of the drawer or with a view to discharging his obligation to the payee. Pothier undoubtedly had in mind payment by someone for the benefit of the debtor, for example by a *negotiorum gestor* who has the intention of administering the affairs of another (*animus negotia aliena gerendi*). This appears from the authorities cited by him in support of his proposition.[98]

Despite the objections to these aspects of the judgment, it must be pointed out that the result was correct, in that the plaintiff bank had indemnified itself

[93] 1984 (4) SA 392 (C), 399 H–I.

[94] *Just Inst*, 3.27.6; *D* 12.6.11.

[95] 1984 (4) SA 392 (C), 405E–406D.

[96] 1959 (1) SA 452 (A), 458 A.

[97] RJ Pothier, *A Treatise on the Law of Obligations* (translated by WD Evans), III.I.1: "It is not essential to the validity of the payment, that it be made by the debtor, or any person authorized by him; it may be made by any person without such authority, or even in opposition to his orders, provided it is made in his name, and in his discharge, and the property is effectually transferred; it is a valid payment, it induces the extinction of the obligation, and the debtor is discharged even against his will." This passage is, with respect, correctly interpreted by Corbett AJA in *Froman v Robertson* 1971 (1) SA 115 (A), 124F–125B.

[98] *D* 46.3.53; 46.3.23; 3.5.38 (39) and 3.5.39 (40). See further JW Wessels, *The Law of Contract in South Africa* (1937), §2130 and §2134 and the authorities cited in DH van Zyl, *Negotiorum Gestio in South African Law* (1985), 11 n 37.

in terms of a notice of countermand, which was signed by the customer/drawer on the understanding that he would have no claim against the bank should the cheque be "inadvertently" paid by the bank. According to the *Shorter Oxford English Dictionary*, "inadvertent" means: "(1) not properly attentive; inobservant; negligent; heedless; (2) Of actions etc: characterised by want of attention; hence unintentional." The bank would thus be indemnified also against its own negligence.[99]

A huge stride forward was taken by Preiss J in *First National Bank of SA Ltd v B & H Engineering*[100] when he held that a banker who had mistakenly paid out on a stopped cheque was entitled to recover the payment from the payee by means of the *condictio sine causa*. It was common cause that the plaintiff bank had acted *bona fide*, but negligently, in making the payment. It was likewise common cause that the defendant was not aware of the countermand when it received the cheque and handed it to its bank for special clearance. The plaintiff's cause of action in the case was unjustified enrichment to which the defendant pleaded that it was not enriched at the expense of the plaintiff. The parties were agreed that, if there was enrichment, the *condictio sine causa* was the appropriate action for the plaintiff to use.

Preiss J referred to the *Govender* case and expressed his disagreement with the finding therein that payment by the bank had the effect of discharging the obligation of the drawer to the payee. In this regard the learned judge said:[101]

> "Rose-Innes J held that the payment of the cheque had been a 'final payment'[102] which had discharged the debt owed by the drawer to the payee. With respect, this may not be so. The drawee bank, it is submitted, was not purporting to discharge an indebtedness owed by the drawer to the payee. Its (mistaken) purpose was merely to obey its mandate. It paid in its own name, not as the agent of the drawer. This being so, the payment did not fall within the rule in *Froman v Robertson*[103] that a payment without authority but in the name of the debtor and in his discharge induces extinction of the obligation."

[99] See further the criticism of JD Sinclair and C Visser, "Recovery of Payment made under a Mistake of Fact" in [1984] ASSAL 383-388 as opposed to the positive comments of JC Stassen, "Countermanded Cheques and Enrichment – Some Clarity, Some Confusion" in (1985) 7 MBL 15; FR Malan, "Price v Neal Revisited" [1992] *Acta Juridica* 131, 145–146; FR Malan, JT Pretorius and CR De Beer (eds), *Malan on Bills of Exchange, Cheques and Promissory Notes in South African Law*, 2nd ed (1994), 360-361. A similar, but distinguishable case is *Saambou Bank Ltd v Essa* 1993 (4) SA 62 (N), discussed by C-J Pretorius, "Mistaken Payments by a Bank on a Countermanded or Dishonoured Cheque – The Condictio Sine Causa and Condictio Indebiti" in (1994) 57 *THRHR* 332.

[100] 1993 (2) SA 41 (T).

[101] *Ibid*, 45G.

[102] 1984 (4) SA 392 (C), 405G–H.

[103] 1971 (1) SA 115 (A).

Preiss J found support for this view in *Barclays Bank v Simms*,[104] although he was careful not to pay undue regard to it since the *condictio sine causa* is foreign to English law. He likewise found support in the following passage from Cowen:[105]

> "I cannot agree that a bank, when paying its customer's cheques, acts as its customer's agent when paying a duly drawn cheque. The bank, although it acts pursuant to the order ('mandate' in one sense of that ambiguous and misleading term) contained in a cheque, pays or 'honours' the cheque as a principal. It does not purport to act as the duly authorised agent of its customer, nor does it purport to be discharging its customer's indebtedness in his name without his authority, within the meaning of the rule formulated by *Pothier* and adopted by the Appellate Division in *Froman v Robertson.*"

The learned judge observed that Cowen's analysis of the legal position was "incontrovertible" and added:[106]

> "I am persuaded thereby that the payment by the plaintiff on a countermanded cheque was not payment effected in its capacity as the drawer's agent. It cannot qualify as a discharge of the drawer's indebtedness . . ."

The learned judge's approach must be welcomed as a refreshingly new insight into a hitherto somewhat nebulous sphere of law, even though it has not received general academic acclaim.[107]

Preiss J's judgment went on appeal and was, unfortunately and incorrectly I believe, overturned in *B & H Engineering v First National Bank of SA Ltd.*[108] EM Grosskopf JA, who delivered the judgment on appeal, accepted that the appropriate remedy was the *condictio sine causa specialis* rather than the *con-*

[104] *Barclays Bank v WJ Simms* [1980] QB 677, discussed *supra*, §6.

[105] Cowen (1983) 16 CILSA 1, 23–24, quoted at 47C–D of Preiss J's judgment.

[106] 1993 (2) SA 41 (T), 47J–48A.

[107] DP Visser, "Unjustified Enrichment" in [1993] ASSAL 229, 234 agrees with Preiss J's approach and says in this regard: "It seems to me that in order for the payment of a cheque to have the effect of discharging a debt, there must be a continuing intention to pay the debt. If the drawer's intention to pay the debt falls away (as manifested by the countermand), there is no intention to pay the debt on anyone's part, because a bank never has the intention to pay a debt when honouring a cheque." A different point of view is expressed by C Visser, "Payment of a Stopped Cheque" in (1993) 1 *Juta's Bus L*, 32–33: "Where the agreement provides that the obligation will be discharged by payment by cheque, the countermand of payment is irrelevant: where the cheque is paid on presentment, the drawer's obligation to the payee is discharged". This is clearly erroneous since it takes no account of the relationship between the bank and customer and the legal effect of countermanding a cheque. See further CJ Nagel, M Roestoff, "Verrykingsaanspraak van Bankier na Betaling van Afgelaste Tjek" (1993) 56 *THRHR* 486 and AE Waring, "Where the Buck Stops" in (1980) 43 *THRHR* 416, 420–422. Waring supports the *Simms* remedy which he believes (422) can be married to the *condictio indebiti* of South African law.

[108] 1995 (2) SA 279 (A).

dictio indebiti.[109] The main issue, in the learned judge's view, was whether the payment by the bank discharged the drawer's debt.[110] In this regard Grosskopf JA stated:[111]

> "The fundamental point is that we are dealing with a contractual relationship between the debtor and the creditor. In law the creditor is entitled to payment in cash but he agrees to accept a cheque. Of necessity this entails that there will be some delay (and, indeed, some uncertainty) in the creditor's receipt of the money, and the law regulates the respective rights of the parties to make provision for this. Once the creditor has received his money from the bank, however, the purpose of the agreement to accept a cheque has been achieved. The creditor has been paid. Why should it matter, as between debtor and creditor, what the arrangements were between the bank and the debtor, and whether the bank has complied with these arrangements?"

I find this statement with respect, somewhat difficult to grasp. It is quite correct that the underlying agreement between the drawer as debtor and payee as creditor is independent of the relationship between the drawer and his bank. It is highly relevant, however, that the legal nature of this relationship is one of mandate, an agreement from which arise well defined rights and obligations. The bank is empowered to act only within the confines of its mandate and, should it fail to do so, it would be in breach of its obligations and act without authority. If the parties to the underlying agreement have chosen to have payment effected by cheque, the bank of necessity becomes involved and its mandate comes into operation. The bank is not the drawer's agent and has no obligation to the payee. When it honours a cheque in terms of its mandate, it is performing its obligations towards the drawer and does not make any performance to the payee. If the drawer should decide to breach its obligation towards the payee by stopping payment for whatever reason, good or bad, the payee cannot compel the bank to disregard the countermand and to honour the cheque in order to have payment effected in spite of the drawer's decision no longer to perform. The "arrangements" between the drawer and the bank are, therefore, particularly relevant in the context of the parties' decision to make use of payment by cheque for purposes of effecting performance by the drawer of his obligations in terms of the underlying agreement.

After pointing out that payment by cheque rather than cash makes practical and commercial good sense, but does expose a creditor to the risk of delay in paying or even of failure to pay the cheque, Grosskopf JA observed that

[109] *Ibid*, 284G–285C.
[110] *Ibid*, 285F.
[111] *Ibid*, 286H–I.

payment by the bank without authority did not necessarily create a risk for the payee. He explained this as follows:[112]

> "An effective debt-extinguishing agreement achieves its purpose when the creditor receives the money owing to him. For this purpose it does not matter whether the payment was, as in the present case, attended by breach of the contract between the Bank and its customer, the drawer. And, indeed, it seems highly undesirable that the payee should be drawn into these matters. He does not normally know what the arrangements are between the bank and the drawer. In particular, he would not usually know whether his payment was authorised by the drawer or not. Indeed, this might be a matter of dispute between the drawer and the bank. Why, for instance, should the payee, who was duly paid, be saddled with the uncertainty and delay of a dispute between the bank and the drawer as to whether a proper countermand had been given?"

The implication of this *dictum* is that the bank's failure to give effect to the countermand of the cheque amounts to a breach of contract between the bank and its customer, which breach is irrelevant as far as the payee is concerned. This loses sight, in my respectful view, of the fact that the countermand as such is an unambiguous indication of the drawer's intention no longer to make performance to the payee and hence to breach the underlying agreement. It cannot simply be ignored.

The learned judge then dealt with certain provisions of the *Bills of Exchange Act* 34 of 1964 before turning his attention to the English authorities, such as the cases of *Cocks v Masterman*[113] and *Barclays Bank v WJ Simms.*[114] He held,[115] with reference to these precedents, that they "do not provide convincing authority for the proposition that a cheque which has been paid according to its tenor in a case like the present was not discharged if the payment is subsequently recovered [*sic*]". This appears to be a *non sequitur*, unless "recovered" should read "countermanded". The statement is clarified, however, when it is succinctly put that "the cheque in the present case was discharged when the Bank paid it".

The subsequent elucidation of this finding by the learned judge[116] is, with respect, unconvincing. It relates first to the inequitable consequences which would be suffered by the creditor/payee of the underlying debt should it not be discharged by payment of the cheque, even if it should be unauthorised. The equities are not reciprocated, it would appear, as far as the debtor/drawer is concerned. Despite his countermand and expressed intention *not* to make

[112] *Ibid*, 287G–H.
[113] (1829) 9 B & C 902.
[114] [1980] QB 677, discussed *supra*, §6.
[115] 1995 (2) SA 279 (A), 290G–J.
[116] *Ibid*, 291B–292D.

performance to the creditor, the bank's mistaken honouring of the cheque is regarded as due performance in terms of the underlying agreement.

Even more inequitable, on the face of it, is the position of the bank. Because of its oversight, which was probably negligent, to put the countermand into operation, it has no authority to debit the account of its customer and, according to the *ratio* in Grosskopf JA's judgment, it has no claim against the payee for mistaken payment or otherwise.

South African law on unauthorised payments by a bank has run full circle: from the doctrine in *Price v Neal* to the flexible approach in *Barclays v Simms* and back again. It could indeed be said that the Appellate Division's decision to deny relief to the bank against the payee has been a retrogressive step.[117] On the other hand it might just have opened the door to a little judicial creativity and innovative thinking.

Whether or not the bank might have an enrichment action against one or the other of the *personae dramatis* is a different question. Grosskopf JA was satisfied that the payee had not been enriched because its debt had been extinguished by payment of the cheque so that its claim against the drawer was likewise extinguished. This did not, however, mean that the bank could not claim against the drawer on the basis of enrichment, since the unauthorised payment to the payee had the effect that the drawer was released from its obligation to the payee and was hence unjustifiably enriched at the expense of the bank.[118]

It is a well established institution of our law that someone may pay the debts of another as an unauthorised administrator or *negotiorum gestor* of the latter.[119] He must then, however, have the intention to manage or administer the affairs of that person (*animus negotia aliena gerendi*).[120] If he does not have this intention, he may qualify for an enrichment action in the form of the "extended" *actio negotiorum gestorum*.[121] This action is available even if he has acted against the express wishes of the *dominus* (*domino prohibente*).[122]

It would not be appropriate to consider this question fully at the present stage, but it can be stated that the plaintiff bank, in the *B & H Engineering* case, would be able to institute an enrichment claim against its customer, as drawer of the cheque which was countermanded and erroneously paid out.

[117] See the critical comments of C-J Pretorius in (1995) 58 *THRHR* 733 as opposed to the approval expressed by FR Malan in (1995) *TSAR* 782. He and JT Pretorius are strongly disapproving, however, in their discussion of *Standard Bank of SA Ltd v Absa Bank Ltd and Another* 1995 (2) SA 740 (T) in (1996) 8 *SA Mercantile LJ* 399.

[118] 1995 (2) SA 279 (A), 294I–295F.

[119] See Van Zyl, *Negotiorum Gestio in South African Law* (1985), 11 and the authorities cited in n 37. See also *supra*, text to n 4.

[120] Van Zyl, 31–40.

[121] Van Zyl, 84–118.

[122] Van Zyl, 105–110.

This enrichment action should, however, in my respectful view be only an alternative remedy to that denied by the Appellate Division in the said case. I reiterate my respectful disagreement with the finding that the bank has no claim against the payee and express the hope that the Supreme Court of Appeal may, at some future stage, amend its views on the subject by granting the bank an enrichment action (be it a *condictio indebiti* or *condictio sine causa*) against the recipient or payee to whom the bank has made an unauthorised payment.

2

Distributing the Burden of Alternative Co-extensive Liabilities: Some Banking Cases Considered

CHARLES MITCHELL*

1. INTRODUCTION

The courts must often decide whether an injured party should be allowed to accumulate recoveries from two or more others who are legally liable for her loss and, if not, whether one of them should bear the whole burden of paying her, or whether they should share this burden.[1] These questions arise

* Lecturer in Law, King's College London. I am grateful to Eva Lomnicka for her comments on a draft of this paper, but I am fully responsible for what follows.

[1] A court which holds that one of them should bear the whole burden of paying for the loss will often say that he is "primarily liable" and that the other is "secondarily liable": see *eg* *Duncan, Fox & Co v North & South Wales Bank* (1880) 6 App Cas 1, 11 (*per* Lord Selborne LC): "[in some cases] there is a primary and secondary liability of two persons for one and the same debt, the debt being, as between the two, that of one of those persons only, and not equally of both"; *Brook's Wharf & Bull Wharf Ltd v Goodman Bros* [1937] 1 KB 534, 544 (*per* Lord Wright MR): "The essence of the rule [that legally compelled payments of another's liability are recoverable] is that there is a liability for the same debt resting on the plaintiff and the defendant and the plaintiff has been legally obliged to pay, but the defendant gets the benefit of the payment, because his debt is discharged either entirely or pro tanto, whereas the defendant is primarily liable to pay as between himself and the defendant"; *cf* T Dugdale, "The Negligent Professional: Liability for a Fair Share?", Chap 4 in P Birks (ed), *Wrongs and Remedies in the Twenty-First Century* (1996), 91 and 103–106 (using the terms "primary" and "subsidiary fault" to express the same idea).

However, the terms "primary" and "secondary liability" have been used in two other different senses in the context of the law of civil obligations, and care must be taken not to confuse any of these usages: (i) The term "primary liability" has been used to describe the liability of a party who is liable regardless of whether any other party is also liable in respect of the same loss, in contradistinction to the "secondary liability" of a party who is liable only in the event of another party's default. Thus, for example, a surety is "secondarily liable" for a guaranteed debt where he has promised to pay only in the event of the principal debtor's default, whereas an indemnity insurer is "primarily liable" for an insured loss where it has promised to pay regardless of whether anyone else is also liable. See *Re Downer Enterprises Ltd* [1974] 1 WLR 1460, 1470 (*per* Pennycuick V-C); J O'Donovan and J Phillips, *The Modern Contract of Guarantee*, 3rd ed (1996), 25–31. (ii) The term "secondary liability" has been used to denote "that form of liability for civil wrongs imposed in civil law in circumstances similar to those in which criminal liability whenever a plaintiff who has been legally compelled to pay an injured party brings an action to recover his payment from a defendant who was also legally liable to her, and whose liability the plaintiff has discharged,[2] on the ground that the defendant has been unjustly enriched at his expense.[3] They also arise whenever a defendant in an action brought by an injured party asserts that the damages payable should be reduced by the amount of a collateral benefit she has previously received from another source.[4]

The parties in these situations do not all seek restitutionary remedies. An award of money paid in the first situation would be a restitutionary award designed to reverse the defendant's unjust enrichment at the plaintiff's expense. But an order that the damages payable by the defendant in the second situation should be reduced would not be designed to reverse unjust enrichment: rather, it would constitute an acknowledgment that the injured

is imposed on persons who aid, abet, counsel or procure a crime": P Sales, "The Tort of Conspiracy and Civil Secondary Liability" (1990) 49 CLJ 491, 502–503. See too *Credit Lyonnais Nederland NV v ECGD* [1998] 1 Lloyd's Rep 19, 46, *per* Hobhouse LJ: "Mere assistance, even knowing assistance, does not suffice to make the 'secondary' party jointly liable as a joint tortfeasor with the primary party."

2 As a general rule, payment or performance of another's liability under legal compulsion will operate to discharge the other's liability: J Beatson and P Birks, "Unrequested Payment of Another's Debt" (1976) 92 LQR 188, 199–200. But there are exceptions to this rule, *eg* a payment by an insurer to its insured will not discharge a third party from liability to the insured for causing the insured loss.

3 The remedy sought by the plaintiff may be an award of money paid to the defendant's use or a contribution award, possibly supplemented by subrogation to whatever securities the defendant may previously have given the injured party to secure his obligation. A contribution claim is essentially a claim for reimbursement of whatever the claimant has been compelled to pay in excess of his own share of a common liability: *Silk v Eyre* (1875) 9 Ir Rep Eq 393, 395 (*per* Chatterton V-C): "[where the claimant son and contributor father were joint debtors] the son was a surety, and the father the principal debtor as to a moiety of these debts"; *Ronex Properties Ltd v John Laing Construction Ltd* [1983] QB 398, 407 (*per* Sir S Shaw): "a claim for contribution [under the Law Reform (Married Women and Tortfeasors) Act 1935] resembles a claim by a plaintiff for money paid by him to the use of the defendant who has been relieved, pro tanto, of his direct liability to the victim of the tort". For general statements of the right to acquire extinguished securities via subrogation to supplement an award of money paid to another's use pursuant to secondary liability, see: *Duncan, Fox & Co v North & South Wales Bank* (1880) 6 App Cas 1, 18 (*per* Lord Selbourne LC); *Re Downer Enterprises Ltd* [1974] 1 WLR 1460, 1468 (*per* Pennycuick V-C); *Becton Dickinson UK Ltd v Zwebner* [1989] QB 208, 216–218 (*per* McNeil J); and see too Mercantile Law Amendment Act 1856, s 5. For general statements of the right to acquire extinguished securities via subrogation to supplement a contribution award, see: *Stirling v Forrester* (1821) 3 Bli 575, 590 (*per* Lord Redesdale); *Ruabon Steamship Co v London Assurance Co* [1900] AC 6, 12 (*per* Lord Halsbury LC); *AE Goodwin Ltd v AG Healing Ltd* (1979) 7 ACLR 481, 489 (*per* Powell J).

4 This may be an action brought by the injured party for her own benefit, or it may be a subrogated action brought in her name, but for the benefit of the party who paid her. In practice, it can be impossible to tell these apart, as English law does not have a "real party in interest rule" of the kind which prevails in many American states, requiring that the name of the party for whose real benefit an action is brought should appear on the face of the record. This is a matter for regret, as in some circumstances, depending on the view which it forms of the parties' respective positions, a court cannot know what order it should make in response to an argument that damages should be reduced unless it knows who is behind the action.

party had had all that she was entitled to, from the "right" person, and that she would therefore be unjustly enriched at the defendant's expense if he were then obliged to pay her as well. These situations have the shared feature, though, that a court cannot know what order to make in response to them unless it first decides whether the injured party should be allowed to accumulate recoveries; and, if not, whether one or more of the parties liable to her should bear the burden of paying her. The purpose of this paper is to suggest that a coherent answer to these questions can be given only if three separate issues are considered in turn, and to illustrate these issues by reference to various cases involving the rights or liabilities of a bank or building society. For the sake of clarity, discussion in this paper is limited to situations where an injured party has the right to recover in respect of his loss from only two others, but in principle the analytical method which this paper advocates should work as well for situations where he has the right to recover from more than two. As the number of parties liable to the injured party increases, though, it will become a more complex undertaking to strike the balance of policy considerations which is required to determine their respective positions.

2. THE THREE ISSUES

To decide whether an injured party should be allowed to accumulate recoveries from two others liable for her loss and, if not, whether one or both of them should bear the burden of paying her, the courts should consider the following three issues in turn: (a) Are the parties co-extensively liable for the loss? (b) Are they alternatively liable for the loss? (c) Should one of them bear the burden of paying for the loss, or should they share this burden?

(a) Are the parties co-extensively liable?

The term "co-extensive" is used here to denote liabilities which are owed by separate parties in respect of the same loss to the same right-holder (whose rights correspond to their liabilities). The term is not used to indicate that their liabilities are of the same degree.[5] Thus, for example, a surety's liability

[5] *Cf Albion Insurance Co Ltd v Government Insurance Office of New South Wales* (1969) 121 CLR 342, 350 (*per* Kitto J): "persons who are under co-ordinate liabilities to make good the one loss (*eg* sureties liable to make good a failure to pay the one debt) must share the burden pro rata." The term "co-ordinate" is used in this passage to indicate that the parties' liabilities are owed in respect of the same loss to the same person, that he may not accumulate recoveries from them, and that the degree of the parties' liabilities is the same: *ie* it indicates that particular conclusions have been reached with regard to each of the three issues set out in this paper. Following

is "co-extensive" with that of a principal debtor, co-sureties and sub-sureties, to the extent that they are all liable to the same creditor in respect of the same debt, although the degrees of their respective liabilities are not all the same. Where the parties' liabilities are not co-extensive because they are owed to different right-holders, no question can arise of restraining one right-holder from enforcing her rights against one of the liable parties on the ground that the other right-holder has previously enforced her rights against the other liable party. And where the parties' liabilities are not co-extensive because they are not owed in respect of the same debt or damage, although they are owed to the same right-holder, she cannot be restrained from enforcing her rights against one of the liable parties on the ground that she has already recovered from the other. In other words, it follows from the fact that the parties' liabilities are not co-extensive that the right-holder(s) to whom their liabilities are owed may accumulate recoveries from both of them, and hence that the liable parties can have no rights inter se to shift all or some of the burden of paying for the right-holder's loss (or right-holders' losses).

In *Bonner v Tottenham and Edmonton Permanent Investment Building Soc*,[6]

Kitto J's dictum in the *Albion Insurance* case, the Australian courts have often attempted to analyse contribution claims in terms of whether or not the liabilities of the parties are "co-ordinate", without always explicitly recognizing the separate and contingent nature of these issues. See *eg Re La Rosa* (1991) 31 FCR 83; *Street v Retravision (NSW) Pty Ltd* (1995) 13 ACLC 757; *Jones v Mortgage Acceptance Nominees Ltd* (23 Feb 1996) (FCA (NSW Dist Reg), Davies J). See too RP Meagher, WMC Gummow, and JRF Lehane, *Equity: Doctrines and Remedies*, 3rd ed (1992), para 1006; K Mason and JW Carter, *The Law of Restitution in Australia* (1995), para 622.

[6] [1899] 1 QB 161. Other cases where the issue of co-extensiveness has been expressly considered by the courts are: *Assicurazioni Generali de Trieste v Empress Assurance Corp Ltd* [1907] 2 KB 814, 820 (*per* Pickford J, in response to the argument of counsel at 817 that the plaintiff reinsurer could only be subrogated to rights that were "incident to the subject of the insurance" and that the wrong done to the reinsured by the insured was "a personal tort not connected with the subject matter of the insurance ... similar to a libel published incidentally in the course of an insurance transaction"): "I think that the money was received in diminution of the loss, and that the case of the libel as suggested is not analogous. The claim was to recover the amount of damages which the defendants had suffered by reason of having to pay the loss, and the amount of the loss was the measure of the damages which the defendants recovered"; *Smith v Cock* [1911] AC 317, 326 (*per* Lord Mersey): "Before there can be any question of contribution there must be a common obligation upon those who are required to contribute. Here there is none. The trusts are not only different in their terms, but each trust requires a separate and independent exercise of the discretion of the trustees of the particular estate as to the sum to be paid by that estate to Alice. When that discretion has been exercised it may be said that a consequent obligation which has no connection with the obligation upon the trustees of the other estate, and cannot therefore afford any ground for contribution."

See too the cases discussed in R Merkin (ed), *Colinvaux's Law of Insurance*, 7th ed (1997), 188–189 (contribution claims between insurers will lie only where they have insured the same risk to the same interest in the same subject matter), and in J O'Donovan and J Phillips, *The Modern Contract of Guarantee*, 3rd ed (1996), 619-620 (contribution claims between sureties will lie only where they have guaranteed the same principal debt owed by the same principal debtor, and will not lie, for example, where they have guaranteed different debts or obligations of the same debtor, or even discrete parts of the same debt).

the plaintiff tenants assigned their lease, and their assignee then mortgaged the lease to the defendant building society. The assignee became bankrupt and the society took possession of the property as sub-tenant. In breach of their contract with the assignee the society then failed to pay any rent. The landlord was unable to recover the rent from the society because no privity of estate existed between them,[7] and so instead it recovered the rent from the plaintiffs under a covenant in the lease. The plaintiffs' claim to recover this payment from the society failed because it had conferred no benefit on the society by paying the landlord in respect of a loss for which the society was not also liable: *ie* the plaintiffs' liability to the landlord was not co-extensive with the society's liability to the assignee. In the words of AL Smith LJ:[8]

> "No contract or privity of estate exists between the plaintiffs and defendants, or between the . . . lessor . . . and the defendants. . . . It is true that [the lessor] could sue the plaintiffs, his lessees, upon their covenant with him in the lease. It is also true that the plaintiffs, the lessees, could sue their assignee . . . upon his covenant with them. It is also true that [the assignee] could sue the defendants, his under-lessees, upon their covenant with him. But how can the plaintiffs sue the defendants?"

(b) Are the parties alternatively liable?

The term "alternatively liable" is used here to indicate that the right-holder to whom the parties' co-extensive liabilities are owed must enforce his rights in the alternative, and must not accumulate recoveries in respect of his loss. As has been said above, it necessarily follows from a finding that the parties' liabilities are not co-extensive that the right-holder(s) to whom they are owed can recover from both of them. But it should not be supposed that the opposite proposition holds good. It does not necessarily follow from the fact that the parties' liabilities are co-extensive that the right-holder to whom they are owed can never accumulate recoveries from them both. On the contrary, it is possible for a right-holder to accumulate recoveries from several co-extensively liable parties if the courts decide as a matter of policy that she should be allowed to do so. Thus, for example, if someone takes out two separate personal accident policies, she can recover on both policies following an insured loss because the courts have decided as a matter of policy to allow parties to accumulate recoveries on separate policies of non-indemnity

[7] *Cf Electricity Supply Nominees Ltd v Thorn EMI Retail Ltd* (1991) 63 P & CR 143 (original tenant's claim against assignee's sub-tenant allowed where sub-tenant had covenanted with landlord to observe obligations of head lease).

[8] [1899] 1 QB 161, 166.

insurance. It follows from a finding that a right-holder can accumulate recoveries from two co-extensively liable parties that they can have no rights inter se to shift the burden of paying for her loss, as in this case they are each liable to pay her in full, regardless of whether the other has paid.

It is inherent in any decision that a payment by one of the parties liable operates to discharge the liability of the other, that the right-holder may not recover from them both. But, again, it should not be supposed that the opposite is true. It does not follow from the fact that a payment by one of the liable parties does not operate to discharge the other's liability that the right-holder must therefore be entitled to recover from the other as well. The courts may decide as a matter of policy to prevent her from doing this, for example by forcing her to relinquish her right of action against the other to the party who has paid: this is what happens when an insurer is subrogated to its insured's subsisting rights of action against a third party. In other words, whilst they sometimes coincide, there is no necessary correlation between the rules which govern the question whether a right-holder can accumulate recoveries in respect of her loss, and the rules which govern the question whether a payment by one co-extensively liable party operates to discharge the liability of the other.

Whether an injured party should be allowed to accumulate recoveries from several co-extensively liable parties is a policy question which the courts have answered in the past by looking at such factors as the nature of the injured party's loss and the nature of the liabilities which are owed to her. For example, the courts' answers have varied according to whether the compensation payable to the injured party has been intended to replace something with a measurable financial value or to compensate her for something with no measurable financial value such as pain and suffering, and according to whether the injured party has paid for the right to be compensated by one or both of the parties liable.[9]

This last factor was recently considered in *Bristol & West Building Soc v May, May and Merrimans (No 2)*.[10] This was one of the latest in a series of cases[11] concerned with the following situation. A building society lends

[9] For discussion of these and other policy considerations, see P Cane (ed), *Atiyah's Accidents, Compensation and the Law*, 5th ed (1993), 322–330. See too Law Commission, *Damages for Personal Injury: Collateral Benefits* (LCCP No 147, 1997), paras 4.30–4.35. But NB the question at issue here is solely whether the injured party should be allowed to accumulate recoveries. It is not whether it would be wrong to allow one of the parties liable to cast the burden of paying her onto the other once it has been decided that she cannot recover twice over, *eg* because he has committed a wrong against her whilst the other is under a contractual obligation to indemnify her.

[10] [1997] 3 All ER 206.

[11] *Alliance and Leicester Building Soc v Edgestop* (13 Jun 1994) Unrep (Ch D: Knox J); *Banque Bruxelles Lambert SA v Eagle Star Ins Co Ltd* [1995] 2 All ER 769, 804 (*per* Phillips J), not considered on appeal to CA: [1995] QB 375, nor on appeal to HL: [1997] AC 191; *Cheltenham and*

money to a borrower to buy property, and the loan is secured by a mortgage over the property. A term of the loan agreement stipulates that the borrower must pay the premiums of a mortgage indemnity guarantee (MIG). The borrower defaults on his repayments, the society exercises its power of sale, and fails to realise the amount of its loan, *inter alia* because at the time of making the loan it supposed the value of the property to be higher than was actually the case. The society accordingly sues the valuer of the property for having negligently or deceitfully valued it in excess of its true value. Alternatively, the society sues its solicitor for having negligently or deceitfully failed to pass on information relevant to the value of the property which it knew or ought to have known about – *eg* a defect in title. The society's action against the valuer or the solicitor is successful, and an order for damages is made. The question then arises whether the MIG proceeds should be brought into account when the amount of damages are assessed.

MIGs are insurance policies under which an insurer typically agrees to pay a mortgagee an indemnity in the event that it exercises its power of sale and the proceeds of sale fall short of the outstanding debt due under the mortgage. The amount payable is typically not equal to, but is calculated by reference to the amount of the mortgagee's loss. Under the Building Societies Act 1986, an advance made by a building society must be secured by a mortgage of a legal estate or, in certain circumstances, an equitable interest in land. Where the amount advanced will exceed the value of the mortgage, the society must satisfy itself that the excess is secured by an additional security of a type prescribed by s 11(2) and (4)(c), and the permitted classes of security include MIGs. In Chadwick J's words,[12] the MIG insurer therefore covenants to pay "that part of the shortfall on realisation of the basic security which is properly attributable to that part of the advance which was in excess of the value of the basic security." It follows from this, as Chadwick J rightly pointed

Gloucester Building Soc v Fleury Manico (date unknown) Unrep (QBD, Anthony Hooper QC, sitting as a deputy High Ct judge); *Portman Building Soc v AB & Co* (25 May 1994) Unrep (QBD: Ian Kennedy J); *Bristol and West Building Soc v Christie* [1996] EGCS 53; *Bristol and West Building Soc v Freeman and Pollard (a firm)*(20 Feb 1996) Unrep (QBD: Judge Jack QC); *Europe Mortgage Co v Halifax Estate Agencies Ltd* [1996], *The Times*, May 23; *National Home Loans Corp Plc v McCarthy-Robinson* (20 Sep 1996) Unrep (Judge Fox-Andrews QC, sitting as an Official Referee); *Platform Home Loans Ltd v Gummer & Singh (a firm)* (31 Oct 1996) Unrep (ChD: Harman J). *Cf Gardiner v Henderson* (1988) 1 Qd R 125, 136 (*per* Ambrose J).

In *Gardner v Marsh & Parsons (a firm)* [1997] 3 All ER 871, the question arose whether the damages payable by the defendant for negligently surveying leasehold property purchased by the plaintiff should be reduced to take account of the fact that plaintiff's landlord had repaired the property pursuant to covenant in lease. The majority of the Court of Appeal held that the repairs were "*res inter alios acta* and therefore collateral to [the defendant's] negligence": *per* Hirst LJ at 886, Pill LJ concurring at 896. Peter Gibson LJ dissented, stating at 893: "Once the property had been put into repair at no cost to the plaintiffs . . . they cannot be allowed to obtain double recovery by an award of damages against the defendants."

[12] *Bristol & West BS v May, May & Merrimann (No 2)* [1997] 3 All ER 206, 213.

out,[13] that in cases where a society suffers loss as a result of negligent or deceitful statements respecting the value of its basic security that loss "cannot form any part of the loss covered by the MIG", which was never intended to provide any security in respect of that part of the society's advance which was made on the strength of the basic security alone. In these circumstances, therefore, the solicitor or valuer cannot have the MIG proceeds brought into account, for the reason that his liability and the insurer's liability are not co-extensive.

In the present case, damages had been awarded against the defendant solicitors which were intended to compensate the plaintiff building society for the whole of the loss which it had suffered following the sale of the mortgaged properties,[14] and part of their liability was therefore co-extensive with the liability of the insurer. Even to this extent, however, Chadwick J refused to order the society to give credit for the MIG proceeds when computing the damages recoverable from the solicitors. He reasoned[15] that the society should have to give credit for the MIG proceeds only if it would otherwise be doubly enriched by accumulating recoveries from the insurer and the solicitors. He decided that there was no risk of this because in the event that the solicitors paid full damages the society would owe a duty to account to the insurer for an amount corresponding to the MIG proceeds, following *Lord Napier & Ettrick v Hunter*.[16] And he concluded that the solicitors should accordingly have to pay full damages.

This analysis obviously depended on the initial premise that the society should not have been allowed to accumulate recoveries from the insurer and the solicitors, and it is a disappointing feature of Chadwick J's judgment that he gave no positive reasons for his decision to take this as his starting point. However, the society did address him on this point, and he did give a negative reason for refusing to adopt its argument that it should have been entitled to accumulate recoveries (although on the view which he took of the case it was unnecessary for him to have done so[17]).

The society's argument ran as follows. It was held in *Bradburn v Great Western Railway*[18] and *Parry v Cleaver*[19] that insurance proceeds are treated as *res inter alios acta* when assessing the damages payable by a tortfeasor

[13] *Ibid*, 213-214; followed in *Bristol & West Building Soc v Fancy & Jackson (a firm)* [1997] 4 All ER 582, 624–626 (*per* Chadwick J).
[14] *Bristol & West Building Soc v May, May, & Merrimans* [1996] 2 All ER 801.
[15] [1997] 3 All ER 206, 215-216.
[16] [1993] AC 713.
[17] [1997] 3 All ER 206, 222.
[18] (1874) LR 10 Exch 1.
[19] [1970] AC 1.

responsible for causing an insured loss. In the latter case, Lord Reid stated that "the real and substantial reason for disregarding them is that the plaintiff has bought them",[20] and an insured should not be penalised for his prudence by there being a reduction of the damages which he would otherwise have received. In this case, the society had effectively paid for the MIG premiums, and the same principle should therefore apply.

Chadwick J rejected this argument on the ground that the society had not in fact paid for the MIG premiums, but had rather required the borrower to do so as part of the loan agreement. With respect, this was unconvincing: there is no reason in principle to distinguish the situation where a society obliges a borrower to pay MIG premiums directly from the situation where a society pays MIG premiums itself and then increases its charges to recoup the cost of this from the borrower. Yet Chadwick J's argument requires that MIG proceeds should be taken into account when assessing damages payable by a third party in the second, but not in the first situation. So far as this distinction is concerned, it is therefore submitted that Scott V-C's remarks on an identical point in *Maes Finance Ltd v AL Phillips & Co (a firm)*[21] are to be preferred. In his view:

> "in a case like the present, where the mortgage transaction required the borrower's funds to be used to effect the policy for the benefit of the mortgagee, where the damages to be paid by the negligent solicitors are to be assessed on the footing that but for the negligence the mortgagee would not have entered into the transaction, and where the mortgagee in calculating his recoverable damages must bring into account the benefits he has received under the transaction, the right question is a much simpler one; namely, do the proceeds of the policy represent part of the benefits received by the plaintiff under the transaction?"

However, even this gloss on the "paid for" argument is really unnecessary to resolve the question, for the reason that the society's argument can be met by a far more fundamental counter-argument, which denies that it constitutes a valid reason to allow accumulation of recoveries at all. This counter-argument was first advanced in response to Lord Reid's original comments in *Parry v Cleaver* by Professor Atiyah:[22]

> "What is at issue is the amount of tort damages, not the question whether the plaintiff should get or keep his insurance payments . . . If a plaintiff collects on a personal accident insurance policy, he receives and keeps his insurance money.

[20] *Ibid*, 14.
[21] (12 March 1997) Unrep (Ch D).
[22] PS Atiyah, "Collateral Benefits Again" (1969) 32 MLR 397, 403 (quoted and discussed in LCCP No 147, paras 4.40–4.46).

The question at issue is how much *more* he should receive in tort damages. To argue that he "has paid" for his insurance payments is beside the point when it is not the insurance payments which are in issue."

(c) Should one of the parties bear the whole burden of paying for the loss, or should they share this burden?

The answer to this question, again, comes down to a matter of policy. Which of the parties should ultimately be made to bear the loss is something the courts can only decide by looking at the nature of the liabilities which the parties owe and the policy considerations which underlie and flow from those liabilities, and by striking a balance between these considerations.[23] It is probably easiest for the courts to do this when the juridical nature of the parties' liabilities is the same – where they are both liable in tort, for example, or liable under similar contracts of insurance or guarantee.[24] When the juridical nature of the parties' liabilities is different, matters can become distinctly complex.

This may be illustrated by an issue which arose in *Wealden Woodlands (Kent) Ltd v National Westminster Bank Ltd.*[25] Here, the plaintiff company gave a mandate to its bank, the defendant, to pay cheques drawn on the com-

[23] *Cf Dutton v Bognor Regis UDC* [1972] 1 QB 373, 397 (*per* Lord Denning MR): "In previous times, when faced with a new problem, the judges have not openly asked themselves the question: what is the best policy to adopt? But the question has always been there in the background. . . . Nowadays we direct ourselves to considerations of policy . . . we look at the relationship of the parties: and then say, as a matter of policy, on whom the loss should fall."

[24] When apportioning the burden of a loss between two tortfeasors under the Civil Liability (Contribution) Act 1978, the courts' approach is to consider both the "causative potency" and the "blameworthiness" of the parties' actions: see *eg Madden v Quirk* [1989] 1 WLR 702, 707 (*per* Simon Brown J); *Downs v Chappell* [1996] 3 All ER 344, 363 (*per* Hobhouse LJ, holding that one tortfeasor's "more serious fault" had "less causative impact" than another's "less serious fault", with the result that they were equally responsible for the victim's loss). But it may be questioned whether a useful conceptual distinction can always be drawn between the "blameworthiness" and "causative potency" of fault-based torts: since the criteria to which the courts refer when assessing the degree of the tortfeasors' blameworthiness can include the causative potency of their actions, the two can at times be inextricably intertwined: *cf* HLA Hart and AM Honoré, *Causation in the Law*, 2 ed (1985), 234: "it is not clear that an apportionment based on fault . . . will lead to different results from one based on causation . . . for the chance of harmful consequences and the probable seriousness of the consequences are relevant to the determination of fault." And these concepts are clearly ill-adapted to assessing the relative liabilities of contract-breakers or parties in breach of an absolute statutory duty, as one breach of contract or breach of statutory duty can be neither more nor less "blameworthy" than another: *Nolan v Merseyside CC* (1982) 133 NLJ 616, 621 (*per* May LJ). But *cf Rippon v Port of London Authority* [1940] 1 KB 858, 866–867 (*per* Tucker J), remarking that it might seem "curious" to decide that responsibility of one party in breach of statutory duty is "in any way different" from responsibility of another for a similar breach, but managing to do so nonetheless.

[25] [1983] *The Times*, March 12; (1983) 133 NLJ 719. These reports are short and do not touch on the aspect of the case which is discussed in the text.

pany's account only if they were signed by two of four authorised signatories, who at all material times were the company's four directors. The bank paid a series of cheques totalling £35,000 which it later transpired were forgeries: one of the directors had forged the signature of another director on the cheques, and used the money to meet the bills of his own business. The company therefore brought a successful action to have its account reinstated to the extent that it had been wrongly debited by the amount of the forged cheques.[26] The question arose *inter alia* whether the company's claim should be reduced to take into account the £5,000 which it had recovered from its insurer on a fidelity policy, which had provided that the insurer would indemnify the company in the event that it suffered loss as the result of frauds perpetrated by its employees. The bank asserted that, "although the insurers might have a claim against the bank by subrogation, no such claim has been made [and the] plaintiffs have, therefore, . . . been compensated for this part of their loss." The company conceded that it had recovered on the policy in respect of some of the cheques, totalling £4,313, and that the amount of the judgment should be reduced by this sum, McNeill J found that there was no "bona fide triable issue on the attribution of the sums making up the insurance payment", accepted that "at the most the judgment sum should be reduced by £4,313", and ordered accordingly.

In effect, the company conceded that the bank's and the fidelity insurers' respective liabilities in respect of the loss to the company of the £4,313 were co-extensive and alternative, and that the burden of paying for this loss should fall on the insurers. Since the insurers made no claim to be subrogated to the company's rights against the bank, it must be assumed that they had made no objection to this concession, but it seems surprising that they made no attempt to argue the third point, and to say that they should have been entitled to subrogation because the burden of paying for the company's loss ought properly to have been borne by the bank.[27]

[26] The company's account was overdrawn at all material times, and the effect of reinstatement was not to bring it into credit. Where a bank is obliged to reinstate an account, and the account is thereby brought into credit, the account holder is entitled to demand that the bank pay over the credit balance: *Limpgrange v Bank of Credit and Commerce International SA* [1986] FLR 36, 47 (*per* Staughton J). Interest is recoverable by the account holder from the date on which it requires the bank to reinstate its account, even though the account is non-interest bearing: *Tai Hing Cotton Mill Ltd v Liu Chong Hing Bank Ltd* [1986] AC 80, 111 (*per* Lord Scarman). If the bank dishonours any of its account-holder's cheques in reliance on a balance struck in consequence of the debits wrongfully made to her account, the limitation period affecting her action for breach of contract will run from the date on which her cheques are wrongfully dishonoured, and not from the date on which the debits are wrongfully entered in the ledger: *National Bank of Commerce v National Westminster Bank* [1990] 2 Lloyd's Rep 514.

[27] If they had not consented to this concession being made, and if in fact the burden of the company's loss should have been borne by the bank, then the insurers might conceivably have

No other Commonwealth cases touching directly on this point have been found,[28] but in a large number of American cases fidelity insurers have attempted to recover via subrogation from banks in similar circumstances.[29] No American case has been found which expressly addresses the issues whether the bank's and the fidelity insurer's liabilities are co-extensive and

been entitled to bring an action for money paid against the bank, by analogy with *Pownal v Ferrand* (1827) 6 B & C 439, the facts of which are discussed in C Mitchell, *The Law of Subrogation* (1994), 93–94. Failing that, the insurers would have been entitled to bring an action for damages against the company, for breach of its duty to safeguard the insurers' right of recovery from the bank: see the authorities cited in C Mitchell, "Defences to an Insurer's Subrogated Action" [1996] LMCLQ 343, 365, n 116.

In a Canadian case, *Cowley v National Life Assurance Co* [1991] ILR 1474, an insured reached a settlement with third parties which left her insurer's subrogation rights out of account. The insurer claimed that the insured's solicitor had been negligent in recommending a settlement on these terms, and sought to recover damages from the solicitor either in its own right or via a subrogated action in the name of the insured. Hickman CJ refused the insurer's direct claim on the ground that there was no solicitor-client relationship between them, and he refused the insurer's subrogated claim on the ground that the insurer's liability to the insured and the solicitor's liability to the insured were not co-extensive, stating (at 1476) that: "any damages which [the insured] may have suffered as a result of [the solicitor's] negligence do not fall within any of the risks against which [the insured] was insured [by the insurer]." This may have been to take an over-restrictive view of the co-extensiveness question, given that his ruling was "without prejudice to any rights which [the insured] may have to look to her solicitor . . . to be indemnified against any judgment which may be obtained by [the insurer] against her."

28 But *cf Registrar General v Gill* (1991) 5 BPR 11,587, affd (16 Aug 1994) Unrep (NSW CA) (solicitor's fidelity insurer subrogated to client's rights against negligent land registrar); *Law Society of NSW v Bruce* (19 July 1996) Unrep (NSWSC: Comm Div, Giles CJ) (solicitor's fidelity insurer subrogated to client's rights against negligent investment adviser). And *cf Canada Deposit Insurance Corp v Prisco* (1991) 2 CPC (3d) 10, leave to appeal refused (1992) 13 CBR 68n (directors of failed bank refused strike out order against deposit insurer's claim to be subrogated to depositors' rights to sue directors for negligent misstatement); *Ernst & Young Inc v Cattanach* (29 June 1995) Unrep (Ont Gen Div, Comm List, MacPherson J) (auditors of failed bank refused strike out order against deposit insurer's claim to be subrogated to depositors' rights to sue auditors for negligence: insurer's claim as subrogee "significantly weaker than its claim in its own right" as it could be in no better position than depositors and a "stretch" required to say that auditors owed duty of care to depositors, but "not so great a stretch as to require being struck out as disclosing no cause of action").

29 See the cases discussed in: Annotation (1932) 77 ALR 1057; SI Langmaid, "Some Recent Subrogation Problems in the Law of Suretyship and Insurance" (1934) 47 Harvard LR 976, 980–983; Comment (1942) 137 ALR 700; Comment (1955) Washington & Lee LR 132; Comment (1960) 44 Marquette LR 194; EA Farnsworth, "Insurance Against Cheque Forgery" (1960) Col LR 284, 316–324; Comment (1965) 43 California LR 85; JD O'Malley, "Subrogation Claims Against Banks on Forged Cheques" (1966) 51 Cornell LQ 441; GE Palmer, *The Law of Restitution* (1978), and Cum Supp by M Eisenstein (1997), para 23.9.

Problems of a similar nature have also arisen in the US when fidelity insurers have come into competition with auditors or company directors liable to insureds for negligently failing to detect the fraudulent activities of the insureds' employees. See J Matson, "Subrogation Claims Against Auditors: What is "The Purest Equity"?" (1979) 6 Ohio NULR 313; GJ Schroeder, "Handling the Complex Fidelity or Financial Institution Bond Claim: The Liability of the Insured's Officers and Directors and Their D & O Carrier" (1986) 21 Tort & Ins LJ 269, 277–294; JJ Hlafcsak, "The Nature and Extent of Subrogation Rights of Fidelity Insurers Against Officers and Directors of Financial Institutions" (1986) 47 U of Pittsburgh LR 727; M Eisenstein, *Cumulative Supplement to Palmer's Law of Restitution* (1997), para 23.9(a).

alternative,[30] but it may be inferred that the American courts think that they are, from the fact that they all cut straight to the question whether the "balance of the equities' between bank and insurer are such that one or other of them should bear the burden of the customer's loss. So far as this issue is concerned, the large majority of the American decisions view the bank as having the "superior equity" to the insurer, unless the insurer can show either that the bank was fixed with knowledge of the fraud committed by the customer's employee, or that it was negligent in failing to detect it. The following reasons of policy have been advanced to support of this view:

(i) The customer selects his employees and is in a better position to monitor their activities than the bank. The burden of paying for losses caused by the employees' fraudulent activities should therefore be borne by the customer, and hence by his fidelity insurer.[31] Similar reasoning underpins the rule contained in the UCC s 4-406, that a customer must examine his

[30] But *cf Standard Accident Insurance Co v Pellachia* (1954) 104 A 2d 288, 302 (*per* Vanderbilt CJ): "where a surety's action against the third party is based on his contractual liability to the insured [one possible solution would be] to allow the insured to recover from both the surety and the third party and thus be doubly indemnified – a situation which the law has always deemed to be contrary to public policy not only by reason of its unfairness but because of its incitement to fraud."

[31] *Louisville Trust Co v Royal Indemnity Co* (1929) 20 SW 2d 71, 72 (*per* Clay J): "As between the employer and the bank, there is much to be said in favour of the position that the loss should fall on the employer who selects an unfaithful agent, and thus vouches for his integrity, rather than on a bank whose officers in many instances are called upon daily to examine and keep account of a large number of checks, a duty which, to say the least, operates a severe strain on ordinary care"; *Washington Mechanics' Savings Bank v District Title Insurance Co* (1933) 65 F 2d 827 (1933), 830 (*per* Martin CJ): "The bonding company, being in the business of guaranteeing for a consideration the faithful conduct of employees, enabled the defaulting employee to hold the position of trust which he occupied." See too *American Alliance Insurance Co v Capital National Bank of Sacramento* (1946) 171 P 2d 449, 453 (*per* Thompson J).

This view of the matter has not recommended itself to the English courts: see *eg Kepitigalla Rubber Estates Ltd v National Bank of India Ltd* [1909] 2 KB 1010, 1025 (*per* Bray J): "[The bank's argument] amounts to a contention that its customers impliedly agreed to take precautions in the general course of carrying on their business to prevent forgeries on the part of their servants. . . . If the bank desire that their customers should make these promises they must expressly stipulate that they shall"; *London Joint Stock Bank Ltd v Macmillan* [1918] AC 777, 795 (*per* Lord Finlay): "It would be no defence to the banker, if the forgery had been that of a clerk of a customer, that the latter had taken the clerk into his service without sufficient inquiry as to his character."

The possibility that a customer might be held vicariously liable for its employee's deceit where the cheque was forged in the course of his employment was touched upon in *Tai Hing Cotton Mill Ltd v Liu Chong Hing Bank Ltd* [1986] AC 80. EP Ellinger and E Lomnicka, *Modern Banking Law*, 2nd edn (1994), 371, comment: "It is true that the employee's fraud, in cases of this type, is contrary to the employer's interests. This aspect, however, is irrelevant, as is demonstrated by the rule in *Lloyd v Grace, Smith & Co* [1912] AC 716. The question is whether the type of fraud here considered is perpetrated in the employee's course of employment. Where the employee's function is to prepare cheques for the employer's signature – as is the case where he is engaged as an accountant or a bookkeeper – the answer may be affirmative." For further discussion, see *Clerk & Lindsell on Torts*, 17th edn (1995), 5.38–5.41.

statements of account and cancelled cheques with reasonable care and promptness, and that breach of this duty will absolve a non-negligent bank from liability to the customer (and hence also to his fidelity insurer).[32]

(ii) The insurer has contracted to bear the loss regardless of whether anyone else might also be liable for it. In the absence of fraud or negligence by the bank, the protection afforded by the insurance coverage should therefore be extended by implication to the bank as well as to the customer.[33] Against this it might be said that in the absence of an express contractual term extending coverage to the bank, it should not be given the benefit of insurance which it has not paid for.

(iii) The insurer has been paid premiums to bear the loss. The insurer would therefore receive a windfall if it were able to shift the burden of paying for the insured loss onto another party.[34] This argument depends on the mistaken belief that subrogation recoveries are not taken into consideration when premium rates are set.[35]

(iv) The insurer has been paid premiums to bear the loss, whereas the bank "receives no benefit from the transaction".[36] It is therefore just that the insurer should have to pay. This argument depends on the mistaken view that

[32] *Roy Supply Inc v Wells Fargo Bank NA* (1995) 27 UCC Rep Serv 2d 1363, 1373 (*per* Sparks, Acting PJ): application of this rule in pre-Code decisions "depended upon notions of reasonableness and relative prejudice." Where a bank and a customer have both acted negligently, however, UCC s 4-406(3) stipulates that the bank must bear full responsibility for the loss, and "it is not for the courts to unsettle the UCC's carefully drawn balance by introducing comparative fault principles drawn from tort law": *Putnam Rolling Ladder Co Inc v Manufacturers Hanover Trust Co* (1989) 10 UCC Rep Serv 2d 14, 20 (*per* Kaye J). See too *New Jersey Steel Corp v Warburton* (1996) 26 UCC Rep Serv 2d 14.

English law places a customer under no wider duty than to take care in the way she draws her cheques and to warn her bank as soon as she actually knows that her signature has been forged; and, in the absence of an express contractual provision to that effect, which has been clearly drawn to her attention, she owes no duty to examine her monthly statements with reasonable care: *Tai Hing Cotton Mills Ltd v Liu Chong Hing Bank Ltd* [1986] AC 80. See too *Canadian Pacific Hotels Ltd v Bank of Montreal* (1988) 40 DLR (4th) 385. But for criticism of the English rule, see EP Ellinger and E Lomnicka, *Modern Banking Law*, 2nd edn (1994), 172–173.

[33] *Bank of Fort Mill v Lawyers Title Insurance Corp* (1959) 268 F 2d 313, 315 (*per* Boreman DJ): "It is the general view that a paid surety has fewer equities than an innocent bank, since the surety company is paid to assume the specific risk." See too *American Surety Co v Bank of California* (1943) 133 F 2d 160, 164 (*per* Stephens CJ).

[34] *New York Title and Manufacturing Co v First National Bank* (1931) 51 F 2d 485, 487 (*per* Gardner CJ): "The plaintiff paid the loan companies only what it contracted primarily to do, but now, retaining the premiums or benefit of its contract, it seeks reimbursement from the bank"; *American Surety Co v Bank of California* (1943) 133 F 2d 160, 164 (*per* Stephens CJ): "the surety company accepted the responsibility for such losses for a compensation, the premiums paid to them, which they have retained."

[35] *Standard Accident Insurance Co v Pellachia* (1954) 104 A 2d 288, 303 (*per* Vanderbilt CJ: "the amounts of recoveries by subrogation are taken into consideration in arriving at the amount of premiums to be charged for surety bonds." This statement accords with the results of the author's own research into this matter: C Mitchell, "Defences to an Insurer's Subrogated Action" [1996] LMCLQ 343, 358.

[36] *Louisville Trust Co v Royal Indemnity Co* (1929) 20 SW 2d 71, 72 (*per* Clay J).

the bank has received no consideration from the customer to bear the loss caused by the employee's fraud. Banks do not provide a free service. The transaction and interest charges they make reflect their overheads.[37] These are likely to include premiums payable to their own insurers for protection against such losses.[38]

[37] *Cf Kepitigalla Rubber Estates Ltd v National Bank of India Ltd* [1909] 2 KB 1010, 1025–1026 (*per* Bray J): "The truth is that the number of cases where bankers sustain losses of this kind are infinitesimal in comparison with the large business they do, and the profits of banking are sufficient to compensate them for this very small risk."

[38] *Cf Standard Accident Insurance Co v Pellachia* (1954) 104 A 2d 288, 303 (*per* Vanderbilt CJ: "cases denying subrogation to a surety of its insured's contractual right against a third party are unrealistic in ignoring the fact that the third party itself is generally insured".

3

Undue Influence and Misrepresentation after O'Brien: *Making Security Secure*

JANET O'SULLIVAN*

1. INTRODUCTION

Fashions in legal thought and practice can be as transient as fashions in popular culture. Just as we reflect with incredulity on the clothes and music of previous decades, in the same way it seems inconceivable that, just twelve years ago, a commentator could have described the doctrine of undue influence as an "infrequently invoked judicial discretion to set aside transactions . . ."[1] Since then, the decisions of the House of Lords in *Barclays Bank Plc v O'Brien*[2] and *CIBC Mortgages Plc v Pitt*[3] have popularised the doctrine to such an extent that it is now one of the most frequently pleaded defences in the armoury of defendants, seeking to resist the claims of lenders to repossess their homes or call in their surety obligations.

Yet despite the vast judicial activity in the field of undue influence (and related vitiating factors, such as misrepresentation and unconscionability), many aspects of the doctrine remain controversial and subject to criticism, both judicial and academic. This paper aims to identify and explore a number of these area of criticism, conscious that, whilst restitution scholars enjoy debating the academic challenges of problem areas, bankers face the practical challenges of doing business and drafting standard documentation and lending guidelines in the face of unsettled legal principles. Has *O'Brien* helped to render security secure?

* Fellow of Selwyn College, Cambridge.

[1] D Tiplady, "The Limits of Undue Influence" (1985) 48 MLR 579.
[2] [1994] 1 AC 180 (hereafter "*O'Brien*").
[3] [1994] 1 AC 200 (hereafter "*Pitt*").

2. STRUCTURE

It is perhaps important first of all to step back from details, and to consider the *structure* of the *O'Brien* doctrine and its place in the legal map of restitutionary relief.

Notice

O'Brien established conclusively that in a three party case, where A applies undue influence (or commits another "equitable wrong") to B which causes B to confer a benefit on C, the issue of whether B can seek relief as against the third party, C, is generally dependent on whether C has *notice*, actual or constructive, of the circumstances which tainted the dealings between A and B. Previously, concepts of agency were relied on, most artificially, so that relief was given against third party banks on the basis that A acted as their agent in his dealings with B. Since *O'Brien*, arguments based on agency will only succeed where there is something exceptional to justify a genuine imposition of agency status to A.[4] Indeed, it is difficult to find a case post-*O'Brien* where agency has been successfully pleaded:[5] a welcome simplification and rationalisation of the law.

Commentators soon realised that this is a peculiar use of the concept of notice. Traditionally, notice determined priority between successive rights, so that, for example, an existing equitable interest in land (such as a beneficial interest under a trust, restrictive covenant or equitable charge) or "mere equity" bound a third party purchaser if that purchaser had notice of the existence of the prior right.[6] Lord Browne-Wilkinson used the language of notice of existing rights binding third parties in his speech in *O'Brien*:[7]

> "A wife who has been influenced to stand as a surety for her husband's debts by his undue influence, misrepresentation or some other legal wrong has an equity

[4] "Although there may be cases where, without artificiality, it can properly be held that the husband was acting as the agent of the creditor in procuring the wife to stand surety, such cases will be of very rare occurrence": *O'Brien* [1994] 1 AC 180, 195.

[5] For example, the wife attempted to rely on agency principles in *Bradford and Bingley Building Society v Chandock* (3 Apr 1966) Unrep (CA) (Lexis transcript), but to no avail. As Nourse LJ explained, "... [the Society] requested Mr Chandock to take Mrs Chandock to a solicitor and to have the matter dealt with by him or her in accordance with the instructions contained in the form of consent. It would be quite impossible on facts such as those to say that the agency principle applied. It would not simply be artificial; it would be nonsensical. Mr Chandock's agency, if any, would have determined at the door of the solicitor's office."

[6] Epitomised in cases such as *Hunt v Luck* [1902] 1 Ch 428 and *Kingsnorth Finance Co Ltd v Tizard* [1986] 1 WLR 783.

[7] [1994] 1 AC 180, 195 (italics added).

> *as against him* to set aside that transaction. Under the ordinary principles of equity, *her right* to set aside that transaction *will be enforceable against third parties* (e.g. against a creditor) if either the husband was acting as the third party's agent or the third party had actual or constructive notice of the facts giving rise to her equity."

However, it is clear that, in *O'Brien* cases, there is no *prior* right in existence at the time the third party bank acquires its interest. There is only ever *one* transaction, the formation of which was tainted by the influence or misrepresentation of a non-party.[8]

Likewise, there is traditionally no way of avoiding notice by taking steps to cure the taint of the prior transaction – by definition, it has already crystallised into existence by the time the third party comes along – whereas the *O'Brien* jurisdiction allows a third party, fixed with *prima facie* notice, nonetheless to avoid being tainted by the influence or misrepresentation by taking certain "reasonable steps".[9]

A jurisdiction that borrows terminology from a context in which its technical meaning is extremely well established, applies it in a different context, and then attempts to stretch the factual characteristics of the new context to fit the label's traditional technical meaning, is bound to cause confusion So, for example, commentators fell into the trap of condemning *O'Brien* as unusable where the land mortgaged is registered, as the system of registered title makes no use of the doctrine of notice.[10] Indeed, the doctrine of notice is so well equipped to do its traditional job (of resolving the priority of successive rights) that courts have been unable to resist the temptation to describe a classic *O'Brien* case in terms of two successive transactions.

Moreover, some have recognised the problem, but treated it as casting doubt on the fundamentals of *O'Brien*, rather than as a by-product of borrowing language inappropriately from traditional notice territory.[11] This approach undermines *O'Brien* entirely. For there is virtually never a genuine prior (or even contemporaneous) transaction between, to use the common

[8] See G Battersby, "Equitable Fraud Committed by Third Parties" (1995) 15 LS 35.

[9] Note Lord Browne-Wilkinson's reference to this point in *O'Brien*. He says [1994] 1 AC 180, 196, "It is plainly impossible to require of banks and other financial institutions that they should inquire of one spouse whether he or she has been unduly influenced or misled by the other."

[10] See M Thompson "The Enforceability of Mortgages" [1994] Conv 140. This argument was convincingly refuted by M Dixon and C Harpum, "Fraud, Undue Influence and Mortgages of Registered Land" [1994] Conv 421 (cited with approval recently by the Court of Appeal in *Barclays Bank Plc v Boulter* [1997] 2 All ER 1002, 1010).

[11] For example, Roch LJ in *Banco Exterior Internacional SA v Thomas* [1997] 1 WLR 221, 232: "I would wish to reserve the question whether the principles in *Barclays Bank v O'Brien* can apply where there is no transaction as between the person said to be the subject of the undue influence or misrepresentation and the person said to have applied the undue influence or to have made the misrepresentation for another case."

O'Brien scenario, husband and wife, merely one transaction between wife and bank. Even an artificial attempt to find a prior agreement between husband and wife, in which the wife agrees that she will stand surety or execute a charge, will fail for absence of any intention to create legal relations (and indeed lack of consideration).[12] There was, for example, certainly no meaningful "transaction" between Mr and Mrs O'Brien.

Recognising the problem, some commentators have suggested an alternative approach, based on a strict liability personal restitutionary claim against the bank, subject where appropriate to the change of position defence.[13] Yet, put very crudely, this sort of reconstruction would raise precisely the same questions and issues using different language. For example, no-one would suggest that every surety transaction is potentially vulnerable, so in some sense the invalidating tendency between A and B would still need to be a logically prior requirement to a claim against the bank. And further, unless the claim is to be rendered invariably unsuccessful by ascribing the defence of change of position to every act of lending in reliance on the "receipt" of the guarantee or security, it will be necessary to identify those cases where the bank is a "wrongdoer" and thus unable to plead change of position.[14] No doubt the most useful and meaningful way of isolating such instances is recourse to concepts of "knowledge", actual or constructive. This would achieve no substantive change (other perhaps than the removal of inappropriate searching for prior transactions) and much confusion – the price of the architectural harmony so beloved by restitution scholars.

On balance, there is nothing fundamentally wrong with the *O'Brien* approach, just its terminology; it would simply be clearer and more accurate to abandon the language of two successive transactions, whilst accepting the basic structure of *O'Brien*. It must be difficult for banks to be confident about setting lending guidelines, and making lending decisions, while sentiments such as those of Roch LJ are still being expressed about the structure of the law, some four years after *O'Brien*. For it does seem that, so far as undue influence is concerned, the structure works in a relatively logical way. The factors that put a lender on notice of potential undue influence – the emotional relationship of trust and confidence, the risk of wrongdoing in certain types of transaction and the absence of financial advantage – are factors which

[12] *Cf* Sparkes, "The Proprietary Effect of Undue Influence" [1995] Conv 250.

[13] Similarly, others (notably E O'Dell, "Restitution, Coercion by a Third Party and the Proper Doctrine of Notice" [1997] CLJ 71) have argued for *O'Brien* to be re-interpreted as an example of the defence of *bona fide* purchase, elevated to a general defence for all personal restitutionary claims. However, this seems contrary to authority, which has hitherto confined the defence to property issues and exceptions to the principle of *nemo dat quod non habet*.

[14] See *Lipkin Gorman v Karpnale Ltd* [1991] 2 AC 548.

(even if wrongly described by reference to a prior transaction) point recognisably to a heightened risk of undue influence.

However, the same regime is also used to give relief against third parties in transactions induced not by undue influence but by other vitiating factors, in particular misrepresentation. In this context, the structure of the law is much more problematic, although it should not be overlooked that *O'Brien* itself was a misrepresentation case, in which the wife's alternative plea of undue influence specifically failed.

Misrepresentation

It is notable that English law is relatively expansive in its willingness to undo transactions entered into as a result of material misrepresentations of fact, where the misrepresentation was made by *the other party to the transaction.* So, where A misrepresents a fact and thereby induces B to contract with him, the transaction is *prima facie* voidable at the suit of B, even if A was wholly innocent and even if B had available to him alternative means of verifying the accuracy of B's statement.[15] However, it seems that, where A misrepresents a fact thereby inducing B to contract *with a third party*, English law generally leaves the transaction between B and C secure, leaving B to seek tortious compensation against A (deceit or, in certain circumstances, negligent misstatement under *Hedley Byrne v Heller*[16]). It is rare indeed for the transaction between B and C to be vulnerable, yet this is the effect of the *O'Brien* rules in certain, very specific, misrepresentation cases.

It could certainly be objected at this point that *O'Brien* merely provides a regime for relief against third parties in those rare cases where the third party has notice of the misrepresentation. Just because such instances are rare, it could be argued, does not make it wrong to impose *O'Brien* liability where appropriate.

There are two responses to this argument. First, it is inconsistent with the normal, intensely restrictive, rules on pre-contract disclosure, and the objective test for contractual terms even where one party is mistaken. The law generally permits a transaction to stand where one party is under a mistake, even where the other party to the transaction is well aware of this mistake, as long as that other party remains silent and makes no misrepresentation or warranty himself.[17] Moreover, it is difficult to find authority which draws a dis-

[15] *Redgrave v Hurd* (1881) 20 Ch D 1.

[16] [1964] AC 465.

[17] Exceptions to the absence of a general duty of disclosure include contracts *uberrimae fidei* and certain unilateral mistake cases where the normal objective principle of contract formation is ousted, as where one party knows that the other is mistaken as to the *terms* of the contract but

tinction between these sorts of uninduced misapprehensions and misapprehensions induced by the misrepresentation of a non-party, and equally difficult to justify any such distinction. For example, if A is selling B his house, and knows or suspects that B believes it to be in good condition when in fact it is subsiding, it should not matter to the susceptibility of the A-B contract whether B's mistake arose spontaneously or was engendered by the misrepresentation of a non-party, C.[18]

Why, then, should a *banking* transaction between, for example, wife and bank, be vulnerable where it was induced by the misrepresentation of the husband? Actual notice of a misrepresentation does not normally oust a contracting party's right to stay silent and uphold the transaction; *a fortiori* mere constructive notice, which appears never to have such an effect in other contexts.

Secondly, even if it is accepted (which seems unlikely) that the risk of misrepresentation is greater in the run up to a surety transaction than in the negotiations preceding any other contract, thereby justifying the imposition of wider relief, it still seems that the *O'Brien* rules on constructive notice are singularly inappropriate to cover cases of misrepresentation. An emotional relationship of trust and confidence, plus disadvantageous terms, hints at a risk of undue influence but surely not of misrepresentation. The law seems to be endorsing greatly enhanced relief whenever misrepresentations are made *in situations where one might have expected to find undue influence*, when there is no good reason why rescission and other equitable relief should be more widely available than normal in such cases.

It is difficult to construct a reasoned or convincing case for allowing rescission of transactions induced by the misrepresentation of a non-party, whether or not the *O'Brien* constructive notice factors are present, since they bear no relation to the risk of misrepresentation by a non-party. Although it might be considered improper to allow a bank to enforce a mortgage or guarantee which was induced by misrepresentation, we should think twice about whether this distaste should be allowed to create an exception to the usual principles of non-disclosure, merely in the interests of structural symmetry with other forms of vitiating factors.[19]

does not correct him (*Smith v Hughes* (1871) LR 6 QB 597). Equitable remedies, such as rectification or (more controversially) rescission, may be available in cases of unilateral mistake, where the non-mistaken party has *actual knowledge* of the mistake (see *Riverlate Properties v Paul* [1975] Ch 133, and *The Nai Genova* [1984] 1 Lloyd's Rep 353), but even this is arguably subject to the requirement that the mistake must be susceptible to relief under *Smith v Hughes*: see Sir G Treitel, *The Law if Contract*, 9th ed (1995), 296.

[18] This point was the subject of much debate at the conference at which this paper was first presented. It is, of course, virtually impossible to demonstrate that there is *no* authority on a particular point!

[19] That is not to say that the law should not impose greater duties of disclosure on creditors in surety transactions, but that is a different issue.

Interestingly, Lord Jauncey of Tullichettle expressed precisely this unease in the recent Scots appeal to the House of Lords in *Smith v Bank of Scotland*,[20] observing:

> ". . . while I can follow the policy reasons for clothing a creditor with constructive knowledge of the risk of undue influence by a husband in the special circumstances of a cautionary obligation. I have the greatest difficulty in seeing why such constructive notice should extend to misrepresentation. There has so far as I am aware never been any suggestion in the law of Scotland that any particular class of persons is more likely to misrepresent in relation to a contract than any other class."

Unfortunately, Lord Jauncey was unable to convince his brethren of this fundamental flaw in the *O'Brien* reasoning and the law of Scotland was duly changed to incorporate *O'Brien* constructive notice of misrepresentation. With respect, English law should instead consider adopting Scotland's former approach to this question.

Having explored some of the structural elements of the *O'Brien* claim, it is now appropriate to look at some of the detailed elements of the regime that have been subjected to criticism or have proved problematic.

3. MANIFEST DISADVANTAGE

In order to raise a presumption of undue influence (although not in cases of actual undue influence), the plaintiff must prove, in addition to the appropriate relationship with the alleged perpetrator of the influence,[21] that the transaction which resulted was "manifestly disadvantageous" to the plaintiff (*National Westminster Bank Plc v Morgan*).[22] Of course, in three-party cases, the facts must support the raising of the presumption as if there were a transaction as between surety and debtor, logically prior to the question of the third party creditor's position, and so manifest disadvantage is no less relevant in *O'Brien* cases than in straightforward two-party cases.[23]

The manifest disadvantage requirement appeared vulnerable after *Pitt*, in which Lord Browne-Wilkinson doubted whether it was consistent with the treatment of fiduciaries who deal with their principals. He said:[24]

[20] 1997 SCLR 765, 769. I am most grateful to Professor Gareth Jones for an early photocopy of the transcript of this case.

[21] Detailed in *Bank of Credit and Commerce International SA v Aboody* [1990] 1 QB 923.

[22] [1985] AC 686.

[23] See *eg Cheese v Thomas* [1994] 1 WLR 129.

[24] [1994] 1 AC 200, 209. See also JRF Lehane, "Undue Influence, Misrepresentation and Third Parties" [1994] 110 LQR 167, 173, and Tiplady (1985) 48 MLR 579.

"I should add that the exact limits of the decision in *Morgan* may have to be considered in the future. The difficulty is to establish the relationship between the law as laid down in *Morgan* and the long standing principle laid down in the abuse of confidence cases: *viz* the law requires those in a fiduciary position who enter into transactions with those to whom they owe fiduciary duties to establish affirmatively that the transaction was a fair one. . . . Unfortunately the attention of this House in *Morgan* was not drawn to the abuse of confidence cases and therefore the interaction between the two principles (if indeed they are two separate principles) remains obscure . . ."

Yet, since *Pitt,* "manifest disadvantage" as a requirement for raising the presumption of undue influence has escaped challenge, perhaps because, in three-party cases, it is essentially reproduced at a later stage, namely as part of the enquiry into the question of whether the third party creditor has constructive notice of the possibility of undue influence having been used to obtain the wife's participation in the transaction. As Lord Browne-Wilkinson explained in *O'Brien*:[25]

". . . a creditor is put on inquiry when a wife offers to stand surety for her husband's debts by a combination of two factors: (a) the transaction is on its face not to the financial advantage of the wife; and (b) there is a substantial risk in transactions of that kind that, in procuring the wife to act as a surety, the husband has committed a legal or equitable wrong that entitles the wife to set aside the transaction."

It was, of course, the absence of any such financial disadvantage on the "face of the transaction" in *Pitt* that proved fatal to Mrs Pitt's claim for relief.[26]

It seems likely that, since the disadvantageous nature of the transaction must in any event be proved to succeed against a third party creditor, there has been no practical impetus for legal advisers to take Lord Browne-Wilkinson's point and seek to remove the manifest disadvantage hurdle from the (logically prior) stage of raising the presumption of undue influence.[27]

So what should be the result, if Lord Browne-Wilkinson's suggested reconsideration of the limits of *National Westminster Bank v Morgan* ever takes place?

[25] [1994] 1 AC 180, 196.

[26] The same applied in *Halifax Mortgage Services Ltd v Stepsky* [1996] Ch 207 and in *Britannia Building Society v Pugh* (10 Jul 1996) Unrep (CA) (Lexis transcript), in which all the documentation described the borrowers as "Mr and Mrs Pugh, trading as property developers", thereby giving no indication to the bank that the business was in fact the husband's own.

[27] Interestingly, Leolin Price QC expressly reserved this point recently in *Dunbar Bank Plc v Nadeem* [1997] 2 All ER 253. The judge observed that, "Mr Price for Mrs Nadeem accepted that as the law currently stands there is a requirement to show manifest disadvantage in class 2 cases, although he did ask me to note that he wished to reserve the point for the future in the light of Lord Browne-Wilkinson's observations in *Pitt*'s case" (264f).

Many commentators have argued that the requirement of manifest disadvantage should be abandoned, or, at the very least, that the burden of proof be reversed, so that the presumption arises from the relationship alone but can be rebutted by proof that the transaction was fair. These arguments are based both on Lord Browne-Wilkinson's observations about fiduciary cases and by reference to the desirability of symmetry between undue influence and other "vitiating" or "unjust" factors. So, the argument runs, there is no requirement of manifest disadvantage to establish other analogous grounds for relief or restitution, such as mistake, misrepresentation or duress, thus undue influence should be brought into line, since at a high level of generalisation all give relief because of the plaintiff's vitiated consent.[28]

These arguments are unconvincing, for two principal reasons. First, they are an example of greater generalisation of classifications obscuring important differences between related categories. In particular, the unique feature of undue influence is the presence of a category of *presumed* undue influence. There are no equivalent categories of presumed mistake, presumed misrepresentation or presumed duress, and the plaintiff must always prove the precise facts on which his claim is based. Moreover, it is entirely appropriate to single out relational undue influence as worthy of such a presumption: it has always seemed to me that the concept of "overborne will", so troublesome and inappropriate in the field of economic duress, is much more meaningful in undue influence cases. If one asked the duress victim, are you doing what you want to do, he would say, through gritted teeth, "No I am not, but I have no realistic choice." He recognises the fact of his own lack of practical volition. The relational undue influence victim, on the other hand, would smilingly assert that he was acting perfectly voluntarily. It is this risk of self-denial that makes the influence from close relationships so potentially harmful and dangerous, demanding a prophylactic regime to isolate and scrutinise risky cases *without* requiring the plaintiff to prove affirmatively that actual influence operated.

Secondly, once the wisdom of the category of *presumed* undue influence is accepted, more is surely needed in order to raise the presumption, reversing the normal burden of proof, than just a relationship between the parties. To require defendants to prove fairness / disprove unfairness would be more than evidentially difficult. It would shed a vital protection for defendants – it is the disadvantageous or unusual nature of the transaction which should "set alarm bells ringing" and prompt the defendant to suggest independent advice

[28] See M Oldham, "Neither a Borrower nor a Lender be: The Life of *O'Brien*" [1995] 7 CFLQ 104, 109, and Birks and Chin, "On the Nature of Undue Influence": ch 3 of Beatson and Friedmann (eds), *Good Faith and Fault in Contract Law* (Clarendon Press, Oxford, 1995).

or other methods of satisfying himself, and subsequently a court, that the plaintiff's involvement in the transaction was free and informed.

Moreover, it is perhaps here that a basis for distinguishing the "abuse of confidence" cases referred to in *Pitt* is found. Despite the instrumental labelling of all persons against whom the presumption of undue influence arises as "fiduciaries",[29] it is clear that the label is rarely appropriate, other than in cases involving, for example, undue influence (actual or presumed) between solicitors and clients where fiduciary status is accorded irrespective of the circumstances of the particular transaction attacked for undue influence. So genuine fiduciaries know, or should know, of the high level of conduct and propriety expected of them throughout, and it is not merely the content of the transaction itself which should alert them to the need look to the other party's interests. There is thus less concern at expecting such genuine fiduciaries to prove the fairness of a given transaction – in a sense, something else sets off the alarm bells.

So where does this leave the requirement of manifest disadvantage (and the related, but logically subsequent, requirement for constructive notice in three-party cases of financial disadvantage on the face of the transaction)? Assuming that the arguments for the retention of manifest disadvantage as a requirement for raising the presumption of undue influence prevail, how has the concept has been interpreted and applied by the courts since *O'Brien*?

The phrase "manifest disadvantage" was adopted by the House of Lords in *Morgan*, as previously the requirement had tended to be described slightly differently. Lindley LJ's definition in *Allcard v Skinner*[30] was"a gift so large as not to be reasonably accounted for on the ground of friendship, relationship, charity or other ordinary motives on which ordinary men act . . ." and this was expressly adopted in numerous subsequent authorities, including *Re Craig*[31] and *Goldsworthy v Brickell*.[32]

It might be thought that Lord Scarman's abbreviation of this concept into "manifest disadvantage" might have led to the loss of some of the concept's meaning and subtlety. However, subsequent courts have provided useful guidance on the meaning of the phrase. For example, Slade LJ in *BCCI v Aboody*[33] explained that

[29] Seen recently in *Mahoney v Purnell* [1996] 3 All ER 61; [1997] 1 FLR 612, where a disadvantageous transaction between an elderly man and his son-in-law, attracting the presumption of undue influence, was described as a "breach of fiduciary duty".

[30] (1887) 36 Ch D 145.

[31] [1971] Ch 95.

[32] [1987] 1 Ch 378.

[33] [1990] 1 QB 923, 964.

> "... a disadvantage would be a manifest disadvantage if it would have been obvious as such to any independent and reasonable persons who considered the transaction at the time with knowledge of all relevant facts."

It is clear then that the objective nature of the original test, judged by reference to the "reasonable" behaviour of "ordinary men", is retained in the more abbreviated "manifest disadvantage" concept. Likewise, the stark word "manifest" might suggest that the flexibility found in the original formulation's reference to gifts and transactions not "reasonably to be accounted for on ordinary motives" has been shed in the modern law. However, this has not proved to be the case. Once again, Slade LJ suggested a workable and sensible definition, namely that

> "... the overall disadvantageous nature of a transaction cannot be said to be manifest, if it only emerges after a fine and close evaluation of its various beneficial and detrimental features. It must be obvious."[34]

Thus, fears that the modern formulation is too inflexible to be applied sensibly to, for example, gifts (are all gifts manifestly disadvantageous or is the size of the donor's estate relevant?) or sales at an undervalue (how manifest is manifest?) are seen to be unfounded, once the extended definition is considered.

Moreover, it seems that the courts are applying this requirement sensitively to plaintiffs and without requiring unduly strict levels of disadvantage. Of course, in some transactions the disadvantage is clearly manifest, such as the extraordinary arrangement in *Credit Lyonnais Bank Nederland NV v Burch*,[35] in which a junior employee charged her modest flat to secure to an unlimited extent all indebtedness, present and future, of her employer's company. Yet the courts also have no difficulty applying the label in less obvious cases, like straightforward surety transactions, where a wife guarantees, or provides security for, the business debts of her husband, even though it might be argued that there can be nothing *manifest* about the disadvantage that flows from such transactions. Indeed, the cases establish very clearly that the courts do look in detail at all the facts of the transaction and circumstances surrounding it, and have not been tempted to require a "screamingly obvious" *Burch* level of disadvantage. Two examples illustrate this tendency.

In *Mahoney v Purnell*,[36] the elderly plaintiff ran a hotel business with his son-in-law. Each held 50% of the shares. The son-in-law suggested that he should buy out the plaintiff's shares and an agreement was executed in March

[34] [1990] 1 QB 964.
[35] [1996] 5 Bank LR 233.
[36] [1996] 3 All ER 61; [1997] 1 FLR 612.

1988 whereby the plaintiff was to receive £200,000 for them, payable over ten years in interest-free instalments. A year later, the son-in-law sold the hotel for £3.27m, whereupon the plaintiff sought rescission of the agreement and/or equitable compensation, alleging presumed undue influence.

The dramatic difference between the sale price of the shares and that of the hotel was not as significant as it appears. The crucial aspect was the proper valuation of the plaintiff's shareholding in March 1988, and the related terms and circumstances of the deal. The judge considered detailed expert evidence of valuation, concluding that the true value of the plaintiff's shares at the relevant date was £267,131. In addition, the purchase price was supposed to include the accelerated repayment of a loan to the plaintiff from the company of £136,618, making a total of £403,749 compared with the price of £200,000. The judge also considered, on the plus side, the plaintiff's release from the company's extensive liabilities and the expedited repayment of his loan, but determined on balance that the transaction was manifestly disadvantageous to the plaintiff. His conclusion was reinforced by the haphazard way the purchase price was determined, without any independent valuation of the plaintiff's shares or the hotel, and the fact that the scheme provided the plaintiff with no security, beyond his son-in-law's personal guarantee, and deprived him of a stake in and control of the business. This level of disadvantage, combined with the relationship of trust and confidence between the parties, raised a presumption of undue influence, which was not rebutted.

The judge was clearly unwilling to take the scheme at face value and felt that Slade LJ's reference to "obvious" disadvantage did not preclude a detailed analysis:[37]

> "Although these reasons are detailed and require an understanding of the details of the scheme, I emphasise that the conclusion of manifest disadvantage is, in my view, obvious once the details are understood. This is not in essence 'a fine and close evaluation' of the various beneficial and detrimental features of the scheme such as would point to a conclusion that any balance of disadvantage was not clear."

A similar level of detailed scrutiny and flexibility was seen recently in *Bank of Scotland v Bennett*,[38] in which a husband gave up a secure job to invest in frozen fish business in south-west Scotland. The wife executed a guarantee and charge over the matrimonial home in favour of the bank, to secure the indebtedness of the fish company. The problem with a straightforward finding of manifest disadvantage was that the wife was also a shareholder in, and

[37] [1996] 3 All ER 61, 84; [1997] 1 FLR 612, 635.
[38] [1997] 1 FLR 801.

officer of, the company, with a shareholding of 11.8%. Could it be said, therefore, that the disadvantage to her was sufficiently obvious?

The judge held that it was, despite her shareholding in the borrowing company. A number of factors persuaded him that a purely formalistic, mathematical approach was inappropriate, including the highly speculative nature of the business, the husband's total lack of experience and the fact that other banks had initially turned the project down on numerous sensible commercial grounds. Moreover, her involvement in the company was entirely artificial – she received no dividends and no salary and took no part in management.

This kind of detailed analysis is, with respect, most welcome and in accordance with the extended definition of manifest disadvantage. The reality of *Bennett* is that the transaction was substantially disadvantageous from Mrs Bennett's point of view – Slade LJ's "independent and reasonable" observer with "knowledge of all relevant facts" would clearly regard her formal position in the company as irrelevant, when compared with the effect of the transaction on her – losing the family's secure source of income and risking their home and security on a peculiarly doomed business venture.

It is also significant that the courts are, generally, taking seriously the need to judge manifest disadvantage as at the time of the transaction and not with the benefit of hindsight. As Slade LJ said in *Aboody*, the disadvantageous nature of the transaction "has to be judged in the circumstances subsisting at the date of the transaction", and this must be appropriate if my rationalisation of the requirement as the defendant's "alarm bells" is the correct one. In one sense, of course, a certain amount of hindsight is built into the enquiry, in that the plea of undue influence is unlikely to be raised unless the transaction proves unsuccessful and, for example, the security or guarantee is enforced (or where, as in *Mahoney*, the relevant asset is subsequently sold at an inflated price on a "frothy market"), but nonetheless the evidence of the case law is that the courts do determine disadvantage at the time of the transaction.[39]

So it seems that the courts have not allowed this requirement to work unduly to the detriment of plaintiffs and in many cases creditors have declined even to argue the point, preferring instead to attack the distinct issue

[39] Occasionally, hindsight has been allowed to creep into the manifest disadvantage reasoning. In *Midland Bank v Greene* [1994] 2 FLR 827, the judge was prepared to decide that a joint mortgage, executed partly to secure the purchase of the matrimonial home, partly to secure the husband's personal indebtedness to the bank, was nonetheless manifestly disadvantageous to the wife, on the basis that "the amount of money that has *in fact turned out to be* secured by the charge, so far at least as Mr Greene is concerned . . . has far outrun the sums that were involved in [the purchase]" (*ibid*, 834; italics added). Yet hindsight here seems unnecessary, since Mrs Greene's assumption of joint liability for all her husband's debts could easily have been regarded as disadvantageous at the time of the transaction, when contrasted with the normal terms of joint borrowing for the purchase of residential property.

of whether the transaction was, on its face, to the financial disadvantage of the surety, necessary for fixing them with constructive notice. Clearly, banks are more likely to succeed if the nature of the transaction is judged at "face" value, as it appeared to them, rather than by reference to all the circumstances prevailing at the time. The courts generally keep the two requirements separate, although the same facts are frequently relevant at both stages.

When considering the "face" of the transaction, some cases fall clearly one side of line, as where the surety derives very little benefit from the transaction (like *Burch,* in which the only conceivable advantage for Miss Burch was to reduce the risk that she would lose her job). Others are obviously the other side of the line, particularly cases like *Pitt* or *Pugh* where there is nothing to reveal to the bank that the transaction is anything other than a joint loan for the joint benefit of both borrowers.

The principal issue in this context has been the appropriate way to treat family cases, where the surety wife has an interest in the success of the debtor husband's business, either a direct interest (*eg* a shareholding in the company) or merely an indirect interest in its success for her livelihood.

Once again, the cases reveal a flexible yet workable approach to this issue. It was established after *O'Brien* that a surety's indirect financial interest in the transaction, however clear this was on its "face", is not sufficient to prevent constructive notice. So for example, the judge in *Goode Durrant Administration v Biddulph*[40] observed that Mrs Biddulph:

> ". . . was dependent upon her husband, his prosperity might well contribute to hers and there is little doubt that his present impoverishment has contributed to her equally being impoverished. To that extent she had, without doubt an indirect interest in the success of the venture . . . But the question in my judgment is not whether or not she had an indirect interest in her husband's prosperity or in the prosperity of the company . . . If that were the question then the finding of constructive notice in the *O'Brien* case would not have been appropriate."

Even where the surety has a *direct* interest in the borrowing company, the courts are willing to examine the totality of facts as they appeared to the creditor. So in *Biddulph* itself, Mrs Biddulph's 2.5% shareholding did not allow the creditor to escape constructive notice, as the bank should nonetheless have noticed the discrepancy between the extensive personal liability being undertaken by Mrs Biddulph for the entirety of the company's indebtedness and the small stake she had in the company. The same approach was used in *Bennett*, in which the judge eschewed a strictly mathematical assessment of the wife's share and asked instead whether her direct financial interest was

[40] [1994] 2 FLR 551, 555.

"out of all proportion" to the liability she was being asked to assume. This is both flexible and workable for banks, as long as the courts continue to take into account only matters apparent to the bank at the date of the transaction.

Subject to this avoidance of hindsight, there seems no good reason to construe the "face" of the transaction narrowly, to cover for example just the loan application and other bank documentation, and the courts have indeed shown themselves to be willing to consider all other information known to the bank. So in *Dunbar Bank v Nadeem*[41] the loan was ostensibly used for securing the joint purchase of a new leasehold interest in the matrimonial home. However, it was in reality proposed and intended as short term security for Mr Nadeem's business debts, which were also secured by the charge and, as the bank knew, amounted at the date of the transaction to approximately 20% of the loan. As the judge observed, ". . . merely because a lending institution makes a joint loan it does not follow that constructive notice of any undue influence is excluded . . . It is a question to be decided on the precise facts of each individual case . . ."[42]

All in all, it seems that the courts have devised a detailed and usable approach to issues of manifest disadvantage and constructive notice. Far from being a legal "problem area",

it is treated as a question of fact, to which a consistent and balanced set of rules is applied. It is to be hoped that the House of Lords resists the temptation to take up Lord Browne-Wilkinson's suggestion of re-thinking this aspect of the doctrine.

However, the same cannot be said of the next issue for consideration, that of the "reasonable steps" a bank must take to avoid being fixed with constructive notice. For here, the law since *O'Brien* has developed in a way that is neither flexible for sureties nor particularly workable for banks.

4. REASONABLE STEPS

Lord Browne-Wilkinson in *O'Brien* made it clear that banks can avoid being fixed with constructive notice of wrongdoing by taking certain "reasonable steps", suggesting the following procedure:[43]

> ". . . in my judgment the creditor, in order to avoid being fixed with constructive notice, can reasonably be expected to take steps to bring home to the wife the risk she is running by standing surety and to advise her to take independent advice.

[41] [1997] 2 All ER 253.

[42] *Ibid*, 270.

[43] [1994] 1 AC 180, 196. Where, exceptionally, the bank knows that the risk of wrongdoing is probable not possible, it must *insist* that the wife is independently advised.

> As to past transactions, it will depend on the facts of each case whether the steps taken by the creditor satisfy this test. However for the future in my judgment a creditor will have satisfied these requirements if it insists that the wife attend a private meeting (in the absence of the husband) with a representative of the creditor at which she is told of the extent of her liability as surety, warned of the risk she is running and urged to take independent legal advice."

However, it rapidly became clear after *O'Brien* that a private meeting between bank and wife was not a popular option for banks seeking to avoid constructive notice.[44] Cases reaching the courts after the judgment in *O'Brien,* but whose facts arose before it, virtually always involved banks which had sent the wife away for some form of legal advice elsewhere, either as a suggestion or as a condition of their entering into the transaction. Post-*O'Brien*, banks have adopted the same approach – the argument being, presumably that, if Lord Browne-Wilkinson was happy for the bank merely to advise the wife to take independent advice, there could be no doubt that going further and *requiring* independent advice would count as reasonable steps.

With hindsight, Lord Browne Wilkinson's suggested regime looks a little unrealistic. In the modern banking world of centralised lenders and computerised transactions, it is not surprising that banks have preferred to make transactions conditional on receipt of confirmation that independent advice has been given, rather than assuming the responsibility of holding a private interview with the wife. Many lenders operate without physical premises, whilst those that have branch offices prefer to divest themselves of the responsibility of seeing the wife, with its attendant risk of adding to her misapprehensions and assuming direct liability towards her.

For this reason, the case law since *O'Brien* on the issue of reasonable steps has tended to focus on the bank's position when some external advice has been given to the surety, with the surety attempting to raise issues of inadequacies in that advice and to argue that such inadequacies prevent the bank's reliance on it from counting as reasonable steps. It is notable that, with rare exceptions, sureties have failed in these attempts, and that the courts have consistently allowed banks to assume that external advice is given properly and to rely on it.

So it is now clear that a bank can rely on the appearance and confirmation of independent advice from a solicitor, even if the husband attends the wife's interview with the solicitor,[45] or if the wife is advised by the solicitor acting also for her husband or the borrowing company,[46] or even if she is sent for

[44] *Midland Bank Plc v Kidwai* [1995] 4 Bank LR 303 was a rare exception, where the bank followed Lord Browne-Wilkinson's regime precisely.

[45] *Massey v Midland Bank Plc* [1995] 1 All ER 929.

[46] *Banco Exterior Internacional v Mann* [1995] 1 All ER 936; *Midland Bank Plc v Serter* [1995] 1 FLR 1034.

advice to the same solicitor acting for both the bank and the husband in the transaction (*Barclays Bank Plc v Thompson*).[47] Moreover, where a solicitor certifies that he has given the wife independent advice, in the form required by the bank, the bank is free to rely on that certification and to assume that the solicitor gave proper advice.[48] It has no duty to enquire into the nature of that advice – deficiencies are a matter between the wife and her solicitor.

This is the case, even where the *bank's* own solicitor gave the advice to the wife. The courts have avoided any suggestion that matters disclosed to the solicitor (*Halifax Mortgage Services Ltd v Stepsky*)[49] or deficiencies in the advice[50] will be imputed to the bank, via its agent the solicitor.

In fact, *Thompson* appears to have gone a good deal further than *Stepsky*. In *Stepsky*, the bank avoided imputed notice (of the true purpose of the loan) because the information came to the knowledge of the solicitor acting for the husband and wife at least a week before the bank instructed him – it was therefore meaningful to rely on section 199 of the Law of Property Act 1925, which provides that matters are only imputed to the principal if they come to the knowledge of the agent whilst acting "as such". In *Thompson*, the court declined to impute to the bank the solicitor's knowledge of deficiencies in the advice he gave the wife, even though he was at all material times also acting for the bank and, indeed, had been instructed by the bank to advise the wife. Simon Brown LJ held that *Stepsky* was not authority for holding that a solicitor who is instructed by a bank to give independent advice to a third party remains the agent of the bank while doing so. His judgment essentially proceeds on the assumption that a solicitor acting for all parties in a transaction can switch out of independent representation of one client and into independent representation of another, depending on the precise piece of work being conducted at the time. As he explained, "knowledge acquired by solicitors whilst tendering independent advice to a signatory does not come to them as agents for the lenders. At that time their professional duty is owed to the signatory alone."[51]

All in all, the courts allow banks to rely utterly on confirmation from any solicitor that he has advised the wife – this will almost inevitably count as "reasonable steps". Indeed, where the bank knows from the beginning of the transaction that the husband and wife are being advised throughout by a solicitor, it seems that no further steps, reasonable or otherwise, are needed.[52]

[47] [1997] 1 FLR 156.
[48] *Bank of Baroda v Shah* [1988] 3 All ER 24, relied on in numerous subsequent cases.
[49] [1996] Ch 207.
[50] *Barclays Bank Plc v Thompson* [1997] 1 FLR 156.
[51] *Ibid*, 166.
[52] See *Bank of Baroda v Rayerel* [1995] 4 Bank LR 333, 338, in which Hoffmann LJ said ". . . in a case in which the bank is dealing with the surety through her solicitor, it is not ordinarily required to take any special steps at all."

A few isolated cases have departed from this standard line, although all can be said to depend on peculiarities in the facts of the case. So for example in *Bank Melli Iran v Samedi-Rad*,[53] the bank did not insist on confirmation of independent advice before lending but were instead content to require a letter confirming that such advice had been given, within seven days after the date of completion. As Morritt LJ observed:[54]

> ". . . I should be most reluctant to conclude that a lender might rely alone on the undertaking of a solicitor that the surety would be separately advised by an unidentified solicitor, when there is no apparent difficulty in requiring and being given at the time of completion a specific assurance or warranty that she has been advised by a named solicitor, for it is a commonplace experience that 'there's many a slip twixt cup and lip'. . . ."

Credit Lyonnais Bank Nederland BV v Burch provided another opportunity for departure from the orthodoxy on reasonable steps. In fact, constructive notice was sealed for the bank because it merely urged Miss Burch to take independent advice by letter, but her reply declining this suggestion should have aroused, rather than allayed, its suspicions about the presence of wrong-doing. However, in an *obiter* passage,[55] Millett LJ went further and suggested (without citing any of the authority referred to above) that the bank would still have been fixed with constructive notice even if it had insisted that Miss Burch be independently advised, because it should have realised that, on the case's extraordinary facts, "no competent solicitor could advise her to enter into a guarantee in the terms she did." In other words, *normally* a third party creditor can assume that the solicitor has discharged his duty, but he "can not make any such assumption if he knows or ought to know that it is false".

The law on "reasonable steps" has thus reached a relatively stable position, but is that position the correct one? It is undoubtedly appropriate that a bank need not scrutinise the advice given to a surety by a truly independent solicitor and ought to be able to rely on confirmation that it has been properly given. Equally, there is no doubt that a bank ought to be able to assume that any solicitor is competent and honest. It is submitted that Millett LJ's dicta in *Burch* go too far in suggesting that, even where a bank receives confirmation from a genuinely independent solicitor that he has advised the surety, there will nonetheless be instances where it may not rely on it, essentially because the bank must realise that no competent solicitor could have advised the surety to proceed. The essence of advice, however vehement, informed

53 [1995] 2 FLR 367.
54 *Ibid*, 375.
55 [1997] 1 All ER 144, 157; [1996] 5 Bank LR 233, 239–240.

and independent, is that it can be ignored by the recipient.[56] Otherwise an "outlaw" class of onerous transactions is created, essentially prohibited by the law, in that no reasonable steps could ever free the bank from notice of presumed wrongdoing.

Nonetheless, it does seem that the current position is unnecessarily favourable to banks and, equally, that it fails to provide equivalent protection for sureties to the regime suggested by Lord Browne-Wilkinson.

In the first place, the concept of *independent* advice in this context has been stripped of all meaning. The Court of Appeal in *Thomson* recently described the advice given to the wife by the solicitor acting also for the bank *and* her husband as "independent", and treated it as satisfying the reasonable steps requirement. Yet advice given to the wife by an adviser acting also for other parties to the transaction carries such an obvious risk that the wife's position will be a very low priority in the context of the transaction as a whole, that it can not be regarded in any meaningful sense as independent. This is recognised in the Solicitors' Professional Conduct Rules, which prevent solicitors acting for more than one party to a transaction where there is any risk of a conflict of interest. Equally, this reality is recognised where legal advice is relied on at the prior stage of rebutting the presumption of undue influence – here it is absolutely clear that the adviser must be genuinely independent and free of any obligation to the influencing party.[57]

There is of course a difference between the role of legal advice in a two-party case, where it is used to demonstrate that the plaintiff entered the transaction with free and informed consent, and its role where a bank insists on confirmation that advice has taken place to avoid constructive notice – here the emphasis is on the "whitewashing" of the bank rather than the removal of the influence. However, if the reasonable steps are not supposed to minimise the risk of undue influence, the law may as well require banks, for example, to make a donation to charity to avoid the taint of constructive notice! Surely, it is time to think again if a regime has been institutionalised as "reasonable" which provides no real guard against undue influence.

Hobhouse LJ recognised this inadequacy in his powerful dissenting judgment in *Banco Exterior v Mann*.[58] Here, the bank required that a solicitor should explain the nature of the charge being explained to the wife and should certify that he had done so. This advice and certification was given by the same solicitor who acted for the husband's company, at a meeting attended by both husband and wife. The majority of the Court of Appeal held that the

[56] See further R Hooley and J O'Sullivan, "Undue Influence and Unconscionable Bargains" [1997] LMCLQ 17.

[57] See *eg Re Coomber* [1911] 1 Ch 723, and *Powell v Powell* [1990] 1 Ch 243.

[58] [1995] 1 All ER 936.

bank was entitled to rely on the solicitor's certification, inevitably citing *Bank of Baroda v Shah*. Hobhouse LJ disagreed, stressing that the steps taken by the bank provided none of the protection for the wife that Lord Browne-Wilkinson's suggested regime envisaged. As he explained, "this approach left open precisely the possibility that materialised. The wife might never receive independent advice."[59]

The gist of Hobhouse LJ's criticism is that *true* independence is necessary if the wife is to be *advised,* rather than merely receive an explanation of the details of the transaction. He said:[60]

> "I do not accept that the requirement that the wife should be separately advised does not visualise that in some circumstances she may be advised not to sign a document. In practical terms, it may be necessary for the independent adviser to say to the wife:
>
> I know that you feel that you have no option but to sign, but you are wrong. You do have a choice and I must advise you that it is not in your interest to sign this document. You should feel under no obligation to do so. You are asking my advice. My advice to you is: Do not sign."

With the best will in the world, it is inconceivable that a solicitor acting also for the bank and/or the borrower will feel able to give such advice. To suggest otherwise would be to countenance the efficacy of a "Chinese Wall" dividing a firm, or even an individual solicitor, where this is regarded as entirely unworkable in every other area of the law.[61]

All in all, the law needs to recognise this reality and remove the institutionalised acceptance of non-independent advice from the reasonable steps regime. So *prima facie* banks should only be entitled to rely on a certification of independent advice if it is given by a solicitor who is not acting for any of the other parties to the transaction. Of course, what we are dealing with here is the avoidance of constructive notice and thus the bank's perception must be critical. Where a solicitor falsely states that he is acting only for the wife, this should not of course taint the bank. However, a bank should generally require certification of genuine independence and should be expected to take the minimal step of comparing the identity of the solicitor acting for the borrower with that of the certifying adviser. *A fortiori* where the bank's own adviser makes the certification.

59 *Ibid*, 948d.

60 *Ibid*, 948g.

61 See *In re a Firm of Solicitors* [1992] QB 959, 971, where Parker LJ observed, ". . . save in a very special case, I doubt very much whether an impregnable wall can *ever* be created and I consider that it is only in very special cases that any attempt should be made to do so."

This appears to be the position in Australia, with no obvious detrimental effect on commerce, or on the use of family sureties or the matrimonial home as security.[62] Inevitably, there will be a small increased cost in requiring the involvement of a fresh adviser, but this is surely outweighed by the likelihood that, very occasionally, a real risk of undue influence may be avoided and litigation prevented.[63]

One other aspect of the current "reasonable steps" regime falls well short of the protection envisaged by Lord Browne-Wilkinson. His suggested regime involved the bank telling the wife "the amount of her potential liability" as surety.[64] This provision of information is lost completely in most of the solicitor's certification cases, where the solicitor advising the wife has only this peripheral involvement in the transaction and is given no information by the bank. The law, however, is clear – the bank need not disclose standard information about the transaction for the provision of external advice to count as "reasonable steps", including for example the current state of the borrower's indebtedness[65] or the existence of prior security.[66]

This is frequently supported by the fact that the bank has a very limited duty of disclosure to sureties, that it risks breaching its duty of confidentiality to the debtor by revealing information to the surety's solicitor and that it can be misleading, for example, to tell the surety of the borrower's current financial position when the security or guarantee covers future indebtedness too, risking possibility liability for the bank to the surety.[67] Yet all these objections could easily be avoided by slight and workable changes to the legal rules and commercial practice of disclosure.

First, it seems incongruous that creditors are obliged to disclose unusual features of the transaction to sureties,[68] but not standard information such as levels of borrowing or the financial history of the debtor. So, for example, the bank in the recent case of *Bank of Scotland v Bennett*[69] was unable to rely in the normal way on the provision of separate legal advice to the wife, because

[62] See M Sneddon, "Lenders and Independent Solicitors' Certificates for Guarantors and Borrowers: Risk Minimisation or Loss Sharing?" (1996) 24 ABLR 5, 21.

[63] For detailed analysis, see Sneddon, *ibid*; also Sneddon, "Unfair Conduct in Taking Guarantees and the Role of Independent Advice" (1990) 13 UNSWLJ 302.

[64] *O'Brien* [1994] 1 AC 180, 199.

[65] *Bank of Scotland v Bennett* [1997] 1 FLR 801.

[66] *Midland Bank Plc v Kidwai* [1995] 4 Bank LR 303.

[67] As Morritt LJ said in *Kidwai*, *ibid*, 307–308, to suggest that the bank should have disclosed to the wife the amount of the existing debt and other salient matters ". . . would cast on the bank the duties of the solicitor or other independent adviser prudent banks advise those in the position of the wife to consult. Not only is the bank not required to do so by the principles expounded by Lord Browne-Wilkinson but it cannot do so because it is interested in the transaction in question and therefore not independent."

[68] *Hamilton v Watson* (1845) 12 C & F 109.

[69] [1997] 1 FLR 801.

of the existence of an unusual agreement whereby another charge was to be ranked in priority to its security, which the bank did not disclose to the wife or her adviser. As the judge said:[70]

> "I do not doubt that, in the ordinary case, a creditor will, as Lord Browne-Wilkinson put it, be 'safe' if the surety is separately advised . . . [But] if the creditor knows of facts relevant to the transaction, which are of a special and peculiar nature, and materially different in significantly disadvantageous respects from what someone in the surety's position might naturally expect, the only way in which the creditor can, in Lord Browne-Wilkinson's words, bring home to the surety the risk she is running . . . is to communicate those facts either to the surety or to the solicitors acting for her."

It seems strange that a bank must pass on unusual information, but not other important features simply because those features are shared by most other transactions of the same type. Both sorts of information are equally material to the surety's position and both are equally difficult for the surety to glean from a debtor who, *ex hypothesi,* is presumed to be applying undue influence or to have made misrepresentations.

Likewise, the argument that a little information is misleading to sureties is also unconvincing. It is patronising to argue that a surety is better off with no information, suggesting that, if a surety is told the current state of indebtedness and is made aware that the charge secures all future indebtedness as well, she will focus only on the first piece of information and be unable to comprehend the significance of the second!

The limited disclosure rules look even more incongruous when viewed alongside the bank's obligation truthfully to answer questions raised by the surety or her adviser.[71] It is only a matter of time before the current bank-favourable rules on "reasonable steps" begin to generate claims by sureties against their solicitors for failing to advise them properly, which is in turn likely to inspire solicitors to raise scores of conveyancing style preliminary enquiries with banks, requesting details of the transaction. It would surely be easier for banks to produce standard disclosure forms, giving specific material pieces of information to sureties and their advisers, rather than becoming inundated with many different forms of solicitors' enquiries. Such forms need only be used in *O'Brien* cases, to avoid the taint of constructive notice, and need play no part in lower risk surety transactions. The argument that this would breach confidentiality to the debtor is unconvincing, since the debtor could simply be requested to waive confidentiality on the specific issues set out in the standard

[70] *Ibid*, 838–839.

[71] See *Hamilton v Watson* (1845) 12 C&F 109, and *Westminster Bank Ltd v Cond* (1940) 46 Com Cas 60.

disclosure form, perhaps by way of a simple clause in the initial offer of loan. Debtors who refuse to comply can expect to be refused finance.

Like the issue of independent advice, the current regime on reasonable steps has institutionalised an acceptance of inadequate provision of information to sureties. It leaves sureties worse off than Lord Browne-Wilkinson envisaged, solicitors (or rather the Solicitors' Indemnity Fund) bearing the brunt of claims from sureties who fail to obtain relief against banks, with very little of substance being achieved to reduce instances of undue influence or other wrongdoing. The position of solicitors vis-à-vis their surety clients is, of course, a separate matter and the next few years can be expected to bring litigation on issues such as the extent of the solicitor's retainer and duty of care, and the possibility of excluding liability towards sureties, whether or not the law on bank disclosure is changed. In the meantime, however, some alteration in the rules on disclosure and what count as "reasonable steps" would surely be beneficial to both sureties and solicitors, without being either administratively unworkable for banks or contrary to principle.

5. REMEDIES – RELIEF ON TERMS?

One final issue which has caused confusion is that of the appropriate remedy, once an *O'Brien* claim of constructive notice has been successfully raised. It is trite law that the claimant is entitled to rescind the transaction, but what precisely does that mean? In particular, can relief be given on terms?

It is appropriate to separate two distinct issues. First, if the surety has derived a benefit from the transaction, must credit be given for this? Secondly, if she would have entered into a similar transaction, but on different terms, even if there had been no wrongdoing (for example, she would have guaranteed a lesser sum), can the transaction be enforced to the extent of those different terms, or must it be rescinded *in toto*?

So far as the first question is concerned, it is now clear that credit must be given for any benefit flowing from the rescinded transaction. On perfectly conventional principles, the surety must make counter-restitution if she wishes to rescind the transaction.[72]

Thus in *Midland Bank Plc v Greene*[73] the husband and wife jointly mortgaged their home to the bank. Part of the loan was used to purchase, first, the

[72] Where *restitutio in integrum* is impossible, the courts are proving increasingly willing to make a monetary award in lieu of rescission – see *Mahoney v Purnell* [1996] All ER 61, 89; [1997] 1 FLR 612, 640, where the award was described as "equitable compensation" but seems to have been assessed on restitutionary, rather than compensatory, principles. See further P Birks, "Unjust Factors and Wrongs: Pecuniary Rescission for Undue Influence" [1997] RLR 72.

[73] [1994] 2 FLR 827.

leasehold interest in the property and, later, the freehold, but the charge also secured all present and future indebtedness of the husband. Having determined that the bank was fixed with constructive notice of the husband's undue influence, the judge had to determine the appropriate relief for Mrs Greene. He began by observing that normally, the court's equitable jurisdiction to avoid a transaction "should be exercised only when the parties can be restored to their position before the transaction. Where that is not possible, then the transaction should be set aside only upon terms that do justice in all the circumstances."[74]

The facts were complicated because, not only had the wife benefitted from the use of the loan to acquire her joint interest in the property, but also a further advance for home improvements had been made three years after the date of the original advance and tacked onto the original security. This home improvement loan was not subject to presumed undue influence and was thus not voidable. On the other hand, the wife was entitled to avoid that part of the security which secured her husband's business debts. The judge, undaunted, ordered that accounts should be taken, with a view to determining the sum (representing the amount used to procure the wife's interest in the property and the amount due on the home improvement account) which the wife would be obliged to pay in order to set aside the mortgage. He rejected the suggestion that he was re-writing the terms of the transaction; on the contrary, he was exercising the well-established equitable jurisdiction to give relief on terms.

Similarly, in *Dunbar Bank v Nadeem*[75] the wife was entitled to rescind the mortgage, which secured both her husband's business debts and the acquisition of the couple's joint interest in the leasehold property charged, provided she repaid to the bank a sum representing the amount used to acquire her half share in the lease, plus interest. This conclusion was again based on the principle that a party who seeks rescission must make counter-restitution.[76] The judge in *Nadeem* expressly distinguished cases of this sort from those of the second type, which do not involve issues of counter-restitution.

The second problem was exemplified in *TSB Bank Plc v Camfield*.[77] Mrs Camfield was induced to stand surety for the debts of her husband's business,

[74] *Ibid*, 835.

[75] [1997] 2 All ER 253.

[76] *Erlanger v New Sombrero Phosphate Co* (1878) 3 App Cas 1218. Precisely the same conclusion was reached in a recent appeal to the High Court of Australia, *Maguire v Makaronis* (1997) 144 ALR 729, where a mortgage in favour of the borrowers' solicitors was rescinded for breach of fiduciary duty, on condition that the loan secured by it must be repaid.

[77] [1995] 1 WLR 430 (hereafter "*Camfield*"). The problem was avoided in *O'Brien* itself (where the misrepresentation was also as to the amount secured) because, by the time the case reached the House of Lords, the amount which Mrs O'Brien would have been prepared to secure had been paid to the bank, originally by order of court.

and to execute a joint mortgage over the matrimonial home, because of her husband's innocent misrepresentation that liability was limited to a maximum of £15,000, when in fact it was unlimited. The bank was fixed with constructive notice of the misrepresentation. Clearly, then, the wife had a right to rescind the transaction, but the bank argued that it should be entitled to enforce it to the extent of £15,000. In other words, as Nourse LJ put it, the bank argued that the wife was "only entitled to have it set aside on terms that she acknowledges that it is a valid security for £15,000."[78]

The Court of Appeal disagreed with the bank, deciding that it had no jurisdiction to order rescission on such terms. Nourse LJ said, "The wife's right to have the transaction set aside *in toto* as against her husband is no less enforceable against the mortgagee."[79]

This solution undoubtedly has the advantage of simplicity, but is it correct?[80] One supporting argument, propounded in *Camfield* by Roch LJ, can be rebutted straightaway. Roch LJ suggested that, because the right to rescind a transaction for misrepresentation is that of the representee not the court, rescission will have taken place before the matter reaches the court, by which time it is too late to impose any terms. He said, "The court is not being asked to grant equitable relief; nor is it, in my view, granting relief to which terms may be attached."[81]

This argument must be wrong. First, it ignores the fact that, although a contract may normally be rescinded by the act of the aggrieved party,[82] it has never been suggested that the restitutionary consequences which flow from rescission are achieved without the intervention of the court. In particular, a mortgage over real property can not be avoided merely by notice from mortgagor to mortgagee: principles of registration of title see to that, if nothing else. Moreover, even if rescission of a mortgage can be achieved without court intervention, it is fallacious logic to say that it can therefore never be rescinded on terms: if the law allows rescission on terms, then they are the terms on which the plaintiff's own act of rescission will take effect and the

[78] *Ibid*, 433.

[79] *Ibid*, 437.

[80] Significantly, the Australian courts reached the opposite conclusion in *Vadasz v Pioneer Concrete (SA) Pty Ltd* (1995) 184 CLR 102, where a guarantee of present and future indebtedness, which had been procured by a misrepresentation that it covered future indebtedness only, was rescinded on terms that the guarantor's liability for future indebtedness be preserved. Arguably, the facts of *Vadasz* are less suitable for relief on terms than those of *Camfield* – relief was being given against the misrepresentor itself, not a mere third party, and it appears that the representation was made fraudulently. Many of the issues raised by *Camfield* and *Vadasz* are discussed in detail by Proksch, "Rescission on Terms" [1996] RLR 71.

[81] *Ibid*, 438–439.

[82] See *Car and Universal Finance Co Ltd v Caldwell* [1964] 1 QB 525.

plaintiff must submit to those terms, even if rescission is triggered by her own act. So this presupposes nothing about the law's prior stance on terms.[83]

There are, however, other arguments to support the stark rule in *Camfield*. In so far as the issue can ever arise, the *Camfield* approach is clearly justifiable in cases of undue influence, where it is rarely going to be meaningful to attempt to determine what transaction the wife would have entered into without undue influence and, in any event, this is surely irrelevant where her consent has been improperly obtained. The only appropriate issue is the feasibility of restoring the *status quo*, subject to counter-restitution.

Moreover, even in misrepresentation cases, it is generally regarded as utterly irrelevant what would have happened had the misrepresentation *been true*.[84] The only appropriate counterfactual in standard two-party misrepresentation cases is, "what would have happened had the misrepresentation *not been made*?" which is inevitably answered, "the representee would not have contracted", since reliance on the representation is required, by definition, for relief. So, for example, the court did not ask what the plaintiff in *Redgrave v Hurd*[85] would have paid for the business had the misrepresented profit figures been true. This approach supports the result in *Camfield*, since it seems that Mrs Camfield would not have agreed to proceed with the transaction if the misrepresentation had *not been made*. In Nourse LJ's words, relief on terms is not appropriate "in a case where it is found, as here, that the wife would not have executed the legal charge if a limit higher than £15,000 had been proposed to her . . ."[86]

Yet, on further reflection, matters are not quite this simple. The appearance of unfairness in a case like *Camfield* arises because, unusually, we *can* determine precisely what Mrs Camfield would have done had the misrepresentation been true, because, unusually, the misrepresentation was as to the *terms* of the transaction she executed. So why not test the fairness of the result by reference to this counter-factual? After all, this is precisely what is now required in cases where damages are sought in negligent misrepresentation cases,[87] and as Hobhouse LJ forcefully explained in *Downs v Chappell*.[88]

[83] Interestingly, Roch LJ's approach found no favour with the judge in *Nadeem*, Robert Englehart QC, who observed that Mrs Nadeem "has not yet made restitution so there can be no question of her already having exercised an entitlement to set the transaction aside by, for example, her pleading": [1997] 2 All ER 253, 272.

[84] *Cf* where the representation is a contractual warranty.

[85] (1881) 20 Ch D 1.

[86] [1995] 1 WLR 430, 437.

[87] As a result of Lord Hoffmann's speech in *Banque Bruxelles Lambert SA v Eagle Star Insurance Co* (also reported as *South Australia Asset Management Corp v York Montague Ltd*) [1997] AC 191.

[88] [1997] 1 WLR 426, 444: "I consider that the appropriate way to give effect to these legitimate concerns is to compare the loss consequent upon entering into the transaction with what would have been the position had the represented, or supposed, state of affairs actually

Perhaps it would be more appropriate to treat third party banks in the same way as defendants in negligent misrepresentation damages cases, than as the misrepresentor is commonly treated in two-party rescission cases – particularly as it is only since *O'Brien* that rescission for misrepresentation reaches as far as third parties via constructive notice.

On the other hand, a further argument in favour of *Camfield* is that, even when the representation is as to one of the terms of the transaction, it is only meaningful to ask what would have happened had the misrepresentation been true where the relevant term misrepresented is as to the amount lent or secured (*ie* the mortgage enforced as to that amount, but not as to the rest). How would relief be structured for other misrepresentations about terms, for example as to the duration of the security or the powers of the mortgagee, or indeed misrepresentations about matters *other* than the terms of the transaction, like the financial position of the creditor? Of course, the courts of equity could cope and have effectively rewritten contracts for common mistake,[89] but in the context of banking transactions this would be surely be unacceptably unpredictable.

Perhaps the real problem is not specific to *Camfield*, but is far wider, namely that the law is not very good at dealing with remedies, both compensatory and restitutionary, where, *but for* the relevant wrongdoing, the plaintiff *would have proceeded with a version of the actual transaction but on different terms* (sometimes called "successful transaction" cases). The law is tailored to remedying cases where the plaintiff would have declined to proceed at all but for the breach, and is equally able to cope with cases where the plaintiff would have acted in precisely the same way, but the intermediate position is rather problematic. It is ignored entirely in straightforward two-party rescission claims for misrepresentation. This is arguably justifiable since the original misrepresentee does not deserve the benefit of such a complex enquiry – after all, it was his representation that prevented anyone ever finding out what terms the plaintiff might otherwise have accepted. But is it right to take this onerous line with third parties, who are merely saddled with constructive notice of another's misrepresentation?

Perhaps the (tentative) conclusion should be, not that *Camfield* is wrong on its terms, but that there is a more fundamental problem with the extension made in *O'Brien* allowing direct relief for a plaintiff against a third party for the misrepresentation of another, based on a spurious and inappropriate test

existed. Assume that there had been no tort because the represented, or supposed, facts were true . . ." (This approach was rejected by the House of Lords in *Smith New Court Securities Ltd v Scrimgeour Vickers (Asset Management) Ltd* [1997] 2 AC 254 for the tort of deceit, but not for negligent advice or misrepresentation).

[89] *Eg Solle v Butcher* [1950] 1 KB 671.

of constructive notice. Arguably, unless and until that is reconsidered,[90] *Camfield* has at least the advantages of simplicity, certainty and consistency with the position of undue influence, although it is no particular credit to our jurisprudence that the court in *Camfield* recognised that the remedy lacked the "morality, perhaps the justice in an abstract sense"[91] of the relief on terms being proposed by the bank!

6. CONCLUSION

Four years after the decision in *O'Brien*, its implications and practical consequences remain as controversial as ever. It seems that some areas which have been subjected to criticism, such as *O'Brien*'s use of the doctrine of notice and the manifest disadvantage requirement for raising the presumption of undue influence, are in fact relatively trouble-free in practice. Conversely, other areas such as the role of external legal advice, the appropriate remedies in *O'Brien* cases and, most fundamentally, the application of the doctrine at all in misrepresentation cases, have yet to be satisfactorily resolved. It remains impossible to regard *O'Brien* as a complete success in its twin objectives of protecting vulnerable sureties and rendering security over the matrimonial home secure.

[90] This seems unlikely to occur given the current attitude of the House of Lords, despite Lord Jauncey's best efforts in *Bank of Scotland v Smith*, *supra* n 20.

[91] [1995] 1 WLR 430, 437, *per* Nourse LJ.

4

Undue Influence and Misrepresentation after O'Brien: *Making Security Secure – A Commentary*

GRAHAM VIRGO*

Janet O'Sullivan is broadly happy with the decision of the House of Lords in *Barclays Bank Plc v O'Brien*.[1] As she herself admits, there is "nothing fundamentally wrong" with that decision. Her comprehensive and careful analysis of the developments following that case does, however, suggest that the judiciary has taken a number of wrong turnings in seeking to clarify the application of the *O'Brien* principle. There are three main issues which arise from her paper.

1. IDENTIFYING THE FEATURES OF THE *O'BRIEN* PRINCIPLE

Whenever the principle identified by Lord Browne-Wilkinson in *O'Brien* is examined and applied, it is vital to be aware both of the rationale which underlies it and what must be established before the principle can be considered to have been triggered. This need for a clear exposition of the principle is something which has been lost in the barrage of cases following *O'Brien*, and this explains why some of the results of those cases are contradictory and unacceptable. This has also been a weakness of a number of the academic commentaries about the case and its implications.

In identifying the rationale and elements of the *O'Brien* principle it is useful to refer to a simple hypothetical case. The simplest and most common context for the *O'Brien* principle to be applicable is where a husband, who owes money to a bank, asks his wife to consent to the matrimonial home, in which she has a beneficial interest, being used as security for further borrowings

* Fellow of Downing College, Cambridge and University Lecturer in the Faculty of Law, University of Cambridge.

[1] [1994] 1 AC 180.

from the bank. Later, the husband is unable to discharge his debts and so the bank seeks to enforce its security against the wife. The wife will wish to rescind the transaction, for example on the ground that she had entered into it as a result of the exercise of undue influence by her husband. The nature of the dispute in such a case is which of two innocent parties, either the wife or the bank, should lose as a result of the bad behaviour of the husband, who is not a party to this dispute. The rationale of the *O'Brien* principle is simply to determine which of these two innocent parties should lose and this requires careful analysis of the conduct of the wife and the bank respectively.

If this rationale of the *O'Brien* principle is borne in mind it is possible to identify and justify the different elements of that principle. If we consider a case where the wife argues that the transaction with the bank should be avoided by reason of undue influence, there are a maximum of five elements which need to be considered before it can be determined whether the wife or the bank should suffer the loss.

(a) Presumption of undue influence: the nature of the relationship[2]

For the wife to establish a presumption that her husband had unduly influenced her into entering into the transaction with the bank, it is necessary for her to show that the relationship between her and her husband was such that she reposed such trust and confidence in him that he was in a position where he could take advantage of his position of influence over her. It is not possible to assume that the relationship between the spouses was of this kind simply from the fact that they were married. The relationship of trust and confidence must be established from the particular facts.

(b) Presumption of undue influence: the transaction was manifestly and unfairly disadvantageous

In addition to the nature of the relationship between the spouses, the wife must also establish that the transaction which she entered into with the bank was manifestly and unfairly disadvantageous to her. This is assessed by reference to an objective test, namely whether a reasonable and independent

[2] If the wife can show that her husband had exercised actual undue influence over her, then it is obviously not necessary to identify any presumption of undue influence and so the first three elements of this test can be ignored. It will, however, usually be easier for the wife to rely on a presumption of undue influence rather than to establish actual undue influence.

person who knew all the facts would consider the transaction to be obviously disadvantageous.[3]

With the rejection of the requirement that the transaction was manifestly disadvantageous for the purposes of establishing actual undue influence,[4] it might be considered that that there is no justification for retaining such a requirement in the context of presumed undue influence. But such an argument would be mistaken, because the simple fact that the relationship between the wife and her husband is one of trust and confidence cannot be sufficient to trigger a presumption that the husband had *unduly* influenced his wife to enter into the transaction with the bank. The fact that the transaction itself was disadvantageous to the wife is of fundamental importance in triggering the presumption, since it is only where the transaction is clearly not in the wife's best interests that it should be presumed that the wife did not exercise a free choice in entering into the transaction.

(c) Rebuttal of the presumption

Once the wife has established the presumption that her husband unduly influenced her, the burden then shifts to the bank to rebut it. To do this the bank must show that the wife did exercise a free choice when she entered into the transaction. One of the best ways of establishing this is by showing that the wife had taken independent legal advice before she entered into the transaction. For this to be sufficient to rebut the presumption, however, the legal adviser must be truly independent and the advice must be informed and competent.[5]

If the presumption of undue influence has been established and cannot be rebutted, then the wife is in a position to set the transaction aside as against the person who unduly influenced her. But, since she had entered into a transaction with the bank which had not unduly influenced her, if she is to rescind this transaction she must establish that the bank was responsible for the undue influence in some way.

(d) Establishing responsibility for the undue influence

The bank will be considered to be responsible for the husband's undue influence, and so bound by it, if the wife can establish that the bank had actual or

[3] *BCCI v Aboody* [1990] 1 QB 923.

[4] *CIBC Mortgages Plc v Pitt* [1994] 1 AC 200.

[5] *Cf* the different interpretation of obtaining independent legal advice in the context of the bank having taken reasonable steps. See point (e) below.

constructive notice of actual undue influence or the circumstances from which undue influence is presumed.[6] Despite the suggestion of some commentators that the doctrine of notice in this context should operate as a defence to the wife's claim to set the transaction aside,[7] and the conclusion of the Court of Appeal that the bank bears the burden of proving that it did not have notice of the wife's equity to set the transaction aside,[8] the better view is that notice forms part of the wife's cause of action in establishing that she can rescind the transaction as against the bank. This is important because it means that the wife bears the burden of proving that the bank had actual or constructive notice of the undue influence.

The introduction of the doctrine of notice to determine whether the bank should be considered to be tainted by the husband's actions has been criticised, primarily because it is assumed that a doctrine which was developed in the context of land law is inappropriate in the context of an *O'Brien* dispute. But such criticism is unfounded. It is, perhaps, unfortunate that Lord Browne-Wilkinson used the word "notice" to describe the relevant test, because of the connotations of the word; but, so long as it is realised that the doctrine of notice has a unique interpretation in this context, because it can be rebutted by proof that the bank had taken reasonable steps, it can do no harm.[9]

(e) The bank has taken reasonable steps

The bank will not be considered to have constructive notice of the undue influence if it can show that it has taken reasonable steps to ensure that the wife had not been unduly influenced. The rationale behind this particular test is simply to determine whether the bank's conduct is such that it should be allowed to enforce the transaction against the wife. We are not at this stage concerned with whether or not the wife had been unduly influenced by her husband.

O'Sullivan correctly observes that the recent cases which have considered what constitutes the taking of reasonable steps are far from satisfactory, primarily because they lean unnecessarily in favour of the interests of the bank rather than the interests of the wife. So, for example, banks will be considered to have taken reasonable steps if they know that their own legal advisers have given financial advice to the wife about the transaction; but such advice can

[6] Alternatively the wife may establish that the husband was acting as the bank's agent, but it is almost unimaginable that such an agency relationship could be identified.

[7] See E O'Dell, "Restitution, Coercion by a Third Party and the Proper Role of Notice" [1997] 56 CLJ 71.

[8] *Barclays Bank Plc v Boulter* [1998] 1 WLR 1. See further Barker, infra, ch 5 .

[9] *Eg* it was recognised in *Barclays Bank Plc v Boulter* [1998] 1 WLR 1 (CA) that the *O'Brien* principle applies regardless of wether the land is registered or unregistered.

hardly be considered to be independent legal advice.[10] The bank will also be considered to have taken reasonable steps if it knows that the wife had received legal advice, even though the bank does not know what the nature of the advice was. It is these decisions on the notion of taking reasonable steps which are most unsatisfactory and the practice of banks in particular should be reconsidered along the lines which O'Sullivan suggests.

2. MISREPRESENTATION

One of the peculiar features of *O'Brien* was that, although the principle identified by Lord Browne-Wilkinson was applicable where the wife entered into a transaction with a bank as a result of actual or presumed undue influence, the case itself involved a wife being induced to enter into the transaction as a result of misrepresentation. This has no serious effect on the analysis which is adopted. Once it has been shown that the husband's misrepresentation had indeed induced the wife to enter into the transaction with the bank, the question whether the wife can rescind this transaction requires her to prove that the bank had actual or constructive notice of the misrepresentation and, if the bank is to enforce the transaction against her, it must then show that it had taken reasonable steps to ensure that the wife freely entered into it.

The cases and academic commentaries following *O'Brien* have assumed that it is right that the same analysis should be adopted regardless of whether the wife wishes to rescind the transaction on the ground of undue influence or misrepresentation. One of the most important aspects of O'Sullivan's paper is that she seeks to challenge this assumption and she asserts that the *O'Brien* principle should be confined to cases where the wife entered into the transaction as a result of undue influence. O'Sullivan supports this conclusion by reference to two alternative conclusions, neither of which is ultimately convincing.

First, she states that the application of the *O'Brien* principle to cases of misrepresentation is inconsistent with the restrictive rules on pre-contract disclosure. But in fact the *O'Brien* principle has little to do with a duty of disclosure before a contract is made. In most cases, rather than creating a duty of disclosure, *O'Brien* has simply created a duty of enquiry. This is because the bank will be able to enforce the transaction with the wife save where it is put on notice to inquire whether or not the wife was being induced to enter into the transaction with it as a result of her husband's misrepresentation. The only exception to this is where the bank has actual notice of the misrepresentation. In such a case it appears that the bank is indeed under a duty to dis-

[10] See *eg Banco Exterior v Mann* [1995] 1 All ER 936.

close this to the wife; for, if the bank knows of the misrepresentation and does not inform the wife, then the bank will not be able to enforce the transaction against her. To this limited extent, therefore, *O'Brien* does indeed effect a shift in the rules about the duty to disclose before a contract is entered into. But this change in the rules is surely justified by reason of the need to balance the interests of two innocent parties to determine which should suffer from the misrepresentation. The fact that the bank knew of the misrepresentation is surely a reason why it should suffer from the husband's misrepresentation rather than the wife.

O'Sullivan's second argument is that a bank will only be found to have constructive notice of the husband's misconduct where there was an emotional relationship of trust and confidence between the wife and her husband, and such a relationship hints at a risk of undue influence and not misrepresentation. But this argument is not convincing. Whilst it may indeed be true that a relationship of trust and confidence is more likely to suggest that the husband had unduly influenced his wife than that he had made a misrepresentation to her, this simply means that it will be more difficult to establish that the bank had constructive notice of the husband's conduct in making a misrepresentation. But this is a question of evidence and not substance. There is no reason in principle why a bank should not be considered to have constructive notice of the husband's misrepresentation.

It follows that it is right that the *O'Brien* principle should apply to cases of misrepresentation as well as to undue influence. Indeed, it would be much more difficult to justify confining the principle to cases of undue influence, when undue influence and misrepresentation are both forms of equitable misconduct and where the issue in both contexts is the same, namely which of two innocent parties should suffer from the misconduct. The doctrines of actual and constructive notice are entirely appropriate in identifying who should suffer from the misconduct, regardless of whether the misconduct was undue influence or misrepresentation.

O'Sullivan's discussion of the application of the *O'Brien* principle to cases of misrepresentation raises another important issue. She assumes that, if the *O'Brien* principle applies to such cases, it only does so in the context of cases where the relationship between the misrepresentor and the misrepresentee is a relationship of trust and confidence. But there is no reason to confine the application of the principle in this way. The principle should be applicable in any case where the misrepresentee enters into a transaction as a result of a misrepresentation from a person who is not a party to the transaction, regardless of the nature of the relationship between the misrepresentor and misrepresentee. In all such cases it should be necessary to consider whether the other party to the transaction had actual or constructive notice of the misrepresentation. It will, of course, be much more difficult to show that that party did have notice where the relationship between the misrepresentor and misrepresentee was not based on trust and confidence and was, for example, a purely commercial relationship. But it does not follow from the fact that this will be difficult to establish that the *O'Brien* principle should be artificially restricted in the way which O'Sullivan suggests.

3. RESCISSION ON TERMS

Once the wife has established that she was induced to enter into the transaction with the bank as a result of undue influence or misrepresentation of which the bank had notice, she will wish to rescind the transaction. Usually the question of rescission in this context causes no problems, but sometimes whether the wife can rescind the transaction is more complicated and this raises the difficult issue of whether the wife can rescind the transaction on terms. As O'Sullivan correctly identifies, there are two different notions of rescission on terms.

(a) Counter-restitution

Where the wife has received benefits under the transaction with the bank then, if she is to rescind the transaction, she should make counter-restitution to the bank of the value of the benefit which she had received. This requirement to make counter-restitution should be a term of the rescission. This should not be a controversial matter and it is increasingly being recognised by the courts.[11]

(b) Avoiding the transaction in part

The alternative notion of rescission on terms concerns whether it is possible for the court to allow the wife to rescind part of the transaction but to order that she is bound by the other part of it. In *TSB Bank Plc v Camfield*[12] it was

[11] See, in particular, *O'Sullivan v Management Agency and Music Ltd* [1985] AC 686, *Mahoney v Purnell* [1996] 3 All ER 61 and *Dunbar Bank Plc v Nadeem* [1997] 2 All ER 253. *Cf* the decision of the Court of Appeal in *Smith New Court Securities Ltd v Scrimgeour Vickers (Asset Management) Ltd* [1994] 1 WLR 1271, where the requirement that the plaintiff must make complete counter-restitution was interpreted strictly. Whilst this question did not arise in the House of Lords, Lord Browne-Wilkinson did suggest that it was open to review: [1997] AC 254, 262.

[12] [1995] 1 WLR 430.

held that this notion of rescission on terms was not recognised in English law.

Whether this decision is correct depends on whether it can be concluded that the wife would have consented to part of the transaction if there had been no misrepresentation or no undue influence, actual or presumed. In many cases it will not be possible to show this; but, if in an exceptional case it is possible to show that she would still have entered into a transaction with the bank, then there is surely no reason why the court should be prevented from ordering rescission on the terms that she is bound by that transaction which she would have freely entered into had there been no undue influence or misrepresentation.

There is surely no objection to such rescission on terms as a matter of principle, since rescission on terms has been recognised previously where the plaintiff wishes to rescind a transaction for mistake.[13] It has even been recognised where the plaintiff has sought to rescind a transaction by reason of presumed undue influence.[14] Rescission on terms is also justified in the particular context of a wife who wishes to rescind a transaction which she entered into with a bank. Where the transaction which the wife entered into is voidable but it can be shown that she would have entered into some aspect of the transaction anyway, it is surely only fair that the transaction is valid to this extent, simply because it cannot be shown that the wife was induced to enter into this aspect of the transaction as the result of misrepresentation or undue influence. The great difficulty with this relates to the need to prove that the wife would have entered into part of the transaction anyway. This will be much easier to establish where the wife was induced to enter into a transaction with the bank as the result of her husband's misrepresentation as to the terms of the transaction. For if the wife thinks she is agreeing to act as a surety for the sum of £10,000 when she is in fact agreeing to secure the sum of £100,000 it is possible to conclude that she had freely agreed to secure the sum of £10,000.[15] Where, on the other hand, the wife was induced to enter into the transaction by reason of undue influence it will be very difficult to establish that she would have freely entered into part of the transaction, simply because undue influence will generally taint the whole transaction.

[13] See *Solle v Butcher* [1950] 1 KB 671 and *Grist v Bailey* [1967] Ch 532.

[14] *Cheese v Thomas* [1994] 1 WLR 129.

[15] This would suggest that the Court of Appeal was wrong in *TSB Bank Plc v Camfield* [1995] 1 WLR 430 to conclude that the transaction in that case could not be rescinded on terms, since the wife thought that her liability was limited to the sum of £15,000 when her liability was in fact unlimited. The transaction should consequently have been rescinded save to the extent of her liability up to the sum of £15,000

5

O'Brien, *Notice and the Onus of Proof*

KIT BARKER*

Barclays Bank Plc v Boulter[1] is the most recent in a series of Court of Appeal cases[2] the task of which has been to interpret the principles laid down by Lord Browne-Wilkinson in *Barclays Bank Plc v O'Brien*.[3] The issue on appeal concerned itself exclusively with the way in which *O'Brien* claims should be pleaded, but the conclusions proffered by the court on this issue have far broader implications. In particular, they have key implications for the way in which restitutionary causes of action are understood in three party cases and for the scope of the defence of bona fide purchase.

A. FACTS AND DECISION

The fact-pattern will be familiar. In 1979, Mrs Boulter signed an all-moneys charge in favour of Barclays Bank over a property which she owned jointly with her husband. By 1993, he had amassed very considerable debts to the bank and defaulted on them. In the following action by Barclays for possession, Mrs Boulter argued by way of defence and counterclaim that the charge had been procured by the husband's misrepresentation and that she was therefore entitled to restitution of her interest in the house. When the case came up for trial in September 1996, before any evidence had been called, the bank raised a procedural objection. Mrs Boulter was intending to argue – but had failed in her pleadings expressly to allege – that the bank was fixed with

* Lecturer in Law, University of Southampton. My thanks to Peter Sparkes, Derrick Dale and Geoffrey Mead for stimulating discussions about this case. None of the views stated here should necessarily be taken as theirs. Any and all errors remain entirely my own.

[1] [1997] 2 All ER 1002 (CA); pet all [1998] 1 WLR 472. Mummery LJ gave the leading judgment. Sir Brian Neill and Leggatt LJ concurred without further comment. The case is also reported now at [1998] 1 WLR 1. Unattributed citations in this chapter are to the All ER report.

[2] *Banco Exterior Internacional v Mann* [1995] 1 All ER 936; *Massey v Midland Bank Plc* [1995] 1 All ER 929; *TSB Bank Plc v Camfield* [1995] 1 WLR 1055; *Banco Exterior Internacional SA v Thomas* [1997] 1 WLR 221.

[3] *Barclays Bank Plc v O'Brien* [1994] 1 AC 180 (HL) (hereafter "*O'Brien*").

constructive notice of the misrepresentation. If she wished to argue the point, the bank contended, she must amend her pleadings and bear the possible consequences in costs. The trial judge agreed, holding that notice was an essential ingredient of her claim and that the purpose of the pleading rules would otherwise be undermined. Whilst he was happy to grant Mrs Boulter leave to amend, amend she must.

This narrow point formed the object of Mrs Boulter's successful appeal. Reversing the judge's decision, the Court of Appeal held that she was entitled to argue the issue of constructive notice at trial without having pleaded it, for two reasons. First (point 1, below), the onus of proof on the issue of notice lay with the bank, not with Mrs Boulter.[4] Indeed, she did not even bear the onus of proving that the bank was put on inquiry as to the misrepresentation.[5] There being no obligation on a party to plead matters which the other party bears the burden of disproving,[6] there was no obligation upon her to raise the issue of notice at all. This was for the bank to do. Second (point 2, below), a party's only obligation is to plead material facts – not matters of law or evidence, or argument.[7] Since notice was not a matter of fact, but rather something towards which the facts might or might not point in a given case,[8] it need not be pleaded specifically. The facts which Mrs Boulter *had* pleaded might be sufficient to enable her to establish it at trial. The implication of this, second, point is that, even if Mrs Boulter *had* born the onus of proving notice, she need not have alluded to it expressly in her defence and counterclaim.

Which of these two points was decisive in the Court's judgment is frustratingly unclear. Mummery LJ took them together and regarded them as mutually supportive of each other,[9] but in fact there is an unresolved tension between them. *Either* Mrs Boulter was exempt from pleading notice because she did not bear the substantive onus of proof; *or* she was exempt because, although she did bear that onus, notice was not a matter that she needed to mention expressly. It could not be for both reasons. The fact that the bulk of the court's judgement is dedicated to point 1 (onus) suggests that this was the main ground of decision. But point 1 was in fact stated as "confirming" point 2,[10] not the other way around; which suggests precisely the opposite conclusion. Not only does this cause confusion as to the true basis of the decision, but both points seem, with respect, to be open to criticism in their own right.

[4] At p 1007h.
[5] At p 1009j.
[6] RSC Ord 18, r 7(3).
[7] At p 1007f–g.
[8] *Ibid.*
[9] At p 1007h. The substantive law on the onus of proof is stated by his Lordship to "confirm" the conclusion predicated by procedure.
[10] *Ibid.*

B. POINT 1: SUBSTANCE: NOTICE AND THE THE ONUS OF PROOF

1. Authority on onus

No prior case had decided the location of the onus of proof in cases of the *O'Brien* type. The court was therefore guided exclusively by a number of extracts from Lord Browne-Wilkinson's speech in that case,[11] by *dicta* in the dissenting judgement of Hobhouse LJ in *Banco Exterior v Mann*[12] and by appeals to what Mummery LJ refers to as "well-established equitable principles,"[13] by which he means the doctrine of bona fide purchase for value without notice.

Unfortunately, none of these provides a particularly solid foundation for the court's conclusions. Whilst there are some parts of Lord Browne-Wilkinson's judgement in *O'Brien* which indeed suggest that the burden is on the creditor to disprove notice,[14] there are an equal number of passages which suggest precisely the reverse.[15] Even in those passages which do suggest that the onus lies with the creditor, the understanding is that this onus only arises once facts have been proven which put the creditor on inquiry of the debtor's impropriety.[16] There is nothing to support Mummery LJ's view[17] – which must consequently be regarded as highly controversial – that the onus lies on the creditor to disprove the existence of such facts, as well as to prove that it has taken reasonable steps to protect the surety, where such facts are shown to exist. One such fact which is known to put the creditor on notice, after all, is the relationship between surety and debtor, and the onus of proving this has always been understood to be on the surety. Another is that the transaction is of a type which carries a particular risk of having been illegitimately procured. Comments in both *O'Brien*[18] and *Pitt*[19] strongly suggest that the surety

[11] [1994] 1 AC 180, 191, 195–196, 199.

[12] [1995] 1 All ER 936, 946.

[13] At p 1007h.

[14] [1994] 1 AC 180, 196 E–F, 198H.

[15] At several points in his speech (see *eg ibid,* 191D,E, 195F,H, 196A–B) Lord Browne-Wilkinson states that the creditor takes subject to the surety's equity "if" it has notice. Contrast these passages with those cited *supra*, n 14, where it is stated that the creditor is affected "unless" it has taken steps to avoid notice.

[16] This is clear from *ibid,* 196E, 197C–D. See also p 198G, where the suggestion is that the onus is cast upon the creditor only when it is (shown to be ?) aware of the cohabitation relationship between surety and debtor.

[17] *Supra*, n 5 and text.

[18] [1994] 1 AC 180, 197C–D.

[19] *CIBC Mortgages Plc v Pitt* [1994] 1 AC 200 (HL), 210–211, *per* Lord Browne-Wilkinson. This analysis seems to offer the only way of rationalising the distinction that is drawn in *Pitt* between surety and joint loan transactions, the former of which are, on their face, more obviously disadvantageous to the wife or cohabitee. See also *Yerkey v Jones* (1940) 63 CLR 649, 675–676, *per* Dixon J, where there is a clear indication that the onus is on the surety to prove the circumstances which ought to give rise to doubt or suspicion on the part of the creditor.

must show the transaction to be of this kind, before the creditor can be called upon to explain a failure to take reasonable steps for her protection.

The rest of the authority referred to by Mummery LJ is equally inconclusive. Hobhouse LJ's comments in *Mann*[20] are clear, but they seem to be addressed towards cases in which the presumption of undue influence has been raised, not, strictly speaking, towards cases of misrepresentation. They are also weakened by being stated to be an interpretation of *O'Brien*, which, as appears from the above, is actually equivocal on onus. The fact that Mrs O'Brien succeeded in her own claim without pleading notice is no more helpful, since no issue was ever taken as to whether or not this should have been done. Equally, the line of authority flowing from *Pilcher v Rawlins*,[21] which states (correctly, I think)[22] that the onus lies on a defendant to make out each element of the defence of bona fide purchase, is of questionable relevance to this type of fact configuration. Although Lord Browne-Wilkinson indeed seems to have been alluding to notice doctrine in its classical form when formulating his principles of recovery in *O'Brien*, the application of that doctrine to *O'Brien*-type facts is decidedly atypical. Bona fide purchase is a defence which applies in favour of those who buy an interest in property from a third party, not, generally, to those who have purchased property (or, for that matter, contractual guarantees) from a claimant.[23] This difficulty is implicitly recognised by Mummery LJ, who accordingly describes *O'Brien* as a non-standard application of notice doctrine.[24] Moreover, his Lordship clearly (in this respect, I suggest, helpfully) states that the *O'Brien* principle applies irrespective of the classification of the relevant property as registered or unregistered;[25] and it is sensible to assume that it applies equally to cases involving the rescission of personal guarantees as to those involving land-charges.[26] Neither of these propositions could be true, were the classical doctrine of bona fide purchase in play. The allusion to that defence seems inapposite and the analogy – tempting though it may be – has led the Court of Appeal astray.

20 [1995] 1 All ER 936, 946.

21 (1872) LR 7 Ch App 259.

22 See *A-G v Biphosphated Guano Co* (1879) 11 Ch D 327; *Re Nisbet and Pott's Contract* [1966] 1 Ch 386; *GL Baker Ltd v Medway Building and Supplies Ltd* [1958] 3 All ER 540; Meagher, Gummow and Lehane, *Equity: Doctrines and Remedies*, 3rd ed (Sydney, 1992), 257–259; Barker, "After Change of Position: Good Faith Exchange in the Modern Law of Restitution" in Birks (ed), *Laundering and Tracing* (Oxford, 1995), 205–209.

23 See Barker, *ibid*, 198–205; Birks, *supra* n 22, at p 333, the cases there cited and *Pilcher v Rawlins* (1872) LR 7 Ch App 259. See *contra* O'Dell [1997] CLJ 71.

24 At p 1008d.

25 At p 1010. The property in both *Boulter* and *O'Brien* was unregistered.

26 This point has never been determined, but there is nothing in Browne-Wilkinson's speech to suggest that it does not. Moreover, there would appear to be no moral or policy distinction between the two cases.

This weakens the foundations of the court's conclusions about onus. Further cracking occurs when some of the cases on which *O'Brien* itself purports to be based are analysed, for most of these are equivocal on onus too;[27] and some of them, including *Bainbrigge v Browne*,[28] suggest that the burden lies upon the surety, if a creditor is to be infected with a third party's impropriety. There is a clear statement by Lord Browne-Wilkinson himself in *Pitt*[29] to the same effect. This is summarily dismissed by Mummery LJ on the basis that that part of Lord Browne-Wilkinson's speech was not concerned with pleading. But the same observation could, I fear, equally well be directed at any of the *dicta* which Mummery LJ himself invokes as the basis for his own conclusions on onus and is therefore a decidedly double-edged sword for his Lordship to wield.

2. Understanding the notice principle

The illustrated and complicating truth is that the issue about onus cannot be resolved satisfactorily by reference to authority alone, because the authorities are not entirely clear. It can really only be determined through a clearer understanding of the notice principle itself and on this we have received little guidance from the Court of Appeal to date. Such guidance is urgently needed, because there are (at least) three different ways of rationalising three-party restitution cases of the *Boulter* configuration, each of which pulls in a significantly different direction. Model 1 results in the onus of proof falling on the creditor. Models 2 and 3 appear to generate the opposite conclusion, though for different reasons. Only a clear choice between them holds out any hope of resolving the issue one way or the other.

Model 1: Strict Restitutionary Liability Subject to Defences

This model conceives of the notice principle as part of a defence of bona fide purchase to a strict liability restitutionary claim by the surety.[30] The latter is

[27] *Turnbull v Duval* [1902] AC 429; *Avon Finance Co Ltd v Bridger* [1985] 2 All ER 281; *Midland Bank Plc v Shephard* [1988] 3 All ER 17. Other cases of the *O'Brien* pattern which are equally inconclusive include: *Bridgeman v Green* (1755) 2 Ves Sen 627; *Kempson v Ashbee* (1874) LR 10 Ch App 15; *Lancashire Loans v Black* [1934] 1 KB 380.

[28] (1881) 18 Ch D 188, 197–198. This is of particular significance, since *Bainbrigge* is stated in *O'Brien* [1994] 1 AC 180, 191E to be the basis of Lord Browne-Wilkinson's notice principle. See also *Thornber v Sheard* (1850) 12 Beav 589, 601, *per* Lord Langdale MR; *Kempson v Ashbee* (1874) LR 10 Ch App 15, 21, *per* Sir James, LJ.

[29] [1994] 1 AC 200, 210A.

[30] See O'Dell [1997] CLJ 71.

entitled to restitution of her proprietary interest in the house because her consent to parting with it was vitiated by some factor (here, misrepresentation) brought to bear upon her will. The analogy is with two-party cases of mistake[31] and other three-party cases of consensual failure, like *Lipkin Gorman v Karpnale*[32] or equitable "tracing claims,"[33] where the law provides a strict restitutionary regime. The enriched creditor is presumptively liable to restore its gain, unless it can make out a defence by proving both that it gave (executed) value and that the value was given in good faith and without notice of the surety's restitutionary right ("equity").[34] Disproving notice is a precondition of the creditor's entitlement to claim transactional security and there is therefore no reason for the surety to raise or plead it.

Model 2: Fault-based restitutionary liability[35]

According to this conception, proof of notice is a necessary feature of the surety's restitutionary cause of action. Although in two-party cases involving mistake or misrepresentation, restitutionary liability is strict, the regime changes when the vitiating factor is brought to bear upon a claimant by a third party. Here, it is incumbent upon the claimant to prove that the recipient knew, or ought to have known about that factor before she will succeed. This is a "pragmatic" restriction placed upon the scope of the claim;[36] the pragmatism lying in the goal of averting excessive transactional disruption. The fault condition hence plays the same role as the defence of bona fide purchase in Model 1 (protecting transactional security), but there is an important difference in that the onus of proof rests with the surety (not with the creditor); and in the fact that even donee creditors can claim immunity from restitutionary claims of the *O'Brien* type, provided they are innocent of the third party's wrongdoing. Since notice forms an essential ingredient of the surety's claim in this model, she is obliged (subject to the resolution of point 2, below) to plead it.

31 *Eg, Barclays Bank Ltd v WJ Simms and Cooke (Southern) Ltd* [1980] 1 QB 677.

32 *Lipkin Gorman (a firm) v Karpnale Ltd* [1991] 2 AC 548 (HL).

33 The inverted commas are included here because tracing is not a claim, but a process which, where applicable, logically precedes a claim. See Birks, *An Introduction to the Law of Restitution* (Oxford, 1985, rev'd 1989), 358.

34 Aside from the defence of bona fide purchase, the creditor could now, of course, claim a defence of change of position: *Lipkin Gorman* [1991] 2 AC 548.

35 See, Birks (ed), *Laundering and Tracing*, 334.

36 *Ibid.*

Model 3: Strict liability restitutionary claim with a contractual overlay

This is identical to Model 1, but with an important overlay. The plaintiff's restitutionary claim is again strict; but, before she can revert to it, she must first set aside the contract that exists between herself and the creditor.[37] She has made a bargain with the bank, according to which it is entitled to her interest in the house and, if she wants the interest back, she must first cut away the bank's agreed entitlement to it. Otherwise, restitution will have the undesirable effect of contradicting the way that risk has been consensually allocated between the parties.

This way of understanding *O'Brien* cases has three consequences. First, in so far as the giving of value by a defendant is relevant, all that is required is for the creditor to show contractual consideration for the guarantee-exchange sufficient to support a simple contract.[38] Second, in all but the rarest of cases, the defence of bona fide purchase is irrelevant and references to it inapposite.[39] Third – and most significantly for current purposes – the onus would seem to be on the surety to do the work to set the contract aside, not on the creditor to show reasons why it should not be.[40] This means that the surety will have to plead and prove the existence of facts which alerted, or (at least) should have alerted,[41] the creditor to the possibility that the contract was not freely made, before she will be entitled to set the arrangement aside.

The court's reference to the bona fide purchase defence suggests that it was endorsing something akin to Model 1, but this is problematic for reasons

[37] See, Barker, *supra* n 22, at pp 203–204; American Law Institute, *Restatement of Restitution* (1937) , s 167 and comment (c) thereto; s 28 (d) and comment (a) thereto; s 70. Where there is a bargain between the transferor and transferee of a benefit, which has been induced by the wrong of a third party, the transferee is not liable to a restitutionary claim unless he had notice of the wrong, because he is "entitled to keep the benefit of the bargain."

[38] *Ibid*, comment (c) to s 167.

[39] *Ibid*. The bona fide purchase defence is confined to those cases in which there is no bargain between creditor and surety, but there is instead some exchange between the creditor and debtor: see comment (e) to s 167. The latter scenario is likely to be rare, since in most surety transactions the bargain is between surety and creditor.

[40] The location of the onus under the *Restatement* is actually unclear. But the normal principle in English contract law is that a contracting party is entitled to rely on his partner's apparent intentions: see *Smith v Hughes* (1871) LR 6 QB 597, 607, *per* Blackburn J; *The Hannah Blumenthal* [1983] 1 AC 854; Treitel, *The Law of Contract* , 9th ed (London, 1995), 1. If those intentions are to be set aside, the onus is on the other party to show a reason for doing so. This conclusion seems to be affirmed in *Chitty on Contracts*, 27th ed (London, 1994), para 2–001, n 6, where the objective principle (as it is commonly called) is stated to prevail unless a "defence" to it can be made out.

[41] There is some doubt as to which of these needs to be proven. The former is sufficient (see *Hartog v Colin and Shields* [1939] 3 All ER 566), but the better view seems to be that the latter will suffice: see *Centrovincial Estates Plc v Merchant Investors Assurance Co Ltd* [1983] Com LR 158, *per* Slade LJ; Collins, *The Law of Contract*, 3rd ed (London, 1997), 214–215.

already stated: the notice principle would not apply in personal guarantee cases and an innocent creditor would apparently have to provide executed consideration[42] in order to make a charge fully secure. The second model of liability is out of kilter with the way that restitutionary causes of action based on consensual failure normally work, because such failures normally describe sufficient reasons in themselves for a plaintiff to have a *prima facie* claim. It also sets up an illogical disparity between liability-regimes in two and three-party cases. And it contradicts its main proponent's customary (and laudable) thesis[43] that issues of transactional security in restitutionary claims are best worked out at the defence stage, not by artificially inhibiting restitutionary causes of action. Model 3 is endorsed in the *Restatement of Restitution*[44] and seems, of the three, to offer the best way forward. Only it has the potential to explain why notice is relevant (a) both in cases involving charges and personal guarantees, (b) both in cases involving registered and unregistered land, and (c) both in cases where the value provided by the creditor is executory and executed. It would also (d) avoid the illogical disparity between two and three-party cases referred to above (endorsing a basic strict-liability regime in both) and (e) explain many of the comments in the older authorities of the *O'Brien* pattern,[45] which suggest that positive reasons have to be shown for a creditor to be legally affected by a third party's wrongdoing. It could not, of course, explain references to notice (should they materialise) where no contract[46] has been made between the surety and the creditor, but such a contract was present in *O'Brien* and it will be, I suggest, in virtually every case. Few sureties assign away their interests in property without an agreement as to the terms according to which they are doing so.

If Model 3 is correct, as I suggest it is, the Court of Appeal's conclusions on onus are seriously open to question. At the very least, the burden must be on a surety to prove facts which ought to have put the creditor on inquiry as to a third party's misrepresentation, before the usual contract of guarantee can be set aside and the proprietary interest in the house reclaimed on that ground. Once such facts have been proven, the onus may then shift to the creditor to show that reasonable precautions were launched for the surety's protection – but not before. To the extent that the Court of Appeal's judgment suggests otherwise, it is to be regretted.

42 Despite the illogic of this, this seems to be the rule: *Hardingham v Nicholls* (1745) 3 Atk 304.

43 See *eg* Birks, *Restitution – The Future* (Sydney, 1993), ch 2, esp at pp 34–42.

44 *Supra* n 37.

45 *Supra* n 28.

46 The same would be true where the contract between surety and creditor was void *ab initio*. In these circumstances, notice would be relevant only to the defendant's entitlement to invoke the restitutionary defence of change of position, or, in the exceptional circumstances referred to in n 39, *supra*, the defence of bona fide purchase.

C. POINT 2: PROCESS: NEED NOTICE BE EXPRESSLY PLEADED?

The Court's second point was that constructive notice need not be pleaded because it is not a matter of fact.[47] Though the judgment is opaque at best, some passages suggest that notice is best viewed as a matter of mixed fact and law: a legal conclusion which the court is led to draw from the facts.[48] This seems correct and the strict position is that such conclusions need not be pleaded.[49] On the other hand, matters of mixed fact and law are in practice regularly included in pleadings. Negligence is a classic example, always pleaded. Moreover, RSC Ord 18, r 12 (4) clearly envisages the pleading of notice in some cases, because it describes a power for the court to order full particulars.

The resulting uncertainty on this issue is probably best resolved in individual cases by reference to the governing purposes of the pleading rules: which include the prevention of surprise at trial, the definition of the issues, and the provision of a fair opportunity to an opposing party to prepare evidence.[50] The particular desire to avoid surprise at trial finds specific expression in RSC Ord. 18, r 8 (1)(b): which states that matters must always be pleaded expressly if failing to do so is liable to have this effect.

Assuming that the burden was, as the cases suggest,[51] on Mrs Boulter to put the bank on inquiry of her husband's misrepresentation, the governing question then becomes: was the bank given a fair opportunity to prepare evidence to meet such arguments and to prove that it had taken reasonable steps to protect her?

The judgment on this is a fine one. On the one hand, Mrs Boulter had pleaded the relationship between herself and her husband; and the fact that she had received no explanation as to the nature and effect of the charge. Both of these facts might pave the way towards a notice-based argument and might legitimately have led the bank to suspect that she intended to raise it. On the other hand, she had not actually mentioned notice and had expressly pleaded agency. The bank's reply and defence to counterclaim understandably proceeded on the latter basis. The bank presumably concluded that she had made a mistake in omitting notice; or that she thought that she was likely to succeed on the agency point alone.[52] Presumably also, Mrs Boulter either had made a

[47] *Supra* n 7.

[48] At pp 1005c–d, 1007g.

[49] Casson, *Odgers on High Court Pleading and Practice*, 23rd ed (London, 1991), 131; RSC Ord 18, r 7(1).

[50] *Bullen & Leake & Jacob's Precedents of Pleadings*, 12th ed (London, 1975), 112–113; *Philipps v Philipps* (1878) 4 QBD 127, 139, *per* Cotton LJ.

[51] *Supra* nn 18, 19.

[52] Given comments in *O'Brien* [1994] 1 AC 180, 193-194, this would have been decidedly optimistic.

mistake of this type, or was a genuine victim of the prevailing uncertainty about the onus of proof, to which we have adverted.

Though the judgement is a difficult one, the trial judge would seem to have been in the best position to assess the merits and demerits of the respective arguments and it is therefore somewhat surprising that the Court of Appeal decided to interfere with his decision. Furthermore, the court's suggestion that notice need *never* be mentioned expressly – even by the party who bears the onus of (dis)proving it – strikes one as wholly counterintuitive. It has the significant potential to leave parties guessing as to the case which is to be argued at trial. This is contrary to the spirit of efficient justice.

D. CONCLUSIONS AND SUGGESTIONS

The instant case raised a very narrow issue, but it has significant implications. It seems likely that the Court of Appeal, out of sympathy for Mrs Boulter in the prevailing environment of uncertainty about the location of the onus of proof and way that claims should be pleaded in *O'Brien* cases,[53] reached the conclusion which was liable to be most advantageous to her in costs. In so doing, however, it has fostered some unfortunate ideas. One of these – that the notice principle derived from *O'Brien* is a novel application of the defence of bona fide purchase – could significantly limit that principle's scope and hence its usefulness. It also leads to inappropriate conclusions on the onus of proof. The idea that creditors bear the onus of pleading and proving the non-existence of facts which might have put them on inquiry about third party impropriety, aside from encountering a certain logical difficulty,[54] ventures just too far down the road of surety-protection and threatens to upset the delicate balance between this value and the value of commercial security. Lord Browne-Wilkinson has always, rightly, been conscious of this balance[55] and it's proper maintainance was probably one of the considerations which caused the Romilly heresy[56] to die an early death.[57] The court's conclusions

[53] It is notable that *Atkin's Encylopedia of Court Forms in Civil Proceedings*, 2nd ed (London, 1996) contains no template for the pleading of *O'Brien*-type misrepresentation claims, where the allegation is one of notice, not agency.

[54] It is difficult to see how a creditor can be "put on inquiry" by facts, which it itself bears the onus of disproving. For a ball to be "put" into one's own court, someone else must first have hit it there.

[55] *O'Brien* [1994] 1 AC 180, 188, 197–198.

[56] This heresy is said to consist in the idea that, where a person (A) obtains a large, voluntary benefit from another (B), the onus is without more cast upon B to prove that A knew and understood what (s)he was doing: *Hoghton v Hoghton* (1852) 15 Beav 278, *per* Lord Romilly.

[57] The heresy has never formally been overruled, but is regarded as bad law: see *Yerkey v Jones* (1940) 63 CLR 649, 678-681; *O'Brien* [1994] 1 AC 180, 193.

on the location of the burden of proof move us one, unfortunate, step back towards this undesirable heresy.

Of the two suggested grounds of decision, the second is the more palatable than the first. That is, it is easier to accept that Mrs Boulter succeeded because, although she bore part of the onus, she had done enough (procedurally) to enable her to seek to discharge it at trial, than it is to accept that an undivided onus fell upon the bank. Unfortunately, however, we are left in some doubt as to which point was decisive. Moreover, even if it was the reasoning on procedure which ultimately held sway, this reasoning has unfortunate repercussions for the efficient administration of justice. If notice need not be mentioned expressly by a surety, creditors can never be sure that the argument is not going to be launched at them at trial. If there is to be sympathy for Mrs Boulter's pleading confusion (which the Court of Appeal evidently felt that there should be), it is difficult to resist the conclusion that this sympathy might have been better expressed not by allowing her appeal, but by exercising subsequent restraint over her liability for the costs of amending her pleadings.

6

Cross-border Security Enforcement and the Conflict of Laws†

GABRIEL MOSS* AND FELICITY TOUBE**

1. INTRODUCTION

The Court of Appeal decision in *Macmillan Inc v Bishopsgate Investment Trust Plc*[1] raised a number of issues which are of importance for lawyers interested in banking, restitution and conflict of laws. The courts at first instance and in the Court of Appeal grappled with questions about a priority dispute in relation to shares. In relation to that dispute, the courts had to deal with the interface between restitution and the conflict of laws. They also had to deal with the relevant choice of law, while not expressing a concluded view as to whether the remedy sought was restitutionary.

In *Macmillan*, the preliminary issue which was taken in the Court of Appeal concerned the question of priority between competing claims to shares between those to whom shares had been legally transferred and other parties who asserted a prior equitable interest. The question of the proper choice of law had added importance, as there were a number of material differences between English and New York laws:

(a) Under English law it is unclear whether (and if so how far) questions of constructive notice are relevant to questions of priority. Under the New York version of the Uniform Commercial Code, a bona fide purchaser for value who takes delivery of a certificated security, including delivery through a paperless transfer system (in New York called the DTC) takes free from any adverse claim of which he had no notice at the time of delivery, whether he subsequently obtains registration or not. The relevant notice cannot merely be constructive notice.

† Some of this material has already appeared in G Moss & F Toube, "Cross-Border Enforcement of Security" (1997) 16 IBFL 1, 9.

* QC.

** Barrister.

[1] [1996] 1 WLR 387 (CA), affg [1995] 1 WLR 978 (Millett J). The House of Lords has declined leave to appeal on the conflicts issue, which was heard by the Court of Appeal as a preliminary issue.

(b) Under English law, a person is required to register the shares in order to perfect title. By contrast, under New York law, the transfer of a certificated security takes place (as between the parties to a transfer and persons claiming under the transferor) when the purchaser, or a person designated by him, acquires possession of the certificate, not when he obtains registration. The certificate so obtained is treated under New York law as a negotiable instrument. It is not so treated under English law.[2]

(c) Special provision is made under New York law for delivery of shares through the DTC system. Such transfers do not require registration with the company. There is no equivalent under English law.

2. THE FACTS

Macmillan arose in the course of unravelling the complex dealings between the public and private sides of the Maxwell empire. Macmillan Inc and various pension funds had equitable ownership of shares from various jurisdictions. The *Macmillan* case itself however, was restricted to questions of priority over shares in Berlitz International Inc ("Berlitz"), which was a company incorporated in New York.

In *Macmillan*, the three relevant defendants (Swiss Volksbank, Credit Suisse and Lehmann Bros) accepted as security shares in Berlitz, amongst other assets. Berlitz shares were a New York stock traded on the New York Stock Exchange. Some of the transfers which were at issue in the case involved the lodging of New York type share certificates in London and some of the transfers concerned share transfers through the DTC in New York. The governing law of the facility in respect of which the shares were given as security was English. The relevant branches of the defendant institutions were located in London. The borrower which gave security was also located in London.

A claim to a prior equitable interest was asserted by Macmillan Inc, a subsidiary of MCC, which was an English stock exchange listed company. Macmillan itself was incorporated, like many corporations in the USA, in Delaware. The question arose as to the choice of law which should govern the question of priorities between Macmillan, the prior equitable owner, and the three financial institutions which claimed that they held shares in Berlitz as security.

[2] See *infra*.

3. FIRST INSTANCE

At first instance, although Millett J accepted that the relevant *obligation* was restitutionary, he identified the relevant *issue* as being that of the priority of proprietary rights. That issue, Millett J held, was governed by the law of the place where the relevant transactions took place, namely New York. The relevant transactions were, the judge held, (i) the paperless share transfer which took place in New York, and (ii) the registration, which also took place in New York, of the transfers of the shares which were commenced by delivery of the share certificates and executed transfer forms in England. He applied New York law but in fact held that the plaintiffs would have failed even under English law.

Macmillan appealed on the ground that the relevant law should have been that with which the obligation to make restitution of the shares had the closest and most real connection, namely English law. It also appealed on various points of New York and English law and on the facts. The Court of Appeal agreed to hear the conflicts issue as a preliminary point.

4. COURT OF APPEAL

(a) The short point of law

The Court of Appeal held that the law governing the priorities was not the law of the place of transfer (the *lex loci actus*), but rather the law of the (deemed) location of the shares (the *lex situs*), which also happened to be New York. In fact the law of the shares themselves was also the law of New York, but it might not have been New York if the relevant register been kept elsewhere.

(b) The three-stage test: characterisation

In the Court of Appeal, the leading judgment was given by Staughton LJ. His Lordship noted that:[3]

> "In any case which involves a foreign element it may prove necessary to decide what system of law is to be applied, either to the case as a whole or to a particular issue or issues."

[3] [1996] 1 WLR 387, 391G.

He divided the task of identifying the correct system of law into a three-stage test to make the proper jurisdiction easier to determine. Staughton LJ identified the following three stages which had to be gone through in order to find the *lex causae*:[4]

> "First, it is necessary to characterise the issue which is before the court. . . . The second stage is to select the rule of conflict of laws which lays down a connecting factor for the issue in question . . . Thus, the formal validity of a marriage is to be determined, for the most part, by the law of the place where it is celebrated; intestate succession to movables, by the law of the place where the deceased was domiciled when he died; and the interpretation of a contract, by what is described as its proper law. Thirdly, it is necessary to identify the system of law which is tied by the connecting factor found in stage two to the issue characterised in stage one."

The answers to each individual stage may well be different in different countries. Staughton LJ correctly noted, following *Dicey & Morris*,[5] that there is a vast theoretical background to this question which has had very little effect upon the actual decisions which have been made by the courts. There has long been academic argument about whether the characterisation should be attempted in respect of the rule of law, the cause of action or the legal issue. Judicial pronouncements have been few and far between, as judges have been willing to avoid the issue if at all possible, and to find some other, more pragmatic way of dealing with the matter.

However, in *Macmillan*, the question had to be faced directly. Staughton LJ stated that he intended that the question of which jurisdiction should be the proper one should be determined by rules of conflict of laws which were "simple and easy to apply".[6] He then went on to give consideration to some fifty cases and gave a judgment of some fourteen pages. At first instance Millett J had accepted the contention put forward by Macmillan that their claim was restitutionary in nature and that therefore the proper law was to be determined by reference to the proper law of the obligation, namely English law. However, as Aldous LJ pointed out, answering the question of characterisation is "not easy".[7]

Like Millett J, the Court of Appeal held that the court should characterise the *issue* before it, rather than the *cause of action*. As Staughton LJ noted, the characterisation of the claim as restitutionary did not really take Macmillan any further. Staughton LJ accepted that the claim was restitutionary in nature, but he stated that the real question at issue was whether the defen-

[4] *Ibid*, 391H–392A.
[5] *Dicey & Morris on the Conflict of Laws*, 12th ed (1993).
[6] [1996] 1 WLR 387, 392G.
[7] *Ibid*, 417G.

dants were bona fide purchasers for value without notice. It was the defence which identified the issue.

(Had the choice of law been determined by the nature of the obligation, the court would have applied Rule 201 as set out by *Dicey & Morris*,[8] namely:

> "The obligation to restore the benefit of an enrichment obtained at another person's expense is governed by the proper law of the obligation.
> The proper law of the obligation is (*semble*)
> If the obligation arises in connection with a contract, its proper law is the law applicable to the contract;
> If it arises in connection with a transaction concerning an immovable (land), its proper law is the law of the country where the immovable is situated (*lex situs*);
> If it arises in any other circumstances, its proper law is the law of the country where the enrichment occurs.")

It appears that this approach is correct in relation to this case. *Macmillan* concerned a battle between two sets of innocent parties, each claiming to have a better *title* to the shares in Berlitz. The relevant issue was therefore one as to the *title* to property, which is usually resolved by the law of the place where the property is situated.[9] However, in other cases, it may be necessary to consider a number of issues, some identified by the pleaded cause of action, and some focused upon in the defence which is served in response to the pleaded claim. It may be that there are different choices of law which apply to different parts of the case.[10] However, in *Macmillan* itself, this difficult question could be, and was, side-stepped by the court.

Auld LJ agreed that the issue should be characterised by reference to the defence of the financial institutions, He warned against characterising issues in terms of categories recognised purely by domestic law – in this case "receipt-based restitutionary claims". Aldous LJ characterised the issue as one of property over shares. This is a characterisation which may be thought to bear closer relation to a characterisation in terms of the cause of action, rather than specifically the issue identified by the other judges.

The differences between the judgments of their Lordships indicates that the manner in which the Court of Appeal dealt with the question of characterisation avoids the fact that, regardless of whether the characterisation which takes place is of the issue or of the cause of action, characterisation tests may be easily manipulated by a court to choose one jurisdiction rather than

[8] *Dicey & Morris*, vol 2, p 1471.

[9] See A Briggs, "From Complexity to Anticlimax: Restitution and Choice of Law" [1996] RLR 88.

[10] See J Bird, "Choice of Law", ch 3 of FD Rose (ed), *Restitution and the Conflict of Laws* (1995).

another. The choice of law which is decided upon by the court rather depends upon how it frames the issue, or indeed the cause of action. Most cases admit of several defined issues, and the manner of definition may affect the eventual choice of law.

(c) The appropriate rule of conflict of laws

In the Court of Appeal, all three judges came to the conclusion that the question of priority should be determined by reference to the *lex situs*, New York. However, the manner in which each of them defined the *lex situs* was slightly different.

Staughton LJ considered the question of the appropriate conflicts rule with an eye to the fact that it was the defence which really defined the issue. The general property rule is that issues as to rights of property are determined by the law of the place where the property is. This same rule applies to chattels. The judge held that negotiable instruments are also governed by the *lex situs*, as they are assimilated to chattels and were treated as tangible movables. Staughton LJ does not appear to have been attracted by the contrary suggestion that to treat shares as similar to tangible movables requires the analogy to be stretched too far. As *Dicey & Morris* notes, "Something with no physical existence can hardly have a location in space".[11]

In reality, the *location* of an intangible must be a *deemed* location, *ie* one which exists as a matter of law rather than of fact. This *location* therefore itself depends on a choice of connecting factors such as place of incorporation, place where the relevant register is kept etc.

Auld LJ agreed that the *lex situs* should be the relevant law, rather than that which governed the chose in action. His Lordship favoured the *lex situs* because it treated shares like other property. He also regarded such a rule as promoting certainty.

Aldous LJ regarded the law governing priority over shares (which he had characterised as the issue) as being the *lex situs*. It appears that his Lordship regarded the *lex situs* as being always the place of incorporation. He reached this conclusion irrespective of whether the relevant shares were registered (as is occasionally the case) in a different jurisdiction, as dictated by the constitutional documents of the company. In fact the relevant case law shows that, in the case of registered shares, where the location of the relevant register is different from the place of incorporation, the location of the shares follows the place of the register and not the place of incorporation.

[11] *Dicey & Morris*, 923.

In reaching its conclusion, the Court of Appeal was affected by its decision that whether the shares were to be characterised as negotiable instruments was a question of domestic English law. Their Lordships concluded that the shares in this case were not so regarded under English law, even though they were so regarded by the law of their *situs*.

Under standard English law doctrines, registered shares are purely intangible. Under the Companies Act 1985, s 185, the share certificate is merely prima facie evidence of title. Share certificates for registered shares are not in English law, in the absence of special usage, regarded as negotiable instruments. Shares are transferred by registration, not by delivery of the certificate.[12]

The situation in New York is very different. The share certificate is in many (although not all) ways regarded as a negotiable instrument, and as a physical embodiment of the shares. Therefore under New York law, shares pass by delivery of the certificate. Registration is not necessary.

Under English law, it is generally regarded as effective to acquire title over tangible movables abroad in the country in which the tangible movable is located.[13] The situation with respect to intangibles is different. The question of priority arising from the creation of a new interest in an intangible depends on the law governing the intangible.[14]

If shares were simply treated in English law as intangibles, the law governing the shares should apply to priority questions. If, however, shares were seen as tangibles, the *lex loci actus* – that is the law of the place where the security interest adverse to the prior equitable interest was created – should apply. Therefore, in the case of a bank taking security over the shares in London, the intangibles rule would mean that its claim to priority over prior equitable owners would depend on the law governing the share in question. If, on the other hand, the tangible movables rules applied, the law of the place where the relevant adverse claim was created would govern the claim to priority.

At first instance in *Macmillan*, Millett J held that shares were neither wholly in the intangible camp nor wholly in the tangible camp. In particular, he accepted that there were separate questions as to priority over the shares as intangibles, on the one hand, and on the other hand over the share certificates as tangibles. Where security was created by delivery of the tangible, the share certificate, Millett J appears to have opted for the tangible movable rule of *lex loci actus*.

[12] Contrast the position in relation to *eg* bearer shares, title to which passes by delivery and which are treated as negotiable instruments for the purposes of priority issues in English domestic law.

[13] *Carnmell v Sewell* (1860) 5 H & N 728; *Winkworth v Christie Manson & Woods Ltd* [1980] Ch. 496; *Inglis v Robertson* [1898] AC 616.

[14] *Le Feuvre v Sullivan* (1855) 10 Moo PC 1; *Kelly v Selwyn* [1905] 2 Ch 117.

There is a further complication which divides English law from New York law on the question of priority, namely the requirement under English law that registration (or possibly something close to it) be achieved in order for title to be perfected, a process described in English law as getting in the legal estate. Under New York law, the equitable/legal mortgage or charge dichotomy is irrelevant. Registration is not required for perfection of title.

In the *Macmillan* case, the share certificate of one particular block of shares was lodged in London. Millett J held at first instance that the question of priorities at this stage was to be judged by English law. After the proceedings had started, the shares were registered in New York. According to Millett J's test, the effect on the question of priorities of the lodging of the certificate for registration in New York was to be judged by New York law. The difficulty was that under New York law this second event was of no significance in relation to priorities. From the point of New York law, priority had already been achieved by delivery of the certificate in London. According to Millett J's test, that first delivery was governed by English law. Under English law, that first delivery did not have the effect of conferring priority on the bank. Millett J refused to accept a result which neither system of law would have reached. He held that the combined effect of the two acts was to give the bank priority under New York law. However, this involved holding that the bank had, by taking the share certificate to New York for registration, altered the applicable law.

The approach of Millett J gave rise to transnational anomalies and difficulties. Suppose, for example, that shares in a New York corporation traded on the New York Stock Exchange were handed half way across the Atlantic on Concorde to a manager of a branch of a bank in London. From a purely technical point of view, since the place of delivery is over international waters, the result may depend on the registration of the plane. That may or may not be the home country of the airline. It would also mean that a bank doing business through a branch in London could find a convenient jurisdiction in some other part of the world which gives easy priority to chargees irrespective of registration over prior equitable interests. The bank could then arrange for share certificates to be couriered to that country and delivered to the bank's agent there. Millett J's approach was contrary to principle and authority and gave rise to anomaly and uncertainty. A banker would not normally keep a record of where a share certificate is delivered and the place of delivery is not normally annotated on the certificate.

The decision of the Court of Appeal avoids any of these problems, as the proper law is the law of the location of the shares, namely the place of registration of shares, which is normally also the place of incorporation and of the jurisdiction whose law governs the shares. This decision provides a measure of certainty and ease of reference. A banker therefore need normally only look at the place of registration/incorporation on the certificate relating to each share to be able to tell what law will govern the question of priorities.

The decision does involve bankers taking legal advice on priority rules under the law of each relevant jurisdiction affecting the shares. However, in the case of registered shares they already need to take advice on rules relating to the perfection of their security in each such jurisdiction and it should not be too onerous to seek advice also on priorities. In many cases there will also be a close link between perfection and priority.[15]

A further advantage of the approach of the Court of Appeal is that there can be no question of the bank which has taken security altering the applicable law by moving the certificate. Moreover, the transnational problem in the *Macmillan* case in relation to the half million block of shares is avoided. English law did not govern the question of priorities merely because the certificate was deposited in England, or continue to govern until the certificate was lodged for registration in New York.

As a postscript for lawyers interested in the conflict of laws, it is also worth noting that Staughton LJ considered and rejected the concept that the correct law was the law which the New York court could apply to the case as a result of the effect of its own rules of conflict of laws (the concept better known as *renvoi*). Auld LJ and Aldous LJ did not really address this question in their judgments, save that Auld LJ noted in passing that the purpose of the rules set down with respect to determining the correct principles in conflict of laws is to "strive for comity between systems".[16]

Interestingly, this is one area upon which the Court of Appeal came to the same conclusion as Millett J, who had held at first instance that *renvoi* was:[17]

> "[a] laudable endeavour to ensure that like cases should be treated alike wherever they are decided [but] it should not be recognised that this cannot be achieved by judicial mental gymnastics but only by international conventions"

Although this approach was practical and avoided the need to make detailed findings on New York law conflicts principles (on which there was considerable contradictory expert evidence), it does give rise to the possibility that the English courts will arrive, in applying foreign law, at results which the foreign court itself would not have arrived at. It is perhaps an example of the sacrifice of any (probably futile) attempt to achieve perfect harmony of result in favour of practicality and cost-effectiveness.

[15] There is much to be said for standardising priority rules in jurisdictions with major stock exchanges in order to facilitate international lending.

[16] [1996] 1 WLR 387, 407C.

[17] [1995] 1 WLR 978, 1008D.

(d) *Re Harvard Securities Ltd*[18]

Harvard bought shares for resale to clients. This case concerned registered American and Australian shares. These were held in blocks by nominees for Harvard. Customers were told that they had bought shares and the sales were recorded by book entries, but no separation of different clients' shares took place. The question for the court was whether Harvard (in liquidation) or the customers had title to the shares.

With regard to the choice of law, the priority question in relation to the Australian shares was determined in accordance with Australian law as the law of the place of the share register. The approach purports to follow and is consistent with the Court of Appeal in *Macmillan*, except that a distinction is drawn between legal and equitable title. This is not a valid distinction for conflict of laws purposes, although it made no difference in the case of Australian shares.

The judgment appears to go fundamentally wrong in relation to the American shares. First, there is the irrelevant distinction between legal and equitable title. Secondly, although it is correctly held that the characterisation issue of whether the shares are negotiable instruments is to be decided in accordance with the *lex fori*, there is the addition of an irrelevant reason, said to be more important, that the share certificates were in England. Thirdly, and worst of all, the English law domestic rule that equitable title can be transferred without registration is used to characterise the American share certificates as "negotiable in equity".[19] This amounts in effect to an impermissible characterisation of the negotiable instrument question in accordance with American law. In English law, the foreign certificate is either negotiable or not, in accordance with the evidence of usage in England. There is no question of negotiability in equity.

In the case of American shares the judgment does not in fact follow *Macmillan* at all, but contradicts it. As a result of a mistaken ruling on characterisation, the wrong choice of law appears to have been made. Following the approach of the Court of Appeal, the share certificates, as in *Macmillan*, should not have been regarded as negotiable instruments and the priority question should have been determined in accordance with the law of the place of registration of the shares, and not the location of the certificates.

[18] [1997] 2 BCLC 368 (Neuberger J).
[19] *Ibid*, 375c.

7

Cross-border Security Enforcement, Restitution and Priorities

NICK SEGAL*

INTRODUCTION

Macmillan Inc v Bishopsgate Investment Trust Plc (*No 3*) raises a number of important issues both in the law of restitution and the law of banking. For the banks involved, the litigation arose out of the conduct of their normal banking business – lending to a group of companies and taking security therefor (hence the banking law issues). For Macmillan, the litigation arose out of a fraud (hence the restitution issues). The heart of the case is the conflict between the rights and interests of banks who hold security taken in the ordinary course of their banking business and those of the innocent victims of fraud seeking to undo the financial consequences of the wrong done to them.

This, of course, is a classic conflict which raises fundamental policy issues concerning the priority to be given to, and the balance to be struck between, the goals of transactional security (the protection of commercial transactions) and the security of property (the protection of vested property rights and interests).[2] These are policy issues which are close to the hearts of bankers. Much of modern banking practice involves the careful and detailed documentation of complex financial transactions; transactional security is a high priority for banks. However, banks frequently become holders of property and proprietary rights, in particular, in the context of taking security to cover credit risk. The protection and preservation of such property rights is also of

* Solicitor, Partner, Allen & Overy.

[1] [1995] 1 WLR 978 (Millett J); affd [1996] 1 WLR 387 (CA).

[2] Denning LJ (as he then was) made the point, as he always did, succinctly, in *Bishopsgate Motor Finance Co Ltd v Transport Brakes Ltd* [1949] 1 KB 322, 336–337: "In the development of our law two principles have striven for mastery. The first is for the protection of property: no one can get a better title than he himself possesses. The second is for the protection of commercial transactions: the person who takes in good faith and for value without notice should get a good title."

fundamental importance to the banking community. Banking law[3] inevitably deals with and seeks to accommodate these policy objectives.

The recognition and balancing of these policy objectives also arises in the law of restitution. However, the precise weight and role to be given to these policy objectives is a matter of some debate. Furthermore, there is a good deal of speculation as to the extent to which the law of restitution is properly concerned with the protection of property rights. The principal significance of the *Macmillan v Bishopsgate* decision in the restitution context is that it raises the question of to the extent to which claims to vindicate subsisting property rights can properly be treated as part of the law of restitution. Both Millett J and two members of the Court of Appeal were prepared to accept that Macmillan's claim should be regarded as being a restitutionary one (albeit that the restitutionary claim was held not be relevant for the purposes of resolving the preliminary conflicts issue). However, no clear explanation was given to support the view that the claim was properly to be treated as restitutionary and, as I discuss below, there are substantial doubts as to whether this view is correct.

The *Macmillan v Bishopsgate* decision also deals with a number of issues relating to the priority of equitable charges. Millett J has some interesting things to say about the doctrine of constructive notice in the commercial context and as to the circumstances in which the holder of an equitable interest/charge (particularly in shares) can take priority over the holder of a prior equitable interest by dealings in the legal title. I will return to these issues after having considered the aspects of *Macmillan v Bishopsgate* which touch and concern the law of restitution.

THE FACTS IN *MACMILLAN* AND THE MANNER IN WHICH THE BANKS' SECURITY INTERESTS AROSE

The basic facts of *Macmillan v Bishopsgate* are as follows. The case arose out of the collapse of Robert Maxwell's business empire and his attempts to use the assets of public companies in the Maxwell Group, and pension funds, to secure the debts of his private companies. Macmillan Inc ("Macmillan"), a Delaware corporation which was a wholly owned subsidiary of Maxwell

[3] Of course, banking law is a secondary, as opposed to a primary, legal discipline which is based on, and uses, the primary legal subjects (including contract, tort and restitution) in the particular context of the activities of banks. Ross Cranston MP, in the Preface to his *Principles of Banking Law* (OUP, 1997) refers to his book as offering "a new framework for banking law. It takes as a given the modern world of the multifunctional bank with international operations ... [and] tries to bring the bulk of legal matters relating to banking activity within the four corners of the picture".

Communications Corporation Plc ("MCC"), sought the return of 10.6 million shares which it had held in a New York corporation, Berlitz International Inc. These shares had been wrongly pledged to various banks as security for indebtedness owed by various Maxwell companies (other than Macmillan or MCC). Macmillan sought to recover the shares from the banks to whom they had been given as security.

In the months prior to his death on 5th November, 1991, Robert Maxwell's group of companies was in serious financial difficulties and he was obliged to provide every increasing collateral in order to avoid breaches of the Group's banking covenants. The arrangements made in relation to the Berlitz shares were part of wide ranging support operation designed to avoid the collapse of the Group. Robert Maxwell needed to be able to use the valuable Berlitz shares as security for the debts of other Maxwell Group companies (which were not associated with, and not for the benefit of, Macmillan or MCC). In order to be able to do this he needed to create the conditions in which the shares could be dealt with and transferred without the direct involvement of Macmillan and in circumstances where the precise ownership of the shares could be hidden.

A number of stages were involved in the process. The first stage (which followed a board meeting of Macmillan at which the Macmillan board, in ignorance of Robert Maxwell's fraudulent purpose, authorised the transfer of the Berlitz shares) involved the transfer of the shares to Bishopsgate Investment Trust plc ("BIT"). BIT was an investment trust controlled by Robert Maxwell which acted as a nominee company holding assets, and acting, on behalf of companies within the Maxwell Group. BIT became the registered stockholder and certificates were issued in its name (at this stage some 21 certificates were issued in BIT's name – as Millett J noted, "the splitting of the stock certificate can have served no useful purpose except to facilitate separate dealings with individual parcels of shares").[4] Subsequently BIT entered into a nominee agreement acknowledging that it held the legal title to the Berlitz shares "as nominee for the account and benefit of Macmillan"; and that it had "no power or right to take any action with respect thereto without the express consent of Macmillan"; and it expressly disclaimed any beneficial interest in the stock. Accordingly, BIT was a bare trustee of the shares and had no authority to dispose of them or to use them as security except at the direction of Macmillan, which direction was never sought or given.

The second stage, in order to facilitate dealings in the shares, involved (in relation to 7.6 million of the shares) the deposit of the shares in the New York Central Depository System ("the DTC"). This was done by BIT in clear

[4] Unreported.

breach of trust and without Macmillan's knowledge or consent. Under the New York Uniform Commercial Code, shares in a New York corporation may be transferred (*inter alia*) by transfer within a central depository system. In such a case the shares are registered in the name of a clearing corporation and may under certain conditions be transferred by the making of appropriate entries to the accounts of the transferor and transferee in the books of the clearing corporation. When shares are deposited with the DTC the certificates are returned to the company's transfer agent and cancelled. The shares are then registered in the name of CEDE & Co ("CEDE"), which is a New York partnership which acts as nominee of the DTC. Accordingly, following their deposit into the DTC the Berlitz shares ceased to be in the registered ownership of BIT and were instead registered in the name of CEDE (which hold them for the account of the DTC agent acting for the Maxwell Group of companies). This was Morgan Stanley. Morgan Stanley was initially told to hold the shares to the order of London & Bishopsgate International Investment Management Plc, a private side company; subsequently Morgan Stanley was instructed to hold the shares to the order of Bishopsgate Investment Management Limited ("BIM"). BIM was a fund manager and the trustee of the common investment fund of the Maxwell Group's pension schemes.

It was in these circumstances that the shares were granted as security to three banks (Shearson Lehman, Swiss Volksbank and Credit Suisse) to secure the obligations owed to them by various private side companies of the Maxwell Group. The security interests in favour of these three banks were created in the following way.

The security in favour of Shearson Lehman arose as a result of the deposit of the share certificates with Lehman Bros in London pursuant to stock lending arrangements between Lehman Bros and BIM. The security was created in England by the deposit of the share certificates in London accompanied by duly executed share transfer forms. Subsequently, the security was perfected in New York by the deposit of the certificates in the DTC system. These shares were initially registered in the name of CEDE and subsequently, but only after the receipt of letters before action and with full knowledge of Macmillan's claim (and a sale by Lehman Bros to its parent Shearson Lehman), were the shares registered in the name of Shearson Lehman.

The security interest in favour of Swiss Volksbank was created in a different manner. Swiss Volksbank had made an advance to Robert Maxwell Group Trading Plc and the obligations of this company were guaranteed by Robert Maxwell Group plc ("RMG"). Berlitz shares were provided to Swiss Volksbank as security for RMG's guarantee. The shares were already deposited in the DTC system at the time that the security was created. The transfer creating the security was effected by means of entries on the books of the DTC in New York, debiting the account of Morgan Stanley and crediting the account of Citibank NA, a nominee company for Swiss Volksbank. Following receipt of letters before action and with full knowledge of Macmillan's claim, Swiss Volksbank was subsequently registered on the share register in New York. Millett J noted the differences between the circumstances in which Swiss Volksbank and Lehman Bros acquired their security interests. He said:[5]

> "The circumstances in which Swiss Volksbank acquired its security interest in the Berlitz shares were very different from those in which Lehman Bros acquired its interest. Lehman Bros acquired its interest in the Berlitz shares from BIT by a series of transactions at a time when BIT was the registered owner of the shares; Swiss Volksbank had no dealings of any kind with BIT. It acquired its interest in consequence of dealings with RMG, by a single transaction, from an unknown transferor, at a time when the shares were in the DTC system and registered in the name of DTC's nominee company. Lehman Bros acquired its security interest in the shares by the physical delivery in England of stock certificates indorsed with duly executed share certificates; Swiss Volksbank acquired its security interest as a result of book entries made in New York".

Credit Suisse took security over two parcels of Berlitz shares. The shares were taken as security for indebtedness owed by RMG. The first parcel (500,000 shares) was pledged by the delivery of share certificates in the same manner as security given to Lehman Bros. Unlike Lehman Bros, however, Credit Suisse had taken no steps to perfect its security at the date of the writ in the action. Following a failed attempt to continue an *ex parte* injunction preventing Credit Suisse perfecting its security, Credit Suisse became the registered owner of these shares. The second parcel of shares (1,000,000) were already deposited in the DTC system at the date when they were pledged to Credit Suisse and the security was therefore taken in the same manner as the security taken by Swiss Volksbank. Long after Macmillan's action had been commenced, Credit Suisse arranged for these shares to be withdrawn from the DTC and registered in the name of its nominee.

MACMILLAN'S CAUSE OF ACTION AND ITS CHARACTERISATION AT FIRST INSTANCE AND IN THE COURT OF APPEAL

Macmillan sought to recover the proceeds of sale of the shares in Berlitz (the shares had been sold with the consent of all parties prior to the hearing) from each of the banks.

[5] [1995] 1 WLR 978, 986E–G.

What was Macmillan's cause of action and what relief did it seek? Macmillan claimed a declaration that it remained beneficially entitled to the shares; a declaration that the defendants held their shares on constructive trust for Macmillan and an enquiry as to compensation, damages for breach of trust and conversion and ancillary relief. Millett J usefully summed at the position as follows:[6]

> "Macmillan seeks both proprietary and personal relief, claiming restitution of the proceeds of sale of the shares and equitable compensation for loss. It originally also claimed damages for conversion but that claim has rightly been abandoned in the course of the trial. Each of the defendants claim to have been, or in the case of shares in Lehman to have derived title through, a bona fide purchaser for value of the shares without notice of Macmillan's interest . . .
>
> The defendants insist that the question at issue is concerned with the priority of competing interests in a chose in action. Macmillan insists that its claim lies in restitution and, being brought by an equitable owner, must be decided in accordance with equitable principles. Even its claim to the return of the Berlitz shares or their proceeds in specie, it submits, which can loosely be described as proprietary, was in truth no more than an invocation of the power of a court of equity, acting in personan as a court of conscience, to require the defendants to take whatever steps were necessary to restore the shares to Macmillan's ownership . . . [The purpose for which Macmillan's claim is to be characterised, in the context of the conflicts issue] is to determine whether the defendants or any of them is under any obligation to Macmillan to restore the relevant Berlitz shares or their proceeds. Such a claim is properly regarded as a restitutionary claim and the liability of the defendants to satisfy the claim as a restitutionary obligation.
>
> . . . *It is manifestly correct to characterise Macmillan's claim as lying in restitution . . . [The present case . . .] is concerned with title, not tracing. There is no doubt that the Berlitz shares in which the defendants claim security interests are the self same shares in which Macmillan's beneficial interest formally subsisted. That is not in dispute. The question is whether any of the defendants has acquired an interest in those shares which is superior to that of Macmillan.*
>
> *In my judgment, Macmillan's claim is properly to be characterised as a restitutionary claim which depends upon establishing a continuing proprietary interest in the subject matter of the claim; each of the defendants claims to have acquired a security interest in that subject matter which is superior to Macmillan's interest; and the question at issue is whether any of the defendants can identify a particular act or event which had the result of extinguishing Macmillan's interest or postponing it to that of the defendant. In my judgment the defendants have correctly characterised the issue as one of priority."*

[6] [1995] 1 WLR 983F-G, 988C-G, 990C-E (emphasis added).

Thus, Macmillan's claim was based on its alleged subsisting equitable interest. Macmillan itself, because of its desire to have the banks judged by English standards as to the notice required to establish a defence against Macmillan's claim, was anxious to play down the proprietary aspect of its claim and wished, instead, to identify and emphasise an obligation to which the banks were subject – which obligation would be governed by English law. Accordingly, Macmillan wished to characterise its claim for the return of the shares (or their proceeds in specie) as being based on equity's in personam jurisdiction to require defendants to restore property received by them, *ie* the claim involved the enforcement of an obligation as opposed to a simple property right. This approach, together with the fact that Millett J was being asked only to determine the conflicts question (so that the defence, as opposed to the claim, in the case was of primary significance) means that some caution is needed when reviewing Millett J's analysis of the cause of action. Nonetheless, and it submitted correctly, Millett J was concerned to be clear about the nature of the cause of action in order to satisfy himself that the banks' defence was an appropriate one.[7]

Millett J noted that because there was no relationship of any kind between Macmillan and the banks there could be no equity between them which would generate an obligation on the banks to return the shares to Macmillan. "In the absence of such an equity, any liability of the defendants to restore the shares or their proceeds to Macmillan or to pay compensation for their failure to do so must be based on Macmillan's continuing equitable ownership of the shares. In the language of restitution, Macmillan's claim must rest upon 'an undestroyed proprietary base'."[8]

Millett J bases himself on "the fundamental distinction" in the law of restitution between unjust enrichment of the defendant which is occasioned by depriving the plaintiff of his property and enrichment which results from a wrong done to the plaintiff by the defendant. This, of course, at least in part, reflects the fundamental divide in the law of restitution between unjust enrichment by subtraction (or autonomous unjust enrichment), where no wrong has to be established, and unjust enrichment by wrongdoing (or dependent unjust enrichment) where the defendant's wrong has to be established and restitution is merely one of several possible remedial responses to that wrong.[9] But some care is required here. Not every case of unjust enrichment by subtraction will involve the transfer of property from plaintiff to defendant (*eg* where

[7] See *ibid*, 989C: "Such a claim cannot succeed against a party who has under the applicable law acquired a title to the shares which is superior to that of Macmillan".

[8] *Ibid*, 989C.

[9] Birks, *An Introduction to the Law of Restitution* (rev ed, 1989) (hereafter "*Birks*"), 23–24, 40–44, 313-315; Burrows, *The Law of Restitution* (Butterworths, 1993) (hereafter "*Burrows*"), 16–17.

services are rendered) and the proprietary base terminology is usually used in the context of a proprietary claim involving tracing and substitutions or intermixture[10] – and Millett J himself has insisted that the case was not about tracing. The point is that the cause of action, and right, relied upon by Macmillan is not necessarily generated by the unjust enrichment of the defendant and it does not follow from the fact that Macmillan relied on "an undestroyed proprietary base" that its claims should be classified as coming within the law of unjust enrichment. Millett J does not justify why he believes that they are. He assumes, for example, that (but does not explain why) the defendant in such circumstances is enriched at the expense of the plaintiff.

Some members of the Court of Appeal were prepared, for the purposes of the case, to accept that Macmillan's claims should be characterised as being based on unjust enrichment. Staughton LJ was "prepared to accept that Macmillan's claim is restitutionary in nature".[11] Auld LJ was more sceptical. He noted, for example, that it was difficult to see what unjust enrichment the banks had received since they gave full value.[12] He then qualified his discussion of the question of which law governed the priority dispute by commenting: "even if the facts could support a claim for unjust enrichment".[13] Aldous LJ was also somewhat sceptical. He noted that the rule in *Dicey & Morris*[14] upon which Macmillan was seeking to rely "is concerned with what has been called unjust enrichment, not a case like the present where the defendants gave value for the shares and the dispute is whether the legal titles they obtained have priority over that of the plaintiffs".[15]

So what exactly was the basis of Macmillan's claim – how was Macmillan's beneficial interest created? As we saw above, the relevant shares were initially transferred from Macmillan to BIT and BIT entered into the nominee agreement acknowledging that it held the shares for Macmillan and disclaiming any beneficial interest in the shares. The effect of this arrangement was probably to result in a new beneficial interest being granted by BIT to Macmillan.[16] Accordingly, it was from this transaction or event that the ben-

[10] See *Birks*, 378-379; and Birks, "Establishing a Proprietary Base" [1994] RLR 83.

[11] But was pleased to find himself in a position where "the considerable learning directed at [the issues relating to the proper characterisation of Macmillan's claims do] not need to be considered in the present case. This part of this appeal is not, in my opinion, the place to confront the law of restitution 'in a logical, consistent and coherent fashion'": *Macmillan v Bishopsgate*, [1996] 1 WLR 387, 398H (CA).

[12] *Ibid*, 409A.

[13] *Ibid.*

[14] *Dicey & Morris on the Conflict of Laws*, 12th ed (1993), Rule 201.

[15] *Ibid*, 418G.

[16] See the speech of Lord Browne-Wilkinson in *Westdeutsche Landesbank Girozentrale v Islington LBC* [1996] AC 669, 706D–F. Lord Browne-Wilkinson says that it is "meaningless" to talk about the transferor retaining an equitable interest where there was no separation of the legal and equitable interests immediately before a transfer. But query whether that is right. See Lord

eficial interest on which Macmillan based its claim was derived; Macmillan's interest was not generated as a response to the unjust enrichment of any of the relevant defendants.

THE ISSUE: ARE PURE PROPRIETARY CLAIMS PART OF THE LAW OF RESTITUTION?

The real issue, of course, is whether pure proprietary claims are properly within the law of restitution. Pure proprietary claims arise where the claimant has never been divested of his property in the assets in question and where there is a passive preservation of existing proprietary rights.[17] Both Millett J and the Court of Appeal consider the question but the underlying issues are not analysed or reviewed.

The question whether pure proprietary claims come within the law of unjust enrichment has been much discussed by commentators, both in the textbooks and in articles. However, the issue has yet to be satisfactorily resolved and there are at least two different views. On the one hand, there are the proponents of the view that pure proprietary claims do not fall within the law of unjust enrichment. This approach is supported, with varying degrees of vigour, by Goff & Jones,[18] Professor Birks,[19] Professor Tettenborn,[20] William Swadling,[21] Kit Barker[22] and John Stevens.[23] On the other hand,

Justice Millett's paper "Equity's Place in the Law of Commerce" (delivered to the Chancery Bar Association in the summer of 1997), where, at p 24, he says that "apparently we may not say that [the transferor] retained [the beneficial interest]; but we can surely agree that he did not part with it". See also S Worthington, *Proprietary Interests in Commercial Transactions* (OUP, 1996), viii–x.

17 It remains an open question whether proprietary claims arising where there is a substitution of one asset for another can properly be said to give rise to pure proprietary claims. Professor Birks has argued that they should not ("the new asset implies a new right"): see Birks (ed), *Laundering and Tracing* (1995), 318–319. William Swadling has questioned this approach: see "Property and Unjust Enrichment" in JW Harris (ed) *Property Problems: From Genes to Pension Funds* (1997) 131–133.

18 Goff & Jones, *The Law of Restitution* (hereafter "*Goff & Jones*") (Sweet & Maxwell, 1993, 4th ed); 73.

19 *Birks*, 14: "The crucial moment to look at is the defendant's receipt of the enriching benefit. If at that moment the law passively preserves pre-existing rights then there is no restitution". See also Birks, "Establishing a Proprietary Base" [1994] RLR 83.

20 Tettenborn, *Law of Restitution in England and Ireland*, 2nd ed (Cavendish, 1996) (hereafter "Tettenborn"), 35–36.

21 WJ Swadling, "Property, Restitution and the Defence of Bona Fide Purchase", in Swadling (ed), *The Limits of Restitutionary Claims: a Comparative Analysis*; also "Property and Unjust Enrichment", in JW Harris (ed), *Property Problems: From Genes to Pension Funds* (1997) and "A Claim in Restitution" [1996] LMCLQ 63. See also [1992] *All ER Rev*, 282–283.

22 Barker, "After Change of Position: Good Faith Exchange in the Modern Law of Restitution", in Birks (ed), *Laundering and Tracing* (1995) 191 (esp 211–214). This is a particularly impressive article.

23 J Stevens, "Restitution or Property? Priority and Title to Shares in the Conflict of Laws" (1996) 59 MLR 741.

there are those who say that pure proprietary claims do fall within the law of restitution. These are (or perhaps more accurately, these at one time included) principally Professor Burrows,[24] Gbolahan Elias[25] and Graham Virgo.[26]

The literature is extensive and the arguments wide ranging. In order to review the merits of the arguments let us consider the reasons put forward for saying that proprietary claims are outside the territory of the law of restitution. There are three main arguments.

(i) The argument from volume

The argument from volume says that it is inappropriate to include pure proprietary claims within the law of restitution since to do so would require the law of restitution to embrace and deal with large areas which are properly confined to the law of property – the creation and transfer of title to property. Goff & Jones note that "it would not be appropriate [in their book on restitution] to discuss every situation in which a proprietary claim can be asserted by a claimant. For that reason we do not discuss in detail a claim that the plaintiff has never been divested of his property in chattels (pure proprietary claims) . . .".[27] Professor Birks expresses the concern that if pure proprietary claims were included within restitution "restitution would be too big".

Professor Burrows, in his *The Law of Restitution*, regards these concerns as being misplaced – restitution can take as read the rules on the creation and transfer of title and pure proprietary remedies can be incorporated within the law of restitution without making the subject unmanageable.[28]

Of course, Professor Burrows is right; but the argument from volume is really only intended, by the proponents of the view that pure proprietary claims lay outside the realm of restitution, to be illustrative of a more general point, namely that regard must be paid to the distinction between the law of property and the law of restitution. Other arguments are put forward as to why this distinction is important and should be respected.

(ii) The no enrichment/unjust factor argument

Pure proprietary claims are based on an assertion by a plaintiff of an existing title to the property which has been lost. The plaintiff relies simply upon the

[24] *Burrows*, ch 13. But see now Burrows and McKendrick, *Cases and Materials on the Law of Restitution* (OUP, 1997), 724.
[25] G Elias, *Explaining Constructive Trusts* (OUP, 1990), 17.
[26] G Virgo, "Reconstructing the Law of Restitution" (1996) 10 TLI 20.
[27] *Goff & Jones*, 73.
[28] *Burrows*, 371.

establishment of his title and the absence of the acquisition of a superior title in the defendant. In these circumstances, it is difficult to see how there is any room for the operation of the "independent cause of action in unjust enrichment".[29] The cause of action in unjust enrichment depends upon proof of a reversible transfer of wealth: the plaintiff must show that (i) the defendant has been enriched/benefited; (ii) that the enrichment was at the plaintiff's expense; (iii) that the enrichment was unjust; (iv) that there are no applicable defences.[30]

In relation to pure proprietary claims, where it is asserted and held that a person (the defendant) is in possession or control of something that is not his, it is difficult to see how he is thereby enriched by its value;[31] or at least the full capital value of the property in question.[32] However, this is not a problem for Professor Burrows, who in *The Law of Restitution* takes a wide view of enrichment and regards retention by the defendant of the plaintiff's property as self evidently enriching to the defendant. He notes that "a defendant cannot rationally refuse to give to give up property and yet claim that it is of no value to him . . . The defendant's gain, by retention of the property, is the plaintiff's loss of that property".

But there is a further, related, point – what is the "unjust" factor which triggers the restitutionary remedy? Professor Burrows regards retention of property belonging to the plaintiff without his consent as an autonomies unjust factor.[33]

However, both in relation to the question of benefit to and enrichment by the defendant and the characterisation of the relevant unjust factor, it has to be said that Professor Burrows' approach in *The Law of Restitution* seems somewhat artificial and strained.

(iii) The defence argument

If pure proprietary claims are within the law of restitution then presumably it follows that the full range of restitutionary defences, such as change of position, will apply. Professor Tettenborn notes that "no one has seriously suggested that actions to recover one's property should be subject to restitutionary defences such as change of position".[34]

[29] See LD Smith, *The Law of Tracing* (OUP, 1997), 293.

[30] See *Burrows*, 7.

[31] See *Tettenborn*, 35. As noted above in the text, this was a concern of Auld LJ in the Court of Appeal in *Macmillan v Bishopsgate*.

[32] It is perhaps easier to see that the person in possession or control of the asset in question is enriched by its use value.

[33] *Burrows*, 363. See also Virgo (1996) 10 TLI 20.

[34] *Tettenborn*, 35.

Now it is true that the principles governing a number of the defences to restitutionary claims are still in the process of being formulated and elaborated. The availability of the change of position defence has only been acknowledged as being available in England relatively recently and its precise ambit is the subject of much debate.[35] Equally, considerable debate rages over the availability and operation of the defence of bona fide purchaser in the law of restitution.[36]

William Swadling argues[37] that there is no defence of bona fide purchase in the law of restitution. Those cases in which the defence is available (their substance is the vindication of property rights) are properly confined to the law of property and have nothing to do with the law of restitution. "In the typical restitution case there is no question but that the transferor had a good title to the property transferred to the restitutionary defendant. The problem is not one of an initial lack of title [but] of a defective or qualified intention to transfer. The principle of *nemo dat* [to which the bona fide purchaser defence is an exception] is in such cases not offended and there is no need for any exception to it to be invoked." It is dangerous to transplant the bona fide purchaser defence from the law of property into the law of restitution (and by implication to bring into the law of restitution claims which are properly confined to the law of property) because the policies of the two legal systems differ. "The law of property favours security of ownership over security of transaction. It only really departs from this view and only in a minority of cases this is because of a concern for the defendant's security of receipt. With the very recent introduction of the defence of change of position the law of restitution can be said to have a general concern for this interest . . .". On his analysis, *Lipkin Gorman v Karpnale*[38] is not a decision on the law of restitution at all. In such cases *ie* pure proprietary claims, there is no unjust factor. Ignorance, the unjust factor proposed by Professor Birks, cannot be justified as a separate unjust factor.

Kit Barker[39] accepts that a clear line needs to be drawn between the law of property and the law of restitution and that pure proprietary claims fall within the former and outside the latter. However, he regards the bona fide

[35] See Barker, *supra* n 22.

[36] See Swadling, *supra* n 21 and Barker, *supra* n22.

[37] See Swadling *supra* n 21, at p 104.

[38] *Lipkin Gorman v Karpnale Ltd* [1991] 2 AC 548. Note, however, Professor Birks' argument that parties whose claims are contingent on tracing do not have a vested and continuing proprietary interest in the assets in question but only a power. Accordingly, claimants who are basing their claim on the tracing process are not relying on a pure proprietary claim. This is why, according to Professor Birks, "all rights which are contingent on tracing are restitutionary . . . [but] a right which persists through a transfer . . . is not generated by unjust enrichment": Birks, "Establishing a Proprietary Base" [1994] RLR 83, 91–92.

[39] Barker, *supra* n 22.

purchaser defence as being available both in relation to pure proprietary claims and in relation to true restitutionary claims. "To leave a defendant immune to a claim in rem to property held, but to fix him with personal liability for its value at the date of receipt would remove the guarantee of security which it was of one objectives of the defence to provide". The defendant purchaser is entitled to protection against pure property claims, restitutionary personal claims and restitutionary proprietary claims – it matters not whether a purchaser's property came with (defeasible) title or with no title at all. If he is operating in good faith and without notice of the plaintiff's rights, considerations of commercial certainty dictate that his transaction should be secure.

Where do such arguments leave the personal liability of third party recipients of misdirected trust funds?[40] Are such claims within, or outside, the law of restitution and is the bona fide purchaser defence available? Tettenborn suggests that the law of restitution ought not to embrace claims for knowing receipt in equity where all that is alleged against the defendant is that he has handled something stolen from the plaintiff in the past but no longer has it. The argument here is that in these circumstances there has been no enrichment of the defendant and any liability should be dependent upon establishing an entitlement to compensation for a wrong, legal or equitable as the case may be. However, in some circumstances the defendant may have received a benefit and enrichment initially (title may have passed to him) but subsequently given it up. In such circumstances it would seem that the conditions for a restitutionary claim would have arisen and the issue is whether an appropriate defence is available. Much confusion continues to exist, in this area, as to whether the defendant's knowledge in personal claims is a precondition to the plaintiff's cause of action or merely relevant for defence purposes.[41] In the case of pure proprietary claims the knowledge of the defendant is an issue relevant to his defence and the burden of proof is on him to establish the availability of that defence. There remains an issue as to whether the law of restitution is similarly configured. Professors Birks has, of course, argued that liability in restitution is strict subject to the availability of defences. If this is the case, and William Swadling is right that the bona fide purchaser defence is not available in the case of restitutionary claims, how do we deal with the position of recipients of misdirected funds?

[40] See *eg* in *Re Montagu's Settlement Trust* [1987] Ch 264; *Powell v Thompson* [1991] NZLR 597; *Eagle Trust Plc v SBC Securities Ltd* [1992] 4 All ER 488; *Cowan de Groot Properties Ltd v Eagle Trust Plc* [1992] 4 All ER 700; *Polly Peck International Plc v Nadir* (No 2) [1992] 4 All ER 769; *El Ajou v Dollar Land Holdings Plc* [1994] 2 All ER 685.

[41] See P Birks, "Persistent Problems in Misdirected Money: A Quintet" [1993] LMCLQ 218, 226.

Of course, pure proprietary claims look as though they might fall within the law of restitution because, in one respect, there is the possibility of a significant overlap. This is because in the case of a pure proprietary claim the plaintiff has, albeit temporarily, lost possession and perhaps some interest in his asset without his consent – in circumstances which might be said to trigger the "ignorance" unjust factor. Now, as noted above, it is argued by some that ignorance is not an unjust factor grounding a claim in restitution. In any event, ignorance (or the absence of consent) is not, in legal terms, the basis of the cause of action in pure proprietary claims. It is the existence of the plaintiff's interest (and the *nemo dat* principle of property law) on which the plaintiff's cause of action is founded. In such circumstances, the plaintiff's proprietary rights are not generated as a response to the unjust enrichment of the defendant but instead arise, and are created, by reason of some other event – there is no requirement to rely on any restitutionary unjust factor and general restitution law defences should not simply be regarded as being available to a defendant in these cases. Of course, this does not mean that, for example, the law of restitution should exclude the defence of bona fide purchaser. It may well be that it is appropriate for the law of restitution to have its own bona fide purchaser defence and for that defence to be equivalent to the defence available in personal and proprietary claims (proprietary claims embracing both pure proprietary claims and restitutionary proprietary claims). This approach has been argued for by Kit Barker and is, in many respects, both elegant and convincing.

THE MEANING OF "NOTICE" IN THE BONA FIDE PURCHASER DEFENCE

Millett J at first instance in *Macmillan v Bishopsgate* was called upon to consider the meaning of notice for the purposes of the bona fide purchaser defence. Much of the (unreported[42]) judgment deals, in enormous detail, with the precise state of mind and information available to each of the three banks at the time that security was created in their favour. In many respects, at least for bankers and their lawyers, these are the most interesting and important parts of the judgment. It is obviously of considerable significance to ensure that banks do not find that they lose their security, or other rights, because they are being judged by unrealistic and inappropriate standards.

[42] The full judgment of Millett J at first instance runs to 638 pages and was not reported not only for reasons for length(!) but also because of an order prohibiting publication (made pursuant to the Contempt of Court Act 1981) in view of the discussion, in the factual parts of the judgment, of a number of individuals who were subject, at the time, to criminal proceedings.

When will banks be taken to be on notice of the rights of third parties so as to be prevented from relying on the bona fide purchaser defence? Millett J, controversially, held that notice in this context included not only actual notice (including wilful blindness or contrived ignorance where the bank deliberately abstains from enquiry in order to avoid learning the truth) but also constructive notice, that is to say notice of such facts as he would have discovered if he had taken proper measures to investigate them.[43] There have, of course, been considerable dicta suggesting that it is inappropriate to extend the equitable doctrine of constructive notice to commercial transactions. As was famously noted by Lindley LJ in *Manchester Trust v Furness*:[44]

> "The equitable doctrines of constructive notice are common enough in dealing with land and estates with which the Court is familiar; but there have been repeated protests against the introduction into commercial transactions of anything like an extension of those doctrines and the protest is founded on perfect good sense. In dealing with estates in land title is everything and it can be leisurely investigated; in commercial transactions possession is everything and there is no time to investigate title; and if we were to extend the doctrine of constructive notice to commercial transactions we should be doing infinite mischief and paralysing the trade of the country . . .".

Despite these sentiments and a range of dicta in subsequent cases based on such an approach, Millett J took the view that constructive notice was relevant even in the context of the banking transactions with which *Macmillan v Bishopsgate* was concerned. He based himself on the following passage from the speech of Lord Browne-Wilkinson in *Barclays Bank Plc v O'Brien*:[45]

> "The doctrine of notice lies at the heart of equity. Given that there are two innocent parties, each enjoying rights, the earlier right prevails against the later right if the enquirer of the later right knows of the earlier right (actual notice) or would have discovered it had he taken proper steps (constructive notice). In particular, if the party asserting that he takes free of the earlier rights of another knows of certain facts which put him on enquiry as to the possible existence of the rights of that other and he fails to make such enquiry or take such other steps as are reasonable to verify whether such earlier right does or does not exist, he will have constructive notice of the earlier right and take subject to it".

This formulation of the doctrine is of general application. But what exactly does "constructive notice" mean in this context? Having worried the life out of banks by saying that constructive notice was relevant, he then makes banks

[43] *Macmillan v Bishopsgate* [1995] 1 WLR 978, 1000D–E. See on the meaning of constructive notice *Snell's Equity*, 29th ed (1990), 51.

[44] *Manchester Trust v Furness* [1895] 2 QB 539, 545.

[45] [1994] 1 AC 180, 195–196.

feel a good deal more comfortable by the meaning he gives to the term. Constructive notice is based on an assessment of what facts would have been discovered had such enquiries and inspections been made as reasonably should have been undertaken. However, in the context of commercial transactions such as the taking of security by the three banks involved in the *Macmillan v Bishopsgate* case, "there is no room for the doctrine of notice in the strict conveyancing sense".[46] This is because in these kinds of transactions it is not the custom and practice to investigate the transferor's title. What enquiries a party ought reasonably to make in any given situation will depend upon the nature of the property which is the subject matter of the transaction in question and the custom and practice associated with it. Thus, for example, Millett J noted that "it is not, however, the practice of lenders, even bank lenders, to check the ownership of US stocks offered to them as collateral against the SEC filings as a matter of course. They only do so when they already have reason to doubt their Borrower's ability to deal with the stock. Even then the information takes several days to obtain and is little real value since it inevitably relates to a date sometime in the past".[47] He also noted that, "while the legal title to shares is a simple matter to verify there is no recognised procedure for investigating the beneficial title . . .".[48] This is the key. Millett J argues that the application of a constructive notice standard cannot depend upon whether the transaction in question is commercial or not but whether there is a recognised procedure for investigating (in the context of mortgages) the mortgagor's title. The creditor ignores such recognised procedures at his peril. As noted, in relation to shares, there was no such procedure so that there was no room for the application of the doctrine of constructive notice in *Macmillan v Bishopsgate*. In the circumstances, therefore, the only test by which the banks were to be judged was one of actual knowledge or suspicion (including a deliberate abstention from inquiry lest the truth be discovered) or a reason to know or cause to suspect. After an exhaustive review of the facts, Millett J was satisfied, in relation to each of the three defendants, that none of the persons concerned with the transactions on behalf of the three defendants knew or suspected or had cause to suspect that the shares were not beneficially owned by the party pledging them by way of security.

If the approach of Millett J is right then it is not the nature of the claim in question which determines the standard of notice by which the defendant will be judged but the nature of the property in which an interest is acquired or claimed.[49]

[46] [1995] 1 WLR 978, 1000.
[47] Unreported.
[48] Unreported.
[49] See the discussion on different standards of notice in Barker, *supra* n 22.

It has to be said that Millett J's approach is not one that will inevitably lead to greater certainty for banks. In many cases there will be some uncertainty as to whether a recognised procedure for investigating title exists and, indeed, what is required by that recognised procedure. As a practical matter, banks may well be best advised to assume that a general standard of reasonable enquiry applies and to proceed on a prudent, cautious, basis.

PRIORITY BETWEEN COMPETING EQUITABLE INTERESTS IN ENGLISH LAW

Millett J had to consider the circumstances in which the holder of a subsequent equitable interest can secure priority over a prior equitable interest by acquiring, or a dealing in, the legal estate. Macmillan, of course, claimed that it had retained the equitable interest in the shares. As a result of the dealings with, and security created over, the shares the banks acquired (in the eyes of English law), initially, equitable interests and then, subsequently, legal interests in the shares (the legal interest arising upon the shares being registered in the name of the bank in question). The issue for consideration (although not ultimately relevant since Millett J held that New York law governed the issue) was whether the banks could rely on the legal interest which they had acquired in order to establish priority over Macmillan.

Millett J noted, following *Snell's Equity*, that the basic rule is that the purchaser must not have received notice of the prior interest prior to its acquisition of the legal estate.[50] However, in *Macmillan v Bishopsgate* none of the banks themselves became the registered holders of the shares before they received notice of Macmillan's claim. Shearson Lehman was only registered on the share register in New York after receipt of letters before action and with full knowledge of Macmillan's claim (albeit that the shares held by it as security had, before such notice, been deposited in the DTC system and were held by CEDE, as registered holder, on behalf of Lehman's nominee). Swiss Volksbank was also only registered on the share register in New York following receipt of letters before action and with full knowledge of Macmillan's claim. Once again, the shares granted to it as security had, before notice, been deposited in the DTC system and were held by CEDE for Swiss Volksbank's nominee. It will be recalled that Credit Suisse had two parcels of Berlitz shares. Security over the first parcel was created by delivery of the share certificates in the same manner as security given to Lehman Bros. However, Credit Suisse did not become the registered owner of these shares until after

[50] Of course, if the bank in question merely has an equitable interest then it has nothing superior to the equity from which it claims to be free; and, as that will be prior in time, it will prevail.

the writ had been issued against it. Accordingly, in all three cases, the banks were not able simply to say that they had acquired a legal interest without notice of Macmillan's claim.

Therefore, the issue arose whether the banks could, nonetheless, take priority to Macmillan's equitable interest. This called for a consideration of the qualifications to the rule that the purchaser must have a legal estate *ie* a consideration of the circumstances in which the acquisition of something less than a legal estate, at a time when the purchaser or mortgagee had no relevant notice, would give priority. Two qualifications to the rule were considered. First, "the better right to the legal estate" and, secondly, "the subsequent acquisition of the legal estate".

Better right to legal estate

A purchaser of an equitable interest without notice will take free from a prior equity if his purchase gave him the better right to a legal estate. It is sufficient if he has the legal estate transferred to a trustee or a nominee for him. The question is then whether or not he or his nominee has notice of the prior equitable interest at the time that the legal estate was acquired by the trustee or nominee. Provided that neither the purchaser nor the trustee/nominee has notice of the prior equitable interest, he will take free from it (he is said to have the better title to the legal estate).

When Lehman Bros deposited the Berlitz shares in the DTC system the effect of so doing was to divest BIT, the former registered owner, of legal title to the shares and to vest it in CEDE as nominee for Lehman Bros. At the time of the deposit of the shares, and the registration of the shares in the name of CEDE, neither Lehman Bros nor CEDE had notice of Macmillan's claim. Therefore, the security acquired by Lehman Bros took priority to the equitable interest of Macmillan.

The position of Swiss Volksbank and Credit Suisse (with respect to the one million parcel of shares) was slightly different. Swiss Volksbank and Credit Suisse initially acquired their security interest as a result of entries within the DTC system. Unlike Lehman Bros, there was no transfer of the legal estate (from BIT to CEDE); instead, CEDE remained the holder of the legal estate and all that happened was that, following the creation of the security, it held the shares for the nominee of Swiss Volksbank and Credit Suisse as opposed to the nominee for the relevant charging company. The creation of the security in these circumstances will involve either a disposition of the chargor's existing equitable interest or the creation of a new equitable interest in favour of the bank taking the security;[51] the legal estate is held (by CEDE) for the bank which has acquired (either the old or a new) equitable interest. Were Swiss Volksbank and Credit Suisse, therefore, to be prejudiced by the fact that the shares over which they were granted security were already in the DTC system and by the fact that there was no new dealing with the legal estate?[52]

Millett J noted that the answer to this question depended upon the correctness or otherwise of dicta in *Assaf v Fuwa*[53] which Meagher, Gummow and Lehane had described[54] as "an impermissible extension" of *Wilkes v Boddington*,[55] which was itself described as "an impermissible extension of the doctrine in tabula in naufragio". Millett J did not need to explore this issue further but it is interesting to consider what the outcome would have been had he had to do so.

The point at issue is that it has been suggested that a subsequent equitable mortgagee can take priority over the holder of a prior equitable interest where he obtains from the holder of the legal estate a declaration of trust over the property in question in his favour or even a deposit of the title deeds (in the case of land) with him. In these circumstances, provided that the holder of the subsequent equitable interest acquired his interest without notice of the outstanding equity, then the normal rules governing equitable priorities would be reversed and he would secure priority. If this approach were correct, presumably, Swiss Volksbank and Credit Suisse would be able to argue that they fell within the rule and therefore secured priority over Macmillan provided that CEDE confirmed that it held the shares on, or executed a declaration of, trust in their favour. Meagher, Gummow and Lehane do not like this solution because they do not see that it is appropriate to extend the basic *tabula in naufragio* doctrine, which requires the getting in of the (paramount) legal estate. A dealing in mere equitable interests should not be enough. Furthermore, *Assaf v Fuwa* suggested that such a principle might apply even beyond the case where there were two competing mortgages and might extend to competition between other equitable claims.

[51] See *Grey v IRC* [1960] AC 1 and *Neville v Wilson* [1997] Ch 144 (CA). See also R Nolan, "The Triumph of Technicality" [1996] CLJ 436.

[52] Of course the DTC system does not apply in England. The Talisman system for settlement of shares traded on the London Stock Exchange involved, for certificated shares, the transfer of the shares to and the registration of shares in the name of a nominee for the exchange (SEPON). No such transfer to a nominee is required for the purposes of CREST (where shares are dematerialised but rights still depend upon registration in the company's (electronic) register). Nonetheless, the problem discussed in the text can arise in any case where shares are held by a nominee and dealings take place only in the equitable interest. Of course, in most cases involving banks, there will be a transfer to a nominee for the bank taking security.

[53] [1955] AC 215.

[54] *Equity: Doctrines and Remedies*, 3rd ed (1992), 233. See also RJ Smith *Property Law* (Longmans, 1996), 195–196.

[55] (1707) 2 Vern 599.

The doctrine of tacking was, of course, abolished by the Law of Property Act 1925, s 94(3) in relation to mortgages. However, here, the dispute was not between two mortgages but between an equitable owner and a subsequent mortgagee. The doctrine, therefore, might still apply. If Millett J had been called upon to decide the matter, I hope, but somehow doubt, that he would have held in favour of Swiss Volksbank and Credit Suisse. It would be a harsh and outmoded (albeit perhaps doctrinally pure) principle that would distinguish between mortgagees according to whether they required a transfer from one nominee to another – a simple change of nominees; Swiss Volksbank and Credit Suisse would, undeniably, have been protected had the shares come out of the DTC system and been transferred from CEDE to another nominee. This seems a very fine distinction upon which to determine a priority dispute.

Subsequent acquisition of legal title

This is the second qualification to the rule that the purchaser must acquire the legal estate and, at that time, not have notice of the prior equity. A mortgagee can acquire priority over a prior equitable interest even though he has notice of it at the time at which he acquires the legal estate provided that he had previously acquired an equitable interest and at that time he had no notice of the prior equity. Tacking allowed the buying in of a legal title which had priority to both the equitable interest of the mortgagee who acquired (the legal) title and the equitable interest of the prior mortgagee. However, the doctrine would not apply where the owner of the later equitable interest acquired the legal estate from a person who committed a breach of trust in conveying it to him.[56] The issue in *Macmillan v Bishopsgate* was therefore whether the banks were able to rely on their subsequent acquisition of the legal interest in the shares (through registration) as giving them priority because their acquisition was without a breach of trust and they had previously acquired an equitable interest without notice of Macmillan's claim.

The banks found authority, in *Dodds v Hills*,[57] which held that in the case of shares, since a subsequent equitable chargee of the shares (whose interest was created after a prior equitable interest, in that case of beneficiary under a trust) could unilaterally acquire the legal interest by lodging with the relevant company the share certificates and stock transfer forms held by it, the legal estate could be got in by a subsequent equitable chargee without breach of trust. The subsequent equitable chargee could, therefore, by getting itself registered, obtain priority.

[56] See *Harpham v Shacklock* (1881) 19 Ch D 207, 214.
[57] (1865) 2 H&M 424.

Millett J had to consider whether *Dodds v Hills* was still good law. He held that it was. He thought it made good commercial sense to facilitate the creation of security over shares without the need for immediate registration. He also thought that it made sense to test whether the bank taking security had notice of the prior equitable interest by reference to the time at which it received the share certificates and stock transfer forms. "As between the transferee who has given value on the one hand and the transferor and those claiming under him on the other, this rather than the time when the transferee actually obtains legal title is to my mind the appropriate time for the question of notice to be tested".[58] The transferor has done everything in his power to vest the legal estate in the transferee/secured creditor and the transferee/secured creditor has it within his own power to get in the legal estate without further recourse to the transferor.

Accordingly, the banks were able to rely on their acquisition of the legal title as giving them priority under the "subsequent acquisition of legal estate" exception.

Did it make any difference that the legal title was got in after notice of Macmillan's claim and, indeed, after the litigation had commenced? The answer was "no". Millett J noted that in *Bailey v Barnes*[59] the legal estate was got in during the litigation but this was expressly held to be immaterial. In *Ireland v Hart*[60] an interlocutory injunction had been granted to preserve the status quo and prevent the getting in of the legal estate. It was clear that, if that injunction had not been granted and the defendant had obtained registration, the outcome of the case would have been different and the defendant would have secured priority. It is an interesting question whether, in these circumstances, it is appropriate to prevent the subsequent transferee/mortgagee from improving its position by taking advantage of this principle. Hoffmann J (as he then was), on the hearing of the application to continue the interlocutory injunction preventing Credit Suisse from becoming registered as holder of the shares charged to it, obviously took the view that there was no basis on which to prevent the transferee/secured creditor becoming registered – the injunction was discharged. This may be a point which has to be dealt with more fully in subsequent litigation.

58 *Macmillan v Bishopsgate* [1995] 1 WLR 978, 1004.
59 [1894] 1 Ch 25.
60 [1902] 1 Ch 522.

8

Tracing and Electronic Funds Transfers

LIONEL D SMITH*

I. INTRODUCTION

This brief paper attempts to answer a single question. The question may be shortly stated, but answering it requires the examination of some profound issues. The question is this: when a case involves a payment by electronic funds transfer (EFT), is it necessary to trace through the payment system?

When the question is stated in this form, many lawyers would instantly say that the answer depends on the type of claim which is being made. If the case involves a payment by EFT, but is pleaded as a case of assault, then tracing is irrelevant. Tracing does not assist in establishing any of the things that need to be established to make out a case of assault. That simple point underlies much of the argument that follows. In other words, to know whether or not tracing is necessary requires us to think about the type of claim being made; and, more importantly, requires us to think about what things need to be established to make out different types of claim.

Some cases say that tracing is necessary, for at least some types of claim. In *Agip (Africa) Ltd v Jackson*,[1] Millett J said that tracing was necessary to establish a common law claim in money had and received, where the defendant received the payment via EFT. The same conclusion was reached by Tuckey J in *Bank Tejarat v Hong Kong and Shanghai Banking Corp (CI) Ltd*.[2] In *Agip*, Millett J also held that tracing was necessary to establish a direct assertion of equitable proprietary rights in traceable proceeds (an "in rem" claim); and to establish a personal equitable claim based on knowing receipt of trust property.[3]

* Fellow of St Hugh's College, Oxford.

[1] [1990] Ch 264, 285C (ChD); affd [1991] Ch 547, 563E (CA); leave to app rfsd 25 March 1991 (HL).

[2] [1995] 1 Lloyd's Rep 239, 245 (QBD: Comm Ct); noted PBH Birks (1995) 9 TLI 91.

[3] [1990] Ch 265, 290GH. See also *El Ajou v Dollar Land Holdings Plc* [1993] 3 All ER 717; [1993] BCLC 735 (ChD); rvsd [1994] 2 All ER 685; [1994] BCLC 464 (CA); remitted [1995] 2 All ER 213 (ChD).

In the modern world it will become increasingly common for cases to involve payments by EFT, and probably by more esoteric means such as cybercash.[4] The question is to what extent a plaintiff needs to be concerned with the law of tracing when faced with such facts.

II. THE NEED TO TRACE

Tracing

In order to decide whether or not tracing is required in a particular case, it is obviously important to know what tracing is. That allows one to understand what it establishes; and that, in turn, allows one to know when it is needed. The word "tracing" is used in different ways, but is probably best confined to the process of establishing that a particular asset was acquired with the value inherent in another particular asset.[5] Analytically distinct is "following," the process of establishing that a particular asset or thing was transferred from one person to another. On this terminology, if a thief steals my car and sells it to the defendant, and I wish to sue the defendant in conversion, there is no need to trace. Tracing could be done; for example, one could trace from possession of the car into the sale proceeds received by the thief. But tracing has no relevance to the claim in conversion against the defendant; it establishes nothing which needs to be established to make out that claim. All that I need to do is to follow the car to show that I held a right to immediate possession of it at the moment the defendant asserted dominion over it.

It should be remembered that tracing itself is not a claim or cause of action, any more than following is.[6] Successfully following a thing from one person to others may increase the range of people against whom certain rights can be asserted. Similarly, successfully tracing value from one form into others may increase the range of assets in which certain rights can be asserted.

Tracing, so understood, *is* required whenever it is necessary to establish that which tracing proves; namely, that a particular asset B was acquired with the value inherent in another asset A. That is necessary in a few different contexts.[7] What those contexts have in common is that tracing is necessary whenever one wishes to establish that, by operation of law, some characteristic which appertained to asset A also appertains or appertained to asset B. Most

[4] This usually refers to payment via the internet, with accounts not necessarily kept in any national currency.

[5] LD Smith, *The Law of Tracing* (Oxford, 1997), 6–10.

[6] *Boscawen v Bajwa* [1996] 1 WLR 328, 334 (CA); *FC Jones (Trustee in Bankruptcy) v Jones* [1997] Ch 159 (CA).

[7] See *The Law of Tracing*, 24–47.

commonly, that characteristic is that the plaintiff held proprietary rights in asset A.[8] If the plaintiff wishes to establish that, by operation of law, she holds or held proprietary rights in asset B, it may be be necessary to show that asset B is the traceable proceeds of asset A. Establishing that she now holds proprietary rights in asset B may be all that the plaintiff wishes to do, if she simply wishes to lay claim to asset B. On the other hand, the plaintiff may wish to show that she held such rights in order to show that a past interference with those rights generated a personal claim.[9]

The example of a conversion claim given above showed that tracing is not always necessary to assert a proprietary right, nor to assert personal rights generated by interference with proprietary rights. The plaintiff who sues the defendant who bought the plaintiff's car from a thief needs to establish her proprietary rights in the car, but presumably does so by some derivative means, showing that she bought the car from an owner. After that, she only needs to follow the car to the point that the defendant committed the conversion. Tracing is only required where there has been some substitution. But any claim which either asserts proprietary rights, or asserts personal rights generated by interference with proprietary rights, will require either following, tracing, or both. Of course, where there has been an EFT, there has inevitably been a substitution. In fact, "tracing" in EFTs is actually a kind of combination of tracing and following. If I send you "money" by wire transfer, then the output of the transfer is a different asset from the input, although tracing may show that the output is the traceable product of the input. Moreover, the asset has moved from one person to another; the substitutions of assets have occurred *en route*.

Tracing, so understood, is *not* necessarily required to establish liability in autonomous unjust enrichment.[10] For example, services might be rendered under the mistaken impression that there is a contract providing for some payment. The person who provided the services may be able to recover their value, on the basis of autonomous unjust enrichment.[11] This presupposes that the plaintiff shows that the defendant was enriched by the services, and that the enrichment was at the expense of the plaintiff; but there is no need to trace, as that word has been defined above. There is no need to show that

[8] One of the other contexts in which tracing is necessary arises where one wishes to establish that certain value was used to pay a debt, in order to establish one's ability to be subrogated to the rights formerly held by the discharged creditor. Subrogation is not addressed in detail herein. See *The Law of Tracing*, 152–154.

[9] *The Law of Tracing*, 285–289.

[10] Contrast K Mason and JW Carter, *Restitution Law in Australia* (1996), 95: "[I]t is absolutely clear that all restitutionary claims (including personal claims) necessarily involve an element of what may be termed 'tracing.' "

[11] *Deglman v Guaranty Trust Co of Canada* [1954] SCR 725; [1954] 3 DLR 785; *Pavey & Matthews Pty Ltd v Paul* (1987) 162 CLR 221.

some asset was acquired with another. Nor is there any need to follow; in the services example, there is nothing to follow. Following and tracing have this in common, that they are concerned with specific assets. Enrichment is a non-specific concept. It is established where a defendant acquires something of value to that defendant; but there is no need (though it will often be the case) that the value reside in a specific asset. "At the expense of the plaintiff" is also a non-specific concept. In the context of autonomous unjust enrichment, it requires that the defendant's enrichment correspond, in some sense, to a deprivation of the plaintiff.

Bearing that in mind, the goal of this paper, as stated above, is to consider whether tracing is required in claims involving EFTs. It will conclude that some of the time, tracing is required. This paper does not address the issue of whether, when it is necessary, it is possible to trace through an EFT. In fact, it appears that it is, although on the orthodox understanding of tracing this assertion requires the support of a rather lengthy argument.[12]

Causes of action

If that is right, then, when a plaintiff needs to show that he holds or held proprietary rights in a particular asset, he needs to follow or to trace, or possibly both. If the plaintiff needs only to show that the defendant was enriched at the (subtractive) expense of the plaintiff, then he may need to do neither. The question then becomes: what does a plaintiff need to establish in order to make out different kinds of claims?

This is a question of the definition of causes of action. A cause of action has been defined as "the fact or combination of facts which gives rise to a right to sue."[13] Another way of putting it is that a cause of action is a set of elements,

[12] *The Law of Tracing*, 243–262. Moreover, in the context of the common law this argument might be thought to depend on another lengthy argument (*ibid*, 162–174) to the effect that, contrary to received wisdom, tracing may be conducted in a common law proceeding through a mixture of value. Even if the received wisdom on mixtures survives, however, it may well be possible to trace through EFT systems in common law claims: see *ibid*, 253–255.

Some commentators have argued that tracing through EFTs is possible on the basis of a simpler argument, derived basically from the causal connection between input and outflow in an EFT: RM Goode, *Commercial Law*, 2nd ed (1995), 496–497; PBH Birks, "Overview," ch 11 in PBH Birks (ed), *Laundering and Tracing* (1995), 302–305. At least on orthodox tracing principles, however, to say that asset B is the traceable product of asset A requires more than just a causal connection between the two. See *The Law of Tracing*, 315–320. It is possible that the result advocated by Goode and Birks would be achieved through the analysis in this paper, without modifying the principles of tracing. Note also that where the defence of change of position comes into play the position may be different, since that defence could operate on causal rather than transactional principles. See *The Law of Tracing*, 37–38; D Hayton, "Equity's Identification Rules", ch 1 in PBH Birks (ed), *Laundering and Tracing* (1995), 1–3.

[13] *Do Carmo v Ford Excavations Pty Ltd* (1984) 154 CLR 234, 245, *per* Wilson J.

the proof of which is individually necessary and collectively sufficient to establish liability. Of necessity, the elements are expressed generically. Thus, one element of the cause of action in battery could be expressed as "an application of force to the person of the defendant"; this generically expressed event could be committed with a fist, a bullet, or indeed a battery.

There is some disagreement about whether there is a cause of action in unjust enrichment.[14] The view that there is says that the various claims which belong to autonomous unjust enrichment are just examples of a single overarching cause of action.[15] Others say that the different claims remain distinct, and that unjust enrichment is just a "principle."[16] Either way, it seems to be agreed that to establish the cause of action in unjust enrichment (on the first view) or any one of the causes of action which are unified by the principle of unjust enrichment (on the other), a plaintiff must show that the defendant was enriched at the (subtractive) expense of the plaintiff. As noted above, that does not necessarily require either tracing or following.[17]

Other causes of action are different. Those which protect proprietary rights require that the existence of such rights be established, whether at the time of trial or at some earlier time when a violation of the rights is alleged to have occurred. These causes of action will require a plaintiff to follow or trace, or do both, in order to establish that the plaintiff held proprietary rights in the relevant asset at the relevant time. For example, consider the equitable claim "in rem," which amounts to a direct assertion of currently held equitable proprietary rights. Since the plaintiff must show equitable ownership of a thing, she must either follow the subject matter of her ownership to its current location, or trace into some other asset and follow that to its current location.

[14] See the discussion in PD Maddaugh and JD McCamus, *The Law of Restitution* (1990), 21–27.

[15] In *White v Central Trust Co* (1984) 7 DLR (4th) 236, 246–247 (CA), La Forest JA said:

> . . . the well recognized categories of unjust enrichment must be regarded as clear examples of the more general principle that transcends them. We are currently in a similar position with regard to unjust enrichment as we are in relation to negligence where we have for some time been abandoning recourse to particularized duties in favour of a generalized duty to one's neighbour, although the process has not yet proceeded as far in the case of restitution.

It is now common in Canada for a case to be pleaded as unjust enrichment, without any reference to traditional categories such as money had and received, recoupment or *quantum meruit*. The process is not so far advanced in the UK: S Hedley, "Unjust Enrichment" [1995] CLJ 578, 580-585.

[16] PBH Birks, *An Introduction to the Law of Restitution*, rev ed (1989), 16–27, rejects the "cause of action" view in favour of a "generic conception." A Burrows, *The Law of Restitution* (1993), 54–56 also rejects a generalized cause of action (but see at 7: "the cause of action principle").

[17] Whether it does sometimes is addressed below.

Two difficult issues must be addressed. The first is the question of which claims are claims in autonomous unjust enrichment, and which are property-protecting claims. The second relates to the way in which autonomous unjust enrichment interacts with causes of action which protect proprietary rights.

1. Classifying claims

If the argument above is correct, then it is very important to know whether a plaintiff's claim is one in autonomous unjust enrichment, or one based on protecting proprietary rights. This is sometimes harder than one might at first think.

(a) *Knowing receipt*

Professor Birks has long argued that a defendant sued in "knowing receipt of trust property" should be strictly liable, subject to defences. This argument is based on the idea that the claim in knowing receipt is a claim in autonomous unjust enrichment. If that is right, then liability should indeed be strict; otherwise there would be a glaring inconsistency between common law actions in unjust enrichment and equitable ones. But it is strongly arguable that the claim in knowing receipt is not a claim in autonomous unjust enrichment at all; rather, it is the equitable analogue of conversion.[18] It is an action which protects interference with equitable proprietary rights. If this is right, then it is not so clear that there is anything wrong with the traditional view that liability in knowing receipt requires some level of knowledge by the defendant. True, there is still an inconsistency between the common law and equity inasmuch as liability in conversion is strict; but the protection of equitable proprietary rights is notoriously weaker than that accorded to legal proprietary rights, as shown by the general equitable doctrine of bona fide purchase.[19]

[18] Birks acknowledges this possibility in PBH Birks, "Equity in the Modern Law: An Exercise in Taxonomy" (1996) 26 UWALR 1, 72. This appears to be the explanation favoured by Burrows: see A Burrows, "Misdirected Money – A Reply" (1990) 106 LQR 20. See also *The Law of Tracing*, 373–374.

[19] It is also true that equity has something that the common law does not, namely a *vindicatio* in the form of the claim "in rem," which could be said to justify a requirement of fault for interference with proprietary rights: see Birks (1996) 26 UWALR 1, 72. It must be admitted that the fault-based approach requires a different explanation for the strict personal claim allowed in *Re Diplock* [1948] Ch 465 (CA); affd [1951] AC 251 (HL), the strongest case in support of Birks's theory. See *The Law of Tracing*, 375 n 21.

If it is correct that knowing receipt is a claim which protects interference with proprietary rights, and is not a claim in autonomous unjust enrichment, then following or tracing or both will always be required to establish a claim in knowing receipt.

(b) *Money had and received*

The action for money had and received is, if anything, more difficult to classify. It appears to have more than one aspect. It certainly *can* be a claim in autonomous unjust enrichment, as where a mistaken payment is made and title to the payment passes to the defendant. It can also be used, however, where title to the payment has not passed.[20] This might be interpreted to mean that claims in autonomous unjust enrichment can be made even where a property-protecting claim is available; this is an issue which will be discussed in the next section. On the other hand, it might be interpreted as showing that there is a conversion-like aspect to money had and received, in which it can protect legal ownership of money.[21] That possibility is consistent with recent authority which shows money had and received as an action protecting a common law proprietary right less than ownership.[22]

If this is right, then, if the argument in this paper is correct, it is not enough to describe a claim as an action in money had and received. The different aspects of this action are so disparate that further analysis is required.

2. Unjust enrichment and property

The interaction between unjust enrichment and property has been discussed frequently in recent literature. There are at least two aspects to this relationship. The first question is whether our law ever creates proprietary rights as a response to subtractive unjust enrichment. This issue is very complicated and much explored.[23] To the extent that proprietary rights are created in response to subtractive unjust enrichment, then it is important to observe that such rights behave like any other proprietary rights. They differ only in their

[20] *Clarke v Shee* (1777) 1 Cowp 197; 98 ER 1041; Lofft 756; 98 ER 903 (KB); *Calland v Loyd* (1840) 6 M & W 26; 151 ER 307 (Exch of Pleas).

[21] *The Law of Tracing*, 334–335.

[22] *Lipkin Gorman v Karpnale Ltd* [1991] 2 AC 548 (HL); *The Law of Tracing*, 332–339. As discussed there at 333, there is another aspect of money had and received, namely the remedial function it serves in "waiver of tort" cases.

[23] See *eg* RM Goode, "Property and Unjust Enrichment" in A Burrows (ed), *Essays on the Law of Restitution* (1991), 215; R Chambers, *Resulting Trusts* (1997); *Westdeutsche Landesbank Girozentrale v Islington London BC* [1996] AC 669 (HL).

provenance. Thus, if a mistaken payment is held on trust by the payee for the payor, then it is possible that a subsequent transferee of the trust property could be liable in knowing receipt.[24] In such a case, the plaintiff might need to establish the cause of action in unjust enrichment in order to establish the creation of the trust; then, processes of following, tracing, or both would be necessary in order to assert ownership of trust property or to establish personal rights generated by interference with the plaintiff's proprietary rights.

The second question, which is analytically distinct, is whether the two types of claim are in some sense mutually exclusive. That is, if a thief steals my car, and thus I can sue him in conversion, can I also sue him in unjust enrichment? It can be argued, on different bases, that the availability of a property-protecting claim excludes a claim in unjust enrichment.[25] On the other hand, one might well say that the thief is enriched by the possession or use value of the car, and that this will support a claim in unjust enrichment regardless of whether or not a property-protecting claim is available.[26]

This second question is potentially complicated by the issue of whether or not the defendant received an enrichment directly from the plaintiff, or rather was a remote recipient. Even if one would allow an unjust enrichment claim where a property-protecting claim is available, it is not clear that unjust enrichment is available against a remote recipient. Assume that a thief steals the plaintiff's car and sells it to the defendant, in such a way that the plaintiff's ownership of the car is preserved. Again, the plaintiff can use conversion against this defendant. It is not so clear that the plaintiff can use unjust enrichment, even if unjust enrichment were available against the thief.

The enrichment of this defendant must be the same as any enrichment of the thief: that is, the use value or possession of the car. But it appears that this enrichment did not come at the subtractive expense of the plaintiff. The defendant did not get his enrichment – namely, possession of the car – from the plaintiff, but from the thief. The plaintiff having lost possession to the

[24] As in *El Ajou v Dollar Land Holdings Plc* [1993] 3 All ER 717; [1993] BCLC 735 (ChD); rvsd [1994] 2 All ER 685; [1994] BCLC 464 (CA); remitted [1995] 2 All ER 213 (ChD).

[25] On one view, the claim in unjust enrichment is excluded because the defendant has not been enriched in the required sense: W Swadling, "A Claim in Restitution?" [1996] LMCLQ 63, 65. On another view, the defendant has been enriched but the claim in unjust enrichment is excluded for policy reasons: RB Grantham and CEF Rickett, "Restitution, Property and Ignorance – A Reply to Mr Swadling" [1996] LMCLQ 463, 465. This latter view amounts to an acceptance of the civilian position that (to varying extents) claims in unjust enrichment are "subsidiary" to other types of claim. See further E Bant, "Ignorance as a Ground of Restitution – Can it Survive?" [1998] LMCLQ 18. For Québec law, see the Civil Code of Québec, art 1494, [1993] RLR at 212, discussed in *Loungnarath v Centre Hospitalier des Laurentides* [1996] RJQ 2498; [1997] RLR §70 (CA) by Chamberland J; more generally, see B Dickson, "Unjust Enrichment Claims: A Comparative Overview" [1995] CLJ 100.

[26] This was the position taken in a public lecture by Professor Birks at the IALS on 16 June 1997.

thief, he cannot lose it again when the thief sells the car to the defendant. When that happens, the defendant is enriched by acquiring possession of the car; but this enrichment comes at the expense of the thief, since it is the thief who transfers possession to the defendant.

Looking at it another way, unjust enrichment is concerned with reversing defective transfers. The thief was enriched at the expense of the plaintiff in this sense, that there was a direct nexus of transfer (of possession) between the plaintiff and the thief (albeit an involuntary transfer from the plaintiff's point of view). This is the same nexus of transfer which exists where there has been a mistaken payment. It can be present whether or not title passed in the transfer of possession. In other words, the question of whether or not there is a nexus of transfer is independent of any question as to title. By contrast, there is no nexus of transfer between the plaintiff and any remote recipient. The enrichment of the remote recipient is not at the plaintiff's subtractive expense.

In the absence of a nexus of transfer, the only nexus between the plaintiff and the remote recipient is that the asset acquired by the latter is owned by the plaintiff.[27] But it is questionable whether one can rely on the plaintiff's proprietary rights to support a claim which analytically does not require any infringement of such rights. In other words, saying that an enrichment is at the plaintiff's expense because the subject matter of the enrichment is owned by the plaintiff is, arguably, to shift from enrichment reasoning to title reasoning. To put this another way: the plaintiff who relies on ownership to support a claim in unjust enrichment is relying on the very thing which is supposed to be irrelevant in such claims. Against the immediate recipient (the thief), the plaintiff does not *rely* on ownership in framing a claim in unjust enrichment. The plaintiff relies merely on the nexus of transfer of possession, and ignores his ownership. But against the remote recipient, in the absence of a nexus of transfer, ownership cannot be ignored. The reason is that the only factor linking the plaintiff to the defendant is the plaintiff's ownership of the thing which the defendant received. But, by assumption, ownership is exactly the enrichment which the defendant does not acquire, and which the plaintiff does not lose, so it can hardly be relied upon to support a claim in autonomous unjust enrichment, which is about reversing defective transfers. The only manner in which the remote recipient is enriched is by acquiring possession of the car; but, as we have seen, that is acquired not from the plaintiff but from the thief. Thus, it may be that such a defendant is, unlike the direct recipient, liable only to property-protecting claims such as conversion.

It is possible for a remote recipient to be liable in unjust enrichment, but the position becomes slightly more complex. In the hypothetical facts so far

[27] According to Burrows, *The Law of Restitution*, 362, this is sufficient to trigger liability in autonomous unjust enrichment.

posited, a thief stole the plaintiff's car and then sold it to the defendant. The receipt of the car was an enrichment of the defendant just as much as it was an enrichment of the thief; but in the case of the defendant, the enrichment was not at the plaintiff's expense in the required sense. Now assume further that the defendant sells the car on, for £1,000. The receipt of the £1,000 by the defendant is an enrichment of the defendant. At first blush it would appear to come even less at the expense of the plaintiff than did the car itself. However, it appears that this enrichment can be seen as coming at the expense of the plaintiff in this sense: it was acquired by giving up something of the plaintiff's. That is, the defendant got the £1,000 by giving up the plaintiff's car; therefore, the defendant acquired this enrichment by doing something which impoverished the plaintiff.[28] If this is right, the defendant can be liable in unjust enrichment in respect of the £1,000. This appears to be the theoretical explanation of how the plaintiff can assert ownership of this £1,000 which is the traceable product of the plaintiff's car.[29] And this reasoning works even against the direct recipient, in respect of substitute assets. Against the thief, tracing is not needed to establish a claim in unjust enrichment based on the acquisition of the car; but if the plaintiff wishes to claim ownership of the sale proceeds received by the thief, tracing is required. It shows that those proceeds, which were an enrichment of the thief, came at the expense of the plaintiff in the relevant sense.

There might appear to be an inconsistency between this analysis and the position taken above that an enrichment is not "at the plaintiff's expense" solely because the plaintiff retained ownership of that enrichment. In my view there is no such inconsistency. The point above is this: an enrichment does not count as "at the plaintiff's expense" merely because the plaintiff retained ownership of the enrichment at the time of receipt by the defendant. The argument now being made is this: an enrichment does count as "at the plaintiff's expense," even though the plaintiff *does not* hold ownership of the enrichment at the time of receipt by the defendant, if that enrichment was acquired through an act which impoverished the plaintiff. An inquiry into the way the plaintiff's position was affected by the transaction in question is always necessary to conclude that a defendant's enrichment was at the plaintiff's expense. Take the simple case of a mistaken payment in which ownership of the payment passes to the defendant. The plaintiff's claim does not depend on retained ownership, and indeed some would say that retained

[28] It is or at least may be true that the impoverishment is only "practical" (as opposed to "legal"), if the plaintiff remains the owner of the car. The defendant has worsened the plaintiff's position by disabling himself from returning possession of the car to the plaintiff. The view taken above is that practical or "use-value" enrichment is a relevant form of enrichment; by analogy, practical impoverishment should be as relevant as legal.

[29] *The Law of Tracing*, 300–301.

ownership would defeat the claim;[30] but it is important that the plaintiff *once* owned the payment, in order to decide that the enrichment was at the plaintiff's expense.

In what way is this defendant liable in unjust enrichment in respect of the £1,000 received in exchange for the plaintiff's car? One might make the defendant personally liable in subtractive unjust enrichment for £1,000. There is some enthusiasm for this in the civilian tradition.[31] The common law does not appear to have worked out this possibility, probably because it offers several other remedies.[32] First, unlike in a civilian system, the unknowing defendant's action is likely to amount to a civil wrong. This will generate a claim for compensation, and possibly a claim for the disgorgement of any enrichment acquired through the wrong. Secondly, the common law (in the wide sense) anyway goes beyond the personal claim in unjust enrichment for the exchange value, by allowing the plaintiff to claim ownership of the exchange proceeds.[33]

To summarize: tracing is not required to show that a defendant was enriched. It may, however, be required to show that an enrichment was acquired at the plaintiff's subtractive expense. It will be so where the enrichment did not come directly from the plaintiff, but rather came from another party in exchange for something of the plaintiff's. Tracing allows the conclusion that an enrichment received by either a remote or a direct (non-remote) recipient counts as having come at the plaintiff's expense, thus supporting a claim in subtractive unjust enrichment; and the facts which usually surround the tracing exercise mean that a proprietary interest in the traceable proceeds will be generated to reverse the unjust enrichment. This proprietary interest can then be asserted against the party who made the exchange, or against subsequent recipients to whom its subject matter may be followed. Pure following, of course, can allow a plaintiff to assert pre-existing proprietary rights, without any need for tracing.

This allows us to generalize as follows: tracing, following or both are necessary when making a claim against a remote recipient. Tracing is necessary

[30] See *supra* n 25.

[31] There is a suggestion of it in the Digest: D.12.1.23 (Africanus); D.12.1.31.1 (Paul). These passages were the subject of some debate among the glossators: see JP Dawson, *Unjust Enrichment*[:] *A Comparative Analysis* (1951), 70–82. German law allows such a claim (BGB §816(1), sentence 1) and, according to Dickson, French law does as well: B Dickson, "Unjust Enrichment Claims: A Comparative Overview" [1995] CLJ 100, 116. Note that in a civilian system, however, the unjust enrichment claim against the remote recipient normally requires that the disposition by that recipient be one which destroys the plaintiff's proprietary rights. This makes it much easier to say that the enrichment came at the plaintiff's expense. As noted above, though, if a practical enrichment is sufficient then it makes some sense that a practical deprivation should be so as well.

[32] See however Burrows, *The Law of Restitution*, 58–59.

[33] *The Law of Tracing*, ch 8.

when making a claim to a substituted asset against a direct recipient. But neither tracing nor following is required to establish a claim in unjust enrichment against a direct recipient, which claim is based on the enrichment received directly from the plaintiff.[34] Tracing is never necessary to establish enrichment; and in the case of a direct recipient, the nexus of transfer from the plaintiff shows that the enrichment was at the plaintiff's expense.

III. TRACING IN ELECTRONIC FUNDS TRANSFERS

If all of this is correct, then what it means is that there is no need to trace in the case of a claim in subtractive unjust enrichment against a direct recipient. On the other hand, if the claim as pleaded involves an allegation that the defendant interfered with the plaintiff's proprietary rights, or is currently interfering with them, then there may well be a need to trace. In such a claim, the plaintiff needs to establish these proprietary rights, and it is this which may require the plaintiff to conduct the exercise of tracing. To put this another way, you only need to trace if your claim turns not just on the enrichment of the defendant at your expense, but rather turns on the defendant's receipt or retention of a particular repository of enrichment, namely, one in which you have rights in the nature of ownership.

This allows us to turn to the consideration of specific cases. In *Bank Tejarat*,[35] there was a claim in money had and received based on a transfer of funds which was induced by fraud. It was argued that tracing was not required, but Tuckey J rejected this proposition, saying that there was no authority for it.[36] In fact, there is a great deal of authority for it. Authority can be found in any case where a mistaken payment is made by a cheque, and a claim in subtractive unjust enrichment is allowed without tracing through the cheque clearing system to show that the funds ultimately received by the payee can be traced from the bank account of the payor. In other words, as argued above, in a case involving a direct nexus of exchange, between plaintiff and defendant, tracing is irrelevant because the plaintiff does not need to show that the defendant received any *particular* enrichment; the plaintiff needs only to show that the defendant was enriched by subtraction from the plaintiff.

But then, it might be asked, was *Bank Tejarat* a two party case? The payment from the plaintiff to the company run by the fraudsters (CAK Ltd) was made by EFT. The claim in money had and received was made against that

[34] As opposed to a claim to a substitute asset acquired with that enrichment.

[35] [1995] 1 Lloyd's Rep 239 (QBD: Com Ct).

[36] At 245.

company's bank, Hong Kong and Shanghai Banking Corp (CI) Ltd ("HKSB"). There were two other banks involved: the plaintiff's bank, Bayerische Vereinsbank ("BV"), and also Dresdner Bank. This last was involved because there was no direct correspondent relationship between BV and HKSB. If a claim had been made against CAK Ltd, could it have been understood as a claim in subtractive unjust enrichment? Or would CAK Ltd have been a remote recipient, meaning that the only type of claim available is one based on interference with proprietary rights? It appears that the case could be seen as a direct transfer from the plaintiff to CAK Ltd, despite the three intervening banks, so that a claim against CAK Ltd could have been framed in subtractive unjust enrichment. The reason is that the intervening banks were all acting as agents for one side or the other.[37] And, as argued above, such a claim would require proof that the defendant was enriched by subtraction from the plaintiff; it would not depend on proof that the defendant received any particular enrichment, and so it would not depend on tracing. The same reasoning applies to the actual claim against HKSB.[38] It also applies to the claim in money had and received made in *Agip.*[39]

What about knowing receipt? Could the plaintiff in *Bank Tejarat* have framed such a claim successfully? We must ask when, if ever, there was a trust. In a case such as *Bank Tejarat*, there could be no trust before the moment of receipt by the defendant. Following *Chase Manhattan Bank NA Ltd v Israel-British Bank (London) Ltd*,[40] a trust to reverse unjust enrichment might have arisen at the moment of receipt. There would be no need to trace to *establish* such a trust; it would arise to remedy an unjust enrichment received by a direct recipient. The litigation in *Chase Manhattan* established that the mistaken payment was held by the defendant as trust property; it did not address

[37] It is not entirely obvious who their principals were, however. It is generally assumed that a payee's bank acts as that payee's agent when receiving a credit transfer. It has been cogently argued that all banks in the chain can best be seen as agents of the payor: R King, "The Receiving Bank's Role in Credit Transfer Transactions" (1982) 45 MLR 369.

[38] Tuckey J asked (245–246) how it was that a plaintiff could deploy the theory (advocated in this paper) that tracing is not necessary in a claim against a direct recipient when it was suing HKSB, which acted as an agent. His point was that the plaintiff wanted to ignore the other two banks in the chain as agents but sue HKSB as a principal. This, however, seems to be generally permissible in unjust enrichment: one is free to sue an enriched agent until that agent has accounted to its principal. See generally M Bryan, "Recovering Misdirected Money from Banks, Ministerial Receipt at Law and in Equity" *infra*, ch 10 in this volume. Indeed, that HKSB had accounted to CAK Ltd provided a reason why the claim against HKSB had to be dismissed in any event (246–247).

[39] [1990] Ch 264; affd [1991] Ch 547 (CA); leave to app rfsd 25 March 1991 (HL).

[40] [1981] Ch 105 (ChD). Some doubt was cast on the reasoning of Goulding J by Lord Browne-Wilkinson in *Westdeutsche Landesbank Girozentrale v Islington London BC* [1996] AC 669 (HL), who took the view that any trust would have arisen later, upon the acquisition of some level of knowledge by the recipient of the payment. The point in the text does not appear to be affected by this view.

the difficult question whether that property remained traceable after the trust arose. But there was no issue about tracing in order to establish the trust initially.[41] What is more, if a trust arises to reverse a subtractive unjust enrichment, it does not appear that the recipient can be liable in knowing receipt. That would be a claim pulling itself up by its own bootstraps. If a defendant is liable in unjust enrichment, there is a personal liability; equity may or may not supplement this by deciding that the substance of the enrichment is held in trust for the plaintiff; but, even if it is, it would be circular to say then that the defendant is personally liable for knowing receipt of trust property. The property is only trust property because the defendant was personally liable (in unjust enrichment). The advantage of establishing a trust to reverse a subtractive unjust enrichment does not lie against the recipient, but rather against subsequent transferees, including a trustee in bankruptcy. These can be forced to surrender the property if the trust survived the transfer,[42] and they may be liable in knowing receipt[43] or knowing assistance.[44]

So if tracing is not needed to establish a personal liability in unjust enrichment on the part of a direct recipient, nor to establish a trust raised to reverse such an unjust enrichment, when is it needed? It is needed when the claim against a particular defendant is based on following to that defendant some asset A in which the plaintiff has proprietary rights, where the plaintiff's rights in asset A can be established only because the plaintiff had rights in some other asset which was used to acquire asset A.

For example, assume that the plaintiff makes a mistaken payment to a payee, in such a way that the plaintiff retains or acquires some proprietary interest in the substance of the value received by the payee. As discussed

[41] In a complicated part of *Bank Tejarat* (247–248) dealing with a claim against HKSB in knowing assistance in a breach of trust, Tuckey J was faced with the argument that (a) no trust could be established unless the plaintiff's payment was traceable to HKSB; (b) it was not traceable in equity unless there was a fiduciary relationship; (c) there could be no fiduciary relationship until a trust arose, which was not before CAK Ltd received the payment; and (d) that was after the payment passed through the EFT system and thus too late to allow tracing when it was needed through that system. On the argument in this paper, (a) is false because there is no need to trace to establish a claim in subtractive unjust enrichment against a direct recipient (whether a trust is alleged to result or not). Parenthetically, it is argued in *The Law of Tracing* (120-130) that (b) is false. Disagreeing with what Millett J said in *Agip*, Tuckey J held that *Chase Manhattan* was inconsistent with (c) and rejected the argument on that footing. On whether such a trust would in any event impose fiduciary duties, see LD Smith, "Constructive Fiduciaries?", ch 9 in PBH Birks (ed), *Privacy and Loyalty* (1997).

[42] As was alleged in *Chase Manhattan Bank NA Ltd v Israel-British Bank (London) Ltd* [1981] Ch 105 (ChD); see also *Attorney-General for Hong Kong v Reid* [1994] 1 AC 324 (PC, NZ) (where however the trust was not to reverse subtractive unjust enrichment but to effect disgorgement of the profits of a wrong).

[43] *El Ajou v Dollar Land Holdings Plc* [1993] 3 All ER 717; [1993] BCLC 735 (ChD); rvsd [1994] 2 All ER 685; [1994] BCLC 464 (CA); remitted [1995] 2 All ER 213 (ChD).

[44] *Agip (Africa) Ltd v Jackson* [1990] Ch 264 (ChD); affd [1991] Ch 547 (CA); leave to app rfsd 25 March 1991 (HL).

above, tracing is not necessary to make the payee personally liable, nor to establish the plaintiff's proprietary rights. Assume further that the payee makes a payment to the defendant by EFT. The plaintiff wants to sue this defendant, either in money had and received or in knowing receipt. The plaintiff has no connection to this defendant unless he can show that he held some rights in the payment received by the defendant. Now tracing through the EFT is required.

Or, return to our earlier example in which a thief steals the plaintiff's car and sells it to the defendant. Assume the defendant sells the car on, receiving payment of £1,000 by EFT. If the plaintiff wishes to lay claim to that £1,000, it is necessary to show that it was the traceable proceeds of the car. That would require tracing through the EFT system.

IV. CONCLUSION

If the arguments here are correct, there is a critical distinction between claims against remote recipients and claims against direct recipients. This paper has focussed on the implications of that distinction in one particular context, namely the need to trace in EFTs. If, however, this distinction is well-founded, then its significance would go beyond tracing, beyond EFTs, and beyond banking law, since it would be a feature of unjust enrichment in general.

9

Assisting a Breach of Duty by a Fiduciary, the Common Law and Money-laundering

MICHAEL TUGENDHAT*

INTRODUCTION

The use of equitable remedies in connection with commercial fraud has given rise to debate as to what must be established if a person who assisted in such a fraud is to be liable to the victim. The debate has been largely concerned with the rules of equity (on what was formerly known as "knowing assistance"). Common law remedies have received little attention. A question commonly discussed is: Is it sufficient to make the assister liable to the victim that his fault was merely one of negligence or must he have been dishonest? This focuses on the " 'sort' of knowledge required"[1] rather than on the subject matter itself, *ie* on how well the assister knows something, rather than what he knows or ought to know. In *Royal Brunei Airlines Sdn Bhd v Tan*[2] the Privy Council concluded that dishonesty on the part of the assister was both a necessary and a sufficient condition for him to be liable in equity on a claim made by a plaintiff beneficiary based on what Lord Nicholls of Birkenhead, delivering the opinion of the Board, called the "accessory liability" principle.

The common law merits more attention than it has received. Professor Birks and Lord Justice Millett both support the development of a logical and coherent structure for this area of the law, embracing both equity and the common law.[3] As Professor Birks noted:[4]

* QC. I am grateful for the comments which I have received on a draft of this paper from Janet Ulph and Jacob Dean. The opinions and errors remain entirely mine.

[1] *Royal Brunei Airlines v Tan* [1995] 2 AC 378, 391.

[2] [1995] 2 AC 378, 392.

[3] Peter Birks: "Civil Wrongs: A New World" in *The Butterworth Lectures 1990-91* (1992) (hereafter "Civil Wrongs"), 99-101; Sir Peter Millett, "Recovering the Proceeds of Fraud", *Ferrier Hodgson's House Magazine*, May-August 1993 (an adaptation of Sir Peter Millett's diagram illustrating this scheme is reproduced in J Glover: *Commercial Equity – Fiduciary Relationships* (Butterworths, 1995), 301).

[4] Birks, "Civil Wrongs", 100–101.

"There is no respectable modern reason why 'knowing assistance' should not be regarded as a tort . . . There is no sense in having an accessory's liability which is openly recognised as such only in equity. Moreover, it is no less important that equity take notice of the law than vice versa".

He added presciently:[5]

"It seems that we have reached a point at which it is likely that doubts on certain points relating to knowing assistance in equity will soon be resolved – not only as to the degree of knowledge but also as to the nature of the principle wrong which can support liability in an accessory. It would be foolish to resolve these matters without attempting to establish the relevant rules at law. Otherwise new inconsistencies are likely to be generated. We need one law on the civil liability of accessories."

Lord Hoffmann[6] has said that

"knowing assistance is essentially a cause of action for fraud, negligence or interference with rights . . . I would wish to see the equitable rules abolished in favour of the development of the common law".

This paper will explore the extent to which the equitable rules and the common law are or can be assimilated. The practical question that arises is whether a plaintiff should in future attempt to prove dishonesty, assuming that that is required if he is to rely on the rules of equity, or whether he should attempt to prove knowledge and intention, or breach of a duty of care in accordance with the requirements of the common law. In other words, are there cases where an assister will be liable under the rules of equity, where he will not be liable under the common law? If the answer is yes (contrary to the arguments in this paper), then equity is fulfilling its traditional function of providing a remedy which is required in circumstances where the common law is unable do so.

In *Royal Brunei* Lord Nicholls emphasised that, in determining whether an accessory should be rendered liable in equity, dishonesty was the crucial test. However, there was a concession that there had been a breach of trust in which the defendant had assisted with actual knowledge. The defendant was not ignorant of any material fact.[7] Consequently, the question whether the defendant must be aware of the trust and its terms was not explored. Nevertheless, it is submitted that *Royal Brunei* should be understood as stat-

[5] Birks, "Civil Wrongs", 101.

[6] Lord Hoffmann, "The Redundancy of Knowing Assistance" in P Birks (ed), *The Frontiers of Liability*, vol 1 (OUP 1994) 27, 29.

[7] [1995] 2 AC 378, 383–384, 393. The defendant was the managing director and controlling shareholder of the trustee company. He was the mind of the trustee. As such it may be that he would have been held strictly liable for the breach of trust whether or not he was dishonest. I am indebted for this comment to Sir Peter Millett.

ing, obiter, that a person will be liable under the rules of equity if he does in fact assist in a breach of trust and is at the same time dishonest, whether or not he knew of the existence of the trustee-beneficiary relationship and (if he does know of it) whether or not he intended to procure its breach. This paper also argues that a person will be liable, under the tort of interference with rights, if he intentionally does an act whereby he in fact assists in a breach of fiduciary duty, provided that he also knows that the property is subject to such a duty and that what he is assisting is a breach of it: it is not necessary that he should know any more about the fiduciary duty than that. However, it may also be that this tort can be extended to cases where the defendant intentionally does an act whereby he in fact assists in a breach of trust, provided that he knows that the person whom he is assisting is breaching an obligation enforceable by civil proceedings (*ie* not limited to a fiduciary duty), even if the assister does not know what the nature of that obligation is or to whom it is owed. It is further argued that in certain cases the assister will be liable for the torts of negligence, or of deceit, either alone, or as a joint tort-feasor with the fiduciary whose duty has been breached.

It is concluded that it cannot yet be said that there is no distinction between the equitable rules relating to knowing assistance and the analogous common law rules.

DISHONESTY AND KNOWLEDGE

In *Royal Brunei* Lord Nicholls pointed out that, for the most part, those who advise and assist trustees will owe to the trustees a duty to exercise reasonable skill and care. This category includes officers and employees of companies in respect of the application of company funds, as well as advisers, consultants, bankers and agents of many kinds. If they fail to exercise that care, they will be liable to make good the loss suffered by the trustees in consequence.[8] This is a liability at common law for a fault which is no more than negligence. The implications of it are discussed below.

Lord Nicholls also drew attention to the close analogy between the rules of equity and the principle recognised by the common law in the torts of knowingly procuring a breach of contract, or knowingly interfering with the due performance of a contract.[9] As is well known, an element of the tort is

> "first that the person charged with the actionable interference knew of the existence of the contract and intended to procure its breach . . ."[10]

[8] [1995] 2 AC 378, 391.
[9] *Ibid*, 387.
[10] *Merkur Island Corp v Laughton* [1983] 2 AC 570, 607; *Lumley v Gye* (1853) 2 E & B 216; 118 ER 749.

It is now recognised that this tort is not confined to interference with contractual rights, but extends to other rights, in particular, in this context, to fiduciary obligations imposed in equity, such as a company director's duty of fidelity to the company or an agent's duty to give an account or to maintain a confidence.[11]

However, while this tort may, as a matter of fact, involve dishonesty, the relevant defining ingredients of it are knowledge of, and intention to interfere with, the right. It follows that the *Baden*[12] scale of knowledge remains of value in relation to such torts.[13] Nevertheless, Lord Nicholls went on to say, in concluding that dishonesty is a necessary and sufficient condition for liability in equity, that

> " 'Knowingly' is better avoided as a defining ingredient of the principle, and in the context of this principle the *Baden* scale of knowledge is best forgotten".

Having drawn the analogy between the tort and the rules of equity, Lord Nicholls appears also to draw a clear distinction between them by recognising knowledge and intent as an ingredient of the former, and avoiding them in favour of dishonesty in the latter. The language of Lord Nicholls in *Royal Brunei*[14] that

> "Acting in reckless disregard of others' rights *or possible rights* can be a tell-tale sign of dishonesty"

bears a strong similarity to that used in cases of criminal fraud.[15] The word "dishonesty" is not used to define a constituent of the analogous torts: the defendant's knowledge and intention are the ingredients of the cause of

[11] *Law Debenture Trust v Ural Caspian* [1993] 1 WLR 138, 150–151; [1995] Ch 152, 163; *Boulting v Association of Cinematograph, Television and Allied Technicians* [1963] 2 QB 606, 627, 648; *Prudential Assurance Co v Lorenz* (1971) 11 KIR 78.

[12] In *Baden v Société Générale SA* [1993] 1 WLR 509, 575–576, para 250, it was submitted that knowledge of a relevant breach of trust can comprise any one of five different mental states which were described as follows: (i) actual knowledge; (ii) wilfully shutting one's eyes to the obvious; (iii) wilfully and recklessly failing to make such inquiries as an honest and reasonable man would make; (iv) knowledge of circumstances which would indicate the facts to an honest and reasonable man; (v) knowledge of circumstances which would put an honest and reasonable man on inquiry. The first three of these states of mind are generally regarded as amounting to dishonesty, the last two to no more than negligence.

[13] As Clarke J has recently said in *Three Rivers DC v Bank of England (No 3)* [1996] 3 All ER 558, 580–581. And see S Gardner, "Knowing Assistance and Receipt" (1996) 112 LQR 56, 67. The Supreme Court of Canada has recently re-affirmed its preference for the test of knowledge and the *Baden* scale: *Gold v Primary Developments Ltd (Gold v Rosenberg)* (1997) 132 DLR (4th) 385; *Citadel General A & S Co Ltd v Lloyds Bank Canada* (1997) *ibid* 411.

[14] [1995] 2 AC 378, 390 (emphasis added).

[15] In *Baden* [1993] 1 WLR 509, 574 Gibson J expressly drew a similar definition of dishonesty from the criminal case of *Reg v Sinclair* [1968] 1 WLR 1246, 1249 ("handing over the whole of the company's assets . . . without a contemporaneous acquisition by the company of the assets promised in return"). See also *Wai Yu Tsang v R* [1992] 1 AC 269, 276-278 and *Scott v MPC* [1975] AC 819.

action, and the defendant may have a defence of justification if he proves that he has acted in defence and protection of an equal or superior right of his own.[16] In the absence of such a justification the defendant's conduct may be dishonest for the purpose of the rules of equity,[17] but it is not clear that knowledge, intention and the absence of justification always amount to dishonesty in this sense. It is the word "malice" which is commonly used in a tort which may (but need not) involve dishonesty, *eg* in malicious falsehood.[18] So, while it cannot be doubted that dishonesty should be a sufficient condition for liability, it has been questioned whether it is necessary.[19]

MONEY LAUNDERING

A context in which these questions arise directly is money laundering. Not all forms of dishonesty involve the misappropriation of other people's property by theft or fraud. Thieves and fraudsters need the assistance of others in their money laundering schemes. Sometimes they obtain it by finding people who are willing to act dishonestly in certain ways, although not to participate in theft. The thieves obtain this assistance by falsely representing that they are engaged in some dishonest activity other than theft. The difficulty this creates for the beneficiary-victim is that the supposed dishonest activity may not involve a fiduciary-beneficiary relationship at all, and so it is impossible to show that the assister knew of the existence of the fiduciary duty or that he intended to procure its breach. Accordingly the victim may not be able rely on the tort of interference with rights, at least as it is at present understood.

The following are some examples of excuses given for participation in different types of commercial fraud. They are drawn or adapted from actual cases. The fraud assumed is that the victim is a company V whose property has been misappropriated by its fiduciary F. F's scheme is to send V's money abroad in order to disguise its source. He obtains the help of an assistant A:

(A) A is a small firm of bankers, accountants or lawyers. They are persuaded by F to help conceal the true payee of certain payments of V's money. A believe it to be V's money and part of a scheme by V to evade tax. A believes taxes are too high and it is morally acceptable to use deception to evade them. The scheme is dishonest: it involves production of false accounts and other documents. But, since it is believed to

[16] *Edwin Hill v First National Finance Corp* [1989] 1 WLR 225. The onus of proof is on the defendant: *ibid*, 228.

[17] *Ie* as defined in *Royal Brunei v Tan* [1995] 2 AC 378, 383, 389–391.

[18] See *Clerk & Lindsell on Torts*, 17th ed (1995) (hereafter "*Clerk & Lindsell*"), para 1–41.

[19] Gardiner (1996) 112 LQR 56, 74–85.

be tax evasion by V, the supposed victim of the scheme is the Inland Revenue (or its foreign equivalent), who are actual or contingent creditors of V, but not beneficiaries of a fiduciary duty owed to them by F or V. A does have knowledge of a fiduciary-beneficiary relationship – namely F's duty to V – but he does not know or intend that V will be deprived of its assets.

(B) A is a director of an English company C which purports to supply goods and services to an Israeli company V, to be paid for by documentary credit. F controls both C and V. F persuades A to inflate the invoices for goods. A believes that he is helping V to avoid Israeli exchange control laws. The scheme involves the production of false documents on which the bank, as well as V, are intended by A to make payments. A is dishonest notwithstanding that he believes that no one will be deprived of his own property, and no creditor left unpaid. The victim is believed by A to be the state of Israel, whose exchange controls will be evaded, and to which no fiduciary duties are owed by F. F in fact uses the scheme to defraud the paying bank, which V cannot reimburse.[20]

(C) A is persuaded by F to let F open and control a bank account in A's name to receive funds which F says are due to himself personally, but which are in fact misappropriated from V. F is a valued business associate of A, and A believes that he is concealing F's assets from F's wife, who has instituted divorce proceedings. The supposed scheme is dishonest and an interference with the administration of justice, but there is no fiduciary-beneficiary relationship known to A, so no knowledge of a breach of any such duty, nor any intention to procure it.

There follows a brief review as to how such examples might be viewed under the following headings:

- equity;
- tort – interference with rights;
- tort – intention to injure the plaintiff;
- joint tortfeasors – negligence, deceit, interference with goods;
- tort – duty of care by the assister;
- crime – money laundering.

EQUITY

In Professor Hayton's words in *Underhill*,[21] "The defendant does not need to know exactly what is going on, so long as he suspects that something dishon-

[20] *Bank Leumi Le Israel BM v Cablefast Ltd and others* (12 Feb 1990) Unrep (QB, Com C, Saville J).

[21] Underhill & Hayton, *The Law Relating to Trusts and Trustees*, 15th ed (1995), 421.

est might be going on". It is submitted that this is correct. It is supported by Millett J in *Agip (Africa) Ltd v Jackson*[22] when he said:

> "In my judgment, however, it is no answer for a man charged with having knowingly assisted in a fraudulent and dishonest scheme to say that he thought that it was 'only' a breach of exchange control or 'only' a case of tax evasion. It is not necessary that he should have been aware of the precise nature of the fraud or even of the identity of the victim. A man who consciously assists others by making arrangements which he knows are calculated to conceal what is happening from a third party, takes the risk that they are part of a fraud practised on that party".

Examples (A) and (B) above are of the kind referred to here.

Commenting on this passage before *Royal Brunei*, Charles Harpum has said:[23]

> "This does seem correct in principle. It would be curious if a person could escape liability by saying: 'Yes, I knew I was assisting the commission of a fraud, but I did not realise that it was this particular fraud and this particular victim' ".

Lord Nicholls' statement of the law contains an approving reference to Mr Harpum's article and to the earlier edition of *Underhill*.[24] While this point did not arise in *Royal Brunei*, Lord Nicholls' formulation of the rules of equity lends support to this statement of the law, although Rimer J has not accepted that *Royal Brunei* should be so interpreted, or that a person could be liable for assisting a breach of trust when he had no knowledge of the existence of the trust.[25] There are analogies in criminal law and tort. Thus, in *R v Thambiah*,[26] Lord Pearce said:

> "One man may abet another by helping to set the stage even before the victim has been found . . . Nice problems may arise when preparations abetting one kind of crime are followed by the execution of a crime of another kind or when the abetting preparations are merely for some criminal but indefinite purpose."

In that case the identity of the intended victim was unknown at the time the assister provided his assistance. It leaves open the question whether the

22 [1990] Ch 265, 295. See also Sir Peter Millett, "Tracing the Proceeds of Fraud" (1991) LQR 71, 84–85.

23 C. Harpum, "The Basis of Equitable Liability", in P Birks (ed), *The Frontiers of Liability*, vol 1 (Oxford, 1994) 9, 15.

24 [1995] 2 AC 378, 389. There is a similar reference to the article by Philip Sales, "the Tort of Conspiracy and Civil Secondary Liability" [1990] CLJ 491.

25 *Brinks Ltd v Abu-Saleh (No 3)* [1995] TLR 533; AJ Oakley, "Is Knowledge Still a Prerequisite to the Imposition of 'Accessory Liability' " (1996) 10 TLI 53. Having represented Brinks Ltd in this litigation, I declare my interest.

26 [1966] AC 37, 46 (PC: *per* Lord Pearce).

assister would have been convicted if he had been deceived by the principal offender into believing that the intended victim had been identified as someone other than the eventual/actual victim. In *Generale Bank Nederland v ECGD*[27] Stuart-Smith LJ considered that the assister in *R v Thambiah* would have been a joint tortfeasor with the principal forger of the cheque in question:

> "What [the assister] did in opening the bank account in a false name and maintaining it was pursuant to and in furtherance of the common design that in due course the fraud would be practised upon the Bank by the actual fraudster".

In *Baden* [28] Gibson J said of the requirement of knowledge:

> "He must know that there was a trust though I do not think it necessary that he should know all the details of the trust: see *eg Foxton v Manchester and Liverpool District Banking Co* (1881) 44 LT 406, 408. He must know of the dishonest and fraudulent design of the trustee. Again, however, I do not think it need be knowledge of the whole design: that would be an impossibly high requirement in most cases. What is crucial is that the alleged constructive trustee should know that a design having the character of being fraudulent and dishonest was being perpetrated. Further, he must know that his act assisted in the implementation of such design."

If read alone, the last two sentences are a correct statement of the law, but the preceding sentences are not now consistent with *Royal Brunei* as it is submitted here that that decision should be understood.

A practice actually adopted by bankers can influence the courts in determining what liabilities the rules of equity should impose upon banks.[29] Tolerance of assistance in breaches of foreign exchange controls and evasion of foreign tax was until recently regarded as consistent with good banking practice. On 10th November 1989 the Bank of England issued a letter to authorised institutions concerning money laundering[30] referring to the *Basle Statement of Principles on Money Laundering*[31] reminding the addressees of the relevant statutes, and saying that the Statement reflected existing best banking practice. The Statement itself says that it is issued "with a view to assisting in the suppression of money-laundering through the banking sys-

[27] [1998] 1 Lloyd's Rep 19. The references to this case in this chapter are all taken from an unapproved transcript of the judgment. This is the view expressed by PS Atiyah in *Vicarious Liability in the Law of Torts* (1967), 301–302.

[28] [1993] 1 WLR 509, 575.

[29] *Barclays Bank v O'Brien* [1994] 1 AC 180, 197–198.

[30] Cresswell *et al, Encyclopaedia of Banking Law* (Butterworths, 1997), H2199.

[31] The Statement is at *ibid*, H2191.

tem, national and international . . ." and to "ensure that business is conducted in conformity with high ethical standards". The Statement then sets out the following at para 3:

"(*b*) *Will banks be required to verify that transactions entered into on behalf of or with foreign customers do not contravene the foreign country's tax or exchange control regulations?* This is not the object of the exercise. Rather, its purpose is to prevent banks from laundering the proceeds of crime . . .

(*c*) *What is included in 'criminal' activities?* The Statement deliberately does not seek to supply a definition . . . However, it can be taken to refer to the obvious major crimes common to all legal systems, such as murder, robbery, embezzlement, fraud and kidnapping, as well as drug-trafficking".

Clearly the evasion of exchange controls and tax were not there included in "major crimes". However, the fallacy of this view has now been recognised by bankers. The current regulatory guidance issued on behalf of the British Bankers' Association and others[32] requires compliance with demanding procedures. It also recognises that: "Evasion of taxation within the UK will usually involve the commission of one or a number of indictable offences under the general criminal code, *eg* false declarations, false accounting, or dishonestly obtaining pecuniary advantage by deception, with the object of escaping or reducing a tax liability". It notes that under the money laundering legislation "criminal conduct" includes any offence wherever committed which would constitute an offence if it had occurred in England and Wales.[33] It notes that breach of overseas exchange controls would not constitute an offence in the UK. However, there seems no reason to doubt that false accounting, or dishonestly obtaining a pecuniary advantage by deception, would constitute "criminal conduct", if such offences were committed with a view to breaching overseas exchange controls.[34] It follows that, in the examples given above, the accessories should be liable under the rules of equity .

TORT – INTERFERENCE WITH RIGHTS

A violation of a legal right committed knowingly provides a cause of action.[35] A recent definition of it is:

[32] *Money Laundering: Guidance Notes for the Mainstream Banking, Lending and Deposit Taking Activities* (Revised February 1995), paras 15-16. This is guidance as referred to in The Money Laundering Regulations 1993 (SI 1993 No 1933), reg 5(3)(a).

[33] *Ibid*, reg 1(7).

[34] *Cf* the finding of deceit in *Bank Leumi v Cablefast* (12 Feb 1990) (Saville J).

[35] *Quinn v Leathem* [1901] AC 495, 510; *Lumley v Gye* (1853) 2 E & B 216; 118 ER 749, *per* Lord Macnaghten. The scope of the tort is unclear, and at least one commentator questions that

> "The necessary ingredients of that tort are (1) existence of the legal right in the plaintiff, (2) knowledge on the part of the defendant of that right and intention to interfere with it, (3) direct and unjustifiable interference with the right by the defendant – direct interference in the sense that it is the necessary consequence of the defendant's actions – and (4) damage (though not necessarily pecuniary loss)".[36]

The analogy between the torts of interference with rights and the rules of equity is based on the fact that both apply to cases where there are three parties: an obligor, an obligee (the plaintiff) and an interferer. But there are also significant differences:

(i) The torts have been developed in the context of activities of an entirely different kind, namely industrial relations and, to a lesser extent, commercial competition (*BMTA v Salvadori*[37]). These cases are generally not concerned with misappropriation of the plaintiff's property, but with contractual, statutory and other non-property rights. By contrast, "knowing assistance" in equity by definition relates to property held subject to fiduciary duties.

(ii) In the trade union cases the interference is procured, rather than assisted or facilitated, by the interferer. The interferer has not assumed any responsibility to the obligor under a contract or otherwise. The obligor participates reluctantly and under threat, if at all. In the equity cases on knowing assistance the instigator is the obligor or, where the obligor is a company, a director or agent. And the interferer commonly has undertaken a contractual or other responsibility, *eg* as banker or solicitor, to the obligor, or to his principal.

(iii) In the commercial cases such as *BMTA v Salvadori*[38] the obligor breaches a restrictive contractual term to which he has agreed and the interferer's involvement is commonly as acquirer of something which the obligor has promised the obligee that he will not sell to the interferer. But for this reason these cases are more closely analogous to the equitable knowing receipt cases than they are to the knowing assistance cases.

In some cases the tort clearly does render the rules of equity redundant, as Lord Hoffmann has said. In *Royal Brunei* itself the defendant director would have been liable for the tort of interfering with the plaintiff's rights under the

it exists separately from the torts requiring intention to injure the plaintiff: see Harvey, *Industrial Relations and Employment Law* (Butterworths, 1997), N [2380].

36 *F v Wirral MC* [1991] Fam 69, 115; *Associate British Ports v TGWU* [1989] 1 WLR 939, 963D.

37 [1949] Ch 556.

38 [1949] Ch 556.

company's contract with it, because he knew of the terms of the trust created by the contract, and he was effectively in control of the company.[39]

So long as the tort is defined by reference to the rights of the obligee, then it will not catch any of the money-laundering examples given above. It is possible that the tort is always so defined only because, on the facts in question in the cases, the interferer knew of the plaintiff's rights. Since this tort does not require an intention to injure the plaintiff,[40] it might be possible that in a future case it could be redefined as follows:

> "(1) existence of the legal *obligation to the plaintiff owed by a third party*, (2) knowledge on the part of the defendant of *the existence of a legal obligation owed by the third party to another* and intention to interfere with it, (3) direct and unjustifiable interference with the *obligation* by the defendant – direct interference in the sense that it is the necessary consequence of the defendant's actions – and (4) damage (though not necessarily pecuniary loss)".

The justification for this redefinition would be that it is not clear that it matters in the commercial cases to whom the obligation is owed, so long as the defendant knows that there is an obligation. And, since the tort protects legally enforceable rights of many types, including contractual, statutory and equitable,[41] it is not clear that it should matter whether the defendant knows the type of obligation he is interfering with, so long as he knows that an obligation exists which is enforceable in civil proceedings, and he intends to interfere with it. The rules of equity focus on the interference with the trustee's duty ("assistance in a breach of trust"), and not on interference with the beneficiary's rights. And in *Royal Brunei*,[42] when making the comparison between the tort and the rules of equity, Lord Nicholls refers to the tort as "interference with the due performance of a contract", which is neutral as between rights and duties. In this way he suggests a closer analogy than appears when the tort is referred to as one of interference with rights.

A tort case which was closely analogous to equitable knowing assistance cases would be one where the acquisition of restricted goods, as in

39 [1995] 2 AC 378, 383. There may be a question as to whether he would have been protected by the doctrine of "corporate identity": *Said v Butt* [1920] 3 KB 597. But application of this rule may be inconsistent with the principle in *Re Hampshire Land Co* [1896] 2 Ch 743 (see *PCW Syndicates v PCW Reinsurers* [1996] 1 WLR 1136, 1143–1144), and see criticisms of the rule in *Bowstead & Reynolds on Agency*, 16th ed (1996) (hereafter "*Bowstead & Reynolds*"), para 9–115 and Lionel Smith, "Constructive Fiduciaries?" in P Birks (ed), *Privacy and Loyalty* (OUP 1997), 259. In *Bank Leumi v Cablefast* (12 Feb 1990) Unrep, Saville J does not mention this point. In *Bank Tejarat v Hong Kong and Shanghai Banking Corp (CI) Ltd* [1995] 1 Lloyds Rep 239, 250, Tuckey J considered that a director would not be personally liable in circumstances that were similar, except that the directors were found not to be dishonest.

40 *Associate British Ports v TGWU* [1989] 1 WLR 939, 963G.

41 *Ibid*, 964C.

42 [1995] 2 AC 378, 387.

Salvadori,[43] was made with the assistance of another person, *eg* a solicitor, and it is that assister who is sued. However, "facilitating the doing of an act" has been said not to be assistance for this purpose: *CBS Songs v Amstrad*.[44] In *CBS* the supplier of goods which, it was foreseen, were likely be used to commit a tort, was not liable as an interferer, or on any of the other bases contended for by the plaintiff. The sub-buyer of shares was not held liable in *Law Debenture*:[45] although he had knowledge of the breach of contract by the seller in selling to the buyer before the sub-sale by the buyer to himself, the sub-buyer did not induce or procure the breach.

There is no authority to the effect that a person should not be liable for the tort of interference with rights if, with the requisite knowledge, he intentionally provides services, *eg* as lawyer or banker, which are instrumental in the disposition of restricted rights or goods. If the agent were not liable this could produce anomalies, both with the criminal law and with the law on joint tortfeasors.[46] On the other hand there is a danger in creating too onerous a duty on the part of, *eg* solicitors, to be owed by them to persons other than their own clients.

Interference with the property rights of another is a tort, but if the property is chattels or intellectual property[47] the victim does not need to invoke the tort of wrongful interference with rights. The torts of wrongful interference with goods and infringement of copyright are ones of strict liability. Since a person who assists another to commit these torts is a joint tortfeasor,[48] the concepts of knowledge, intention and dishonesty are relevant to his liability only to the extent that they would be relevant to the liability of the person whom he assists.

The cases on interference with rights contain some discussion of the defendant's knowledge and intention. As to knowledge, in *Stratford v Lindley*[49] Lord Pearce said:

> "It is no answer to a claim based on wrongfully inducing a breach of contract, to assert that the defendants did not know with exactitude all the terms of the contract. The relevant question is whether they had sufficient knowledge of the terms to know that they were inducing a breach of contract".

Perhaps the question should be whether the defendants had sufficient knowledge of the obligation to know that they were inducing a breach of an obligation enforceable in civil proceedings.

43 [1949] Ch 556.
44 [1988] AC 1013, 1058.
45 [1993] 1 WLR 138, 148
46 See below under "Joint Tortfeasors".
47 *Byrne v Statist* [1914] 1 KB 622.
48 See below under "Joint Tortfeasors".
49 [1965] AC 269, 332.

This citation illustrates the continuing relevance to torts of at least the first three stages of the *Baden* scale of knowledge. If the defendant is genuinely mistaken about the facts (however carelessly), he cannot be liable. If he knows the facts, it is no defence that he might be mistaken about the legal effect of those facts.[50] The fact that a person has the means of knowledge may, but need not, lead to the inference that he has actual knowledge. But it is important to keep the two separate.[51]

Knowledge and intention are inevitably matters on which there is rarely direct evidence and on which inference is common. In many money laundering cases, the assister often has not asked for evidence that his client or friend is indeed dealing only with his own personal property. Nor, generally, has the assister asked for confirmation directly from the fiduciary's named principals or partners that they have authorised the dishonest transaction. He can then hardly complain if the judge infers that he believed there to be a fiduciary relationship and that he intended to interfere with it.[52]

In such cases the court may draw an inference that the defendant was wilfully blind, and then it will be unnecessary to consider whether there is any distinction between the rules of equity and the torts of wrongful interference. But there will be some cases where the question whether there is a distinction will arise. Examples (B) and (C) above are ones where the assister is not a professional agent. There are from time to time striking cases where a defendant who is admittedly engaged in dishonest activities gives evidence, and is believed by the judge, when he says that he simply did not suspect something which the judge thinks a less naive person would have thought obvious.

TORT – INTENTION TO INJURE THE PLAINTIFF

Intent to injure a particular individual who is the plaintiff is a necessary element in every tort of conspiracy[53] and of interference with the performance of a contract by unlawful means.[54] The identity of the plaintiff is rarely in question in the reported cases, and it does not follow that the individual intended to be injured has to be known to the defendant by name. So long as it is understood that the defendant has to know either the exact identity of the

[50] *Pritchard v Briggs* [1980] Ch 338, 413-415; *Sillitoe v McGraw-Hill Book Co (UK) Ltd* [1983] FSR 545, 557.

[51] *Bristol and West Building Soc v Mothew* [1997] 2 WLR 436, 447D.

[52] Cf Sir Peter Millett's account of the evidence in an unnamed case given in a book review at [1993] LMCLQ 415.

[53] *Quinn v Leathem* [1901] AC 495, 535; *Lonrho v Fayed* [1992] 1 AC 448.

[54] On the other hand it is not necessary to prove actual breach of an obligation. On this account Mr Gardner suggests that this tort might provide a remedy to a beneficiary even where no breach of trust has occurred: (1996) 112 LQR 56, 68.

plaintiff, or at least his relationship with the obligor, these torts will not catch the examples of money-laundering given above.

One reason for the absence of authority on this point is that the cases on intention to injure rarely involve infringement of property rights. In the case of torts whereby property rights are infringed, tortfeasors generally do not care who is the owner of the property. Thieves intend to injure the owner of the stolen goods, but they do not care who he is. But in cases of theft of chattels the wrongdoers are joint tortfeasors in the tort of wrongful interference with goods, and an averment of conspiracy is mere surplusage.[55] The money laundering examples given above are all ones where there is an agreement to use means which the obligor and the interferer each believe to be unlawful (although for different reasons), and where the interferer intended to injure a person who has rights to receive, or to be informed of, the money which is being diverted. As a matter of principle it is difficult to see why it should matter that the defendants are ignorant or mistaken as to who that person is, so long as they intend to injure that person, whoever he or she is.

In tort it is generally sufficient if the defendant acted intentionally, and it is immaterial that he was unaware that in law the act was wrongful.[56] In principle, therefore, if the tortfeasor did intend to injure and realised that his act was unlawful, it should be no excuse if he was mistaken as to the nature of the unlawfulness.[57] In so far as it is permissible to draw analogies between the tort of conspiracy to injure and the crime of conspiracy to defraud,[58] the cases in crime suggest that the victim may be identified by broad descriptive language.[59] Similarly, a person is guilty of handling if he dishonestly receives goods knowing or believing them to be stolen.[60] He does not have to know the identity of the owner.

In *Merkur Island Corp v Laughton*[61] the plaintiff shipowners complained of

[55] *Sorrell v Smith* [1925] AC 700, 716.

[56] *Unilever Plc v Gillette (UK) Ltd* [1989] RPC 583, 609; and see *Clerk & Lindsell*, paras 1–41, 17–06.

[57] Here the tort of conspiracy may differ from the crime, because in the crime of conspiracy the agreement is to commit an offence, and the precise nature of the offence will therefore be crucial.

[58] Lord Nicholls appears to have drawn from the criminal law by using words in relation to the taking of risks and dishonesty which are strikingly similar to the words used in the criminal cases referred to in the next note: [1995] 2 AC 378, 390.

[59] *Welham v DPP* [1961] AC 103, 123, 133-134; *Wai Yu Tsang v R* [1992] 1 AC 269, 273 (conspiracy "to defraud the bank and its existing and potential shareholders, creditors and depositors, by dishonestly concealing in the bank's accounts the dishonouring of the United States dollar cheques in the sum of US$124m, which had been purchased by the bank"); *R v Landy* (1981) 72 Cr App 237; *Adams v The Queen* [1995] 1 WLR 52 (conspiracy "to defraud any one or more of [EHL], its subsidiary companies and others in that they did agree to use dishonestly a system of disguising the source and utilisation of moneys from legitimate inquiry . . .).

[60] Theft Act 1968, s 22.

[61] [1983] 2 AC 570.

wrongful interference with the contract between themselves and the charterers of their vessel. The unlawful means was the act of the defendant union in procuring tugmen and lock-keepers to break their contracts of employment with the operators of the tugs and locks. The purpose of this action was undoubtedly to bring pressure to bear on the plaintiffs to improve their crew's conditions of employment. The pressure was brought by immobilising the plaintiff's ship. One point of contention in the case was whether the defendant knew of the owner's contract with the charterer. In a passage of the judgment in the Court of Appeal, approved by Lord Diplock, Lord Donaldson MR said:[62]

> "... the defendants must in my judgment be deemed to have known of the almost certain existence of contracts of carriage to which the shipowners were parties. The wholly exceptional case would be that of a ship carrying the owner's own goods. Whether that contract or those contracts consisted of a time charter, a voyage charter or one or more bill of lading contracts or some or all of such contracts would have been immaterial to the defendants. Prima facie their intention was to immobilise the ship and in so doing to interfere with the performance by the owners of their contract or contracts of carriage – immobilising a laden ship which had no contractual obligation to move would have been a pointless exercise, since it would have brought no pressure to bear on the owners".

The principle that men are in general to be taken as intending the direct consequences of their acts applies in this field of the law.[63]

Adapting the approach in *Merkur* to a case of assistance in a breach of duty, it may be argued that the defendant must be deemed to have known of the almost certain existence of fiduciary obligations by which the person requesting assistance was bound. Sole traders dealing only with their own funds, without partners, principals or corporate vehicles, are now the "wholly exceptional case" in the context of commercial transactions involving large sums of money. The novelty comes in saying that the nature of the fiduciary's duty is "immaterial". A dishonest transaction by a fiduciary is likely to be one which is also a breach of his fiduciary duty. The assister is unlikely to have any assurance (*ie* other than that of the person requesting assistance) that the possible beneficiaries have authorised the transaction. Any assurance given by the person requesting assistance will not normally be reliable, since he is presenting himself to the proposed assister as person who is engaged in dishonesty. A judge will therefore often conclude that the assister's intention is to interfere with the duties of the fiduciary which he believes to exist. In *Merkur* the defendants were ignorant of the identity of the parties to the contracts of

62 *Ibid*, 591E–G, 609A–B. *Cf Emerald Construction v Lowthian* [1966] 1 WLR 691.
63 *Crofter Hand Woven Harris Tweed Co v Veitch* [1942] AC 435, 452.

carriage, but they were taken to know that the contracts in question were contracts of carriage. The case does not go so far as to say that it would not have mattered if there had been no contracts of carriage at all, but, say, a contract to sell the ship for scrap.

In *Merkur* the defendant's liability was not confined to the first contract with which he interfered. That case showed that he might be liable for a chain of contracts where the relevant knowledge and intention can be established. Thus, an interferer who interferes with the duty owed by a director to his company may also be liable for the interference with the fiduciary duty owed by the company to the beneficial owner of property of which the company is the legal owner and trustee. However, the extension of the law in *Merkur* has raised concerns: the defendant should not be liable for every interference which is a necessary and foreseeable consequence of his illegal act.[64]

JOINT TORTFEASORS – NEGLIGENCE, DECEIT, INTERFERENCE WITH GOODS

Joint tortfeasors are two or more persons who act in concert with one another pursuant to a common design.

> "Certain classes of persons seem clearly to be 'joint tortfeasors': The agent who commits a tort within the scope of his employment for his principal, and the principal; the servant who commits a tort in the course of his employment, and his master; two persons who agree on common action, in the course of, and to further which, one of them commits a tort".[65]

Certain preliminary observations must be made. First, breaches of a duty of care arise in both contract and tort concurrently.[66] So a person who breaches his duties to his principal or employer may be liable to his principal, not only for breach of fiduciary duty, but also for breach of contract and tort. A person who assists in such a breach of a contractual duty may therefore be liable to the principal as a joint tortfeasor, whether or not the claim is (or could be) framed against the fiduciary in contract or in tort, or in equity.[67]

[64] Harvey, *Industrial Relations and Employment Law* (Butterworths, 1997), para N [2231].

[65] *The Koursk* [1924] P 140, 155; *CBS v Amstrad* [1988] AC 1018, 1057. Where a person delegates the performance of a duty to an independent contractor who performs it negligently, the two may also be joint tortfeasors: *Jones v Manchester Corp* [1952] 2 QB 852, 869E; *Clerk & Lindsell*, para 4–56.

[66] *Henderson v Merrett Syndicates Ltd* [1995] 2 AC 145. A person may assume a duty in tort that is wider than the one which had been assumed by contract: *Sumitomo Bank v BBL* [1997] 1 Lloyds Rep 487, 513.

[67] That the decision in *Henderson v Merrett* [1995] 2 AC 145 would spread liability to joint tortfeasors, and give rise to rights of contribution not available between negligent contract

And if the assister is liable as a joint tortfeasor, he may be liable without dishonesty.

The cases brought against assisters show an undue emphasis on breach of fiduciary duties, as opposed to duties of care arising in equity and at common law. This has obscured the full range of bases under which an assister may be made liable to a victim. Not every breach of duty by a fiduciary is a breach of fiduciary duty: the distinguishing obligation of a fiduciary is that of loyalty.[68] Duties which are properly called fiduciary attract remedies which are peculiar to the equitable jurisdiction and are primarily restitutionary (involving a disgorgement of enrichment) rather than compensatory.[69] The rules of law formed to attach liability to an assister are compensatory in nature, not restitutionary.

The range of duties owed by a fiduciary depend crucially on the kind of fiduciary that he is. Fiduciary duties (and the rules relating to their breach) derive from the equitable rules on trusts. A trustee holds money or property for another. The trustee normally has the legal title, but the property belongs in equity to the beneficiary, whose rights are enforceable under the rules of equity, and not at common law. On the other hand, agency and employment are essentially common law notions. While an agent or employee may hold the legal title to his principal's property as trustee for his principal, his fiduciary duty does not depend on this. It is more likely that the legal title to property under the care of the agent will be held by the principal. It follows that, unlike the trustee, the agent's duties will be in contract, in tort, and as a bailee, as well as fiduciary.[70]

If the fiduciary is a trustee holding the legal title to the property, then in misappropriating it he is not committing a tort, but at most a breach of fiduciary duty. Hence, to address the liability of an assister, there is a need for the rules of equity formerly known as "knowing assistance", or for a separate tort of interference with rights.

But if property is owned by a company or other principal, and the misappropriation is by a director or agent, then (whoever has the legal title) the

breakers, was adverted to in argument in that case, and by Lord Goff of Chieveley: see [1995] 2 AC 145, 151, 162, 185H, 195E. But the scope of this extension of liability remains to be determined.

[68] *Bristol and West Building Soc v Mothew* [1997] 2 WLR 436, 448B, 449G.

[69] *Ibid*, 449F. Breaches of fiduciary duties may not be regarded as torts (*cf Kitechnology v Unicor* [1995] FSR 763, 776), which may raise problems of jurisdiction under Art 5(3) of the Brussels Convention on Jurisdiction and the Recognition of Judgments in Civil and Commercial Matters 1968 (as amended) and the Lugano Convention on Jurisdiction and the Enforcement of Judgments in Civil and Commercial Matters made between the States of the EC and the States of the EFTA 1988.

[70] *Bowstead & Reynolds*, para 1–026.

director or agent may commit a breach of his common law duty to act with reasonable skill and care. As Lord Nicholls said in *Royal Brunei*:[71]

> "This question, it should be remembered, is directed at whether an honest third party who receives no trust property should be liable if he procures or assists in a breach of trust of which he would have become aware had he exercised reasonable diligence. Should he be liable to the beneficiaries for the loss they suffer from the breach of trust? The majority of persons falling into this category will be the hosts of people who act for trustees in various ways: as advisers, consultants, bankers and agents of many kinds. This category also includes officers and employees of companies in respect of the application of company funds. All these people will be accountable to the trustees for their conduct. For the most part they will owe to the trustees a duty to exercise reasonable skill and care. When that is so, the rights flowing from that duty form part of the trust property. As such they can be enforced by the beneficiaries in a suitable case if the trustees are unable or unwilling to do so . . .".

There may then be no need for "knowing assistance" or the separate tort of interference with rights. In the case of chattels, the director or agent may be liable under the tort of wrongful interference with goods (which he may commit without dishonesty, or even negligence), and, in the case of other property, there may be a breach of his duty of care (which, again, may be committed without dishonesty). He may at the same time commit a breach of his fiduciary duty of loyalty, but that adds little. A person assisting a director or agent in the tort of wrongful interference with goods may be liable to the principal as a joint tortfeasor. His liability will then not depend on dishonesty, even if the act is also a breach of fiduciary duty owed to a principal. The tort does not always require knowledge or intention.

It is useful to note the various torts for which a fiduciary might be liable to his principal or employer in the course of money-laundering. The false documents that are likely to be produced include invoices or payment orders by which the victim's innocent accountant or banker is induced to make payments. The document may be false in identifying a payee to whom no money is properly payable, or in overstating the amount that is payable, or in stating

[71] [1995] 2 AC 378, 391. This is not the place to explore the precise nature of the duty of a director, which has been considered in this context in *Selangor United Rubber Estates Ltd v Cradock (No 3)* [1968] 1 WLR 1555, 1574G. See also *Re D'Jan of London Ltd* [1994] 1 BCLC 561. For the duty of bankers see *Lipkin Gorman v Karpnale* [1989] 1 WLR 1340, 1378B. In *Agip v Jackson* [1990] 1 Ch 265 a claim which did not depend on dishonesty could presumably have been brought by Baker Oil, in the Isle of Man, against Mr Jackson and Mr Griffin. Agip had an unsatisfied judgment against Baker Oil, which was in liquidation (p 282F). Mr Jackson and Mr Griffin, as sole directors (p 278D), would presumably have been liable in any action brought by Baker Oil, as were the directors in *Selangor*: they paid away the entire assets of Baker Oil for no consideration, leaving it with a debt to Agip which it could not pay.

that it is payable at a date earlier than the due date.[72] Such documents will contain misrepresentations. In the case of the dishonest fiduciary, the tort will amount to deceit. But it may not be necessary to put it so high. Where there is a duty to take care in making a statement, a false statement may be a breach of that duty. Officers of a company, and agents generally, are under a common law duty to use skill and care, and to keep the principal informed about matters which are of his concern.[73] An agent has a duty to pay over money held to the use of the principal even at common law.[74] A person in a position of responsibility may also owe a duty at common law to safeguard the assets of his principal and even to take steps for the prevention and detection of fraud. Examples (A) and (B) given above would be breaches of these common law duties. Liability attaches without the need to allege dishonesty, even if dishonesty is obviously present in fact. It is no defence that the victim was not intended to make a loss as a result of the misrepresentation.

Accountants and others who assist in the issuing and processing of such false documents, and preparing accounts on the basis of them, may often have no belief, and no grounds to believe that the documents are true,[75] even if they do not know or believe them to be false. They may be careless, not dishonest. If they are careless and intend to assist the guilty agent to induce the victim's innocent agents to act on the documents, that should be sufficient for the assister to be liable as joint tortfeasor in the agent's tort of negligence. If an assister were dishonest that might make him a joint tortfeasor in the agent's tort of deceit.[76]

In the case of *Royal Brunei*, whether or not there was an alternative claim in tort for negligence might have depended on whether the obligation to pay the money into a separate account were held to be a strict contractual obligation, or an obligation to take reasonable care.[77] Suppose a similar type of case where the contractual duty is clearly that, until the money is accounted

[72] In *Bank Leumi v Cablefast* (12 Feb 1990) Unrep – Example (B) above – Saville J held that the purported sale was in substance a transfer of money in breach of Israeli exchange control, that A impliedly misrepresented to the bank that the transaction was a genuine sale, and so was liable to the bank for deceit, even though he had not intended the bank to lose. *Cf United City Merchants v Royal Bank of Canada* [1983] 1 AC 168, where the price was overstated as part of an evasion of exchange controls, and the bill of lading was backdated to achieve conformity with a letter of credit.

[73] *Bowstead & Reynolds* Art 42, paras 6–016 to 6–016, 6–019.

[74] *Ibid*, Art 53, para 6–098.

[75] *Cf Agip v Jackson* [1990] Ch 265, 294 where, with the assistance of accountants, $10m was transferred over two years from an oil company with a branch in Tunis to a jewellery business in France. There was a finding of dishonesty (p 295); but, even if the Judge had accepted that the accountants were not dishonest, there was sufficient ground for a finding of breach of duty of care.

[76] *Generale Bank Nederland NV v ECGD* [1998] 1 Lloyd's Rep 19, 36, *per* Stuart-Smith LJ commenting on *R v Thembiah* [1966] AC 37.

[77] *Barclays v Fairclough* [1995] QB 214, 223, 227.

for to the principal, the agent should take care of it by applying it (less his commission) for specified purposes. Suppose the agent also acts for other principals, some of whom permit him to use all proceeds of sale as his own, so that to them the agent is no more than a creditor in respect of money he has received. It follows that cheques and other payments remitted to the agent have to be sorted, and commission calculated, to work out exactly what credits are available for what purposes. The agent's accountant (who is an employee) and his bankers (who are independent contractors) are informed of all this and undertake to perform the sorting task, and the agent delegates this task to them. Honestly, but carelessly, the accountant and bankers each misdirect into the agent's own account monies which should have been applied only to the specified purposes. The agent is also honest, but he too is careless, and fails to notice the obvious mistakes. He then becomes insolvent. Clearly the agent is in breach of his contractual duty to take care of the money. It would appear to follow from *Henderson v Merrett*[78] that, independently of the contract, the agent is liable in tort for breach of his duty of care, and the accountant and bankers are each joint tortfeasors with the agent in relation to the mistake each has made. As joint tortfeasors they may be sued by the principal. On this analysis the allegation of a fiduciary duty adds nothing. Even in cases where there is dishonesty (*eg* because the agent and his bankers both know that there is a serious risk, which they have no right to take, of the money being lost to the principal, or as in Example (A) above), there is still a breach of a duty of care, and resort to the rules of equity is unnecessary.

What amounts to assistance for this purpose does not appear clearly from the authorities. Assistance has been said not to include facilitation,[79] but this seems difficult to reconcile with the classic statement that "All persons in trespass who aid or counsel, direct, or join, are joint trespassers".[80] The word "facilitates" is now used in the Criminal Justice Act 1988 s 93A, and there is everything to be said for facilitation to give rise to civil liability if it is sufficient to give rise to criminal liability (discussed below). However, *Generale v ECGD*[81] is authority that "mere assistance, even knowing assistance, does not suffice to make the 'secondary party' jointly liable as a tortfeasor with the primary party". In that case Hobhouse LJ also says that: "The criminal law for obvious policy reasons goes further than the civil law". Hobhouse LJ refers

[78] [1995] 2 AC 145.

[79] *PLG Research Ltd v Ardon International* [1993] FSR 197, 239.

[80] *Petrie v Lamont* (1842) Car & Marsh 93, 96; and compare the Accessories and Abettors Act 1861, s 8 ("Whosoever shall aid, abet, counsel or procure the commission of any indictable offence . . . shall be liable . . . as a principal offender"); *NCB v Gamble* [1959] 1 QB 11; *Ackroyds v DPP* [1950] 1 All ER 933 (travel agents convicted of aiding the unlawful carriage of passengers).

[81] [1998] 1 Lloyd's Rep 19.

to the rules of equity as enunciated in *Baden*, and tentatively suggests that they are akin to the common law principles of agency or joint enterprise. It does not appear from the unapproved version of the judgment whether or not *Royal Brunei* was cited.

If the assister is not liable as a joint tortfeasor, but is liable only if he has committed the tort of interfering with rights, then there may be an extremely important distinction between tort and the analogous rules of equity: the rules of equity clearly do catch agents who advise and assist, but do not induce, a breach of duty.[82]

It is also interesting to note that people can be joint tortfeasors where one of them is honest and the other is not, *eg* an auctioneer who innocently helps a thief sell stolen goods.[83] In tort dishonesty is rarely an ingredient, and in any event an objective test must be applied: ignorance of the law is no defence. What is required is a common design to do an act which is in fact a tort, whether or not the defendants realise it is unlawful. As Mustill LJ said in relation to infringement of patent:[84]

> "Nor . . . is there any need for a common design to infringe. It is enough if the parties combine to secure the doing of acts which in the event prove to be infringements".

It follows that, when Lord Nicholls said in *Royal Brunei* that a dishonest assister may be liable when the trustee himself is not, he was going some way to assimilating the position in equity with that in tort.

TORT – DUTY OF CARE BY THE ASSISTER

Even where the legal title to assets is held by a trustee, there is certainly one, and possibly two, routes whereby a person who assists in the breach of trust may be held directly liable to the victim for the tort of negligence, without the need for a joint tortfeasor.

Where assets are held on trust by a corporate trustee, that company may sue the assister in contract or tort because, even though it has no beneficial interest in the asset, the company is the victim of its agent's fraud as much as the beneficiary.[85] The beneficiary will obtain the benefit of any claim against

[82] See Sales [1990] CLJ 491, 507–510; Lionel Smith: "Constructive Fiduciaries?" in Peter Birks (ed), *Privacy and Loyalty* (OUP, 1997), 259.

[83] *RH Willis and Son v British Car Auctions Ltd* [1978] 1 WLR 438 and *Bowstead & Reynolds*, Art 116.

[84] *Unilever Plc v Gillette (UK) Ltd* [1989] RPC 583, 609.

[85] *Baden* [1983] 1 WLR 509, 574C–D, para 244; *Brink's-Mat v Noye* [1991] 1 Bank LR 68.

the assister. The assister may be sued in contract or tort by the beneficiary in a case where the trustee is unable or unwilling to sue.[86] Although liability on this basis requires no greater fault than negligence, it is not, of course, negligence in the sense of a breach of duty of care owed by the assister directly to the victim-beneficiary.

However, the existence of this right might well make it unnecessary for the law to recognise a duty of care owed directly by the assister to the victim-beneficiary.

Nevertheless, in *Royal Brunei*[87] Lord Nicholls also envisaged the possibility that the assister might be liable to the beneficiary for breach of a duty of care in tort owed directly by the assister to the beneficiary. While Lord Nicholls does not say what he has in mind here, it may be that he was thinking of the cases of liability in negligence where there is no reliance, *eg White v Jones*,[88] in which he was concerned while sitting in the Court of Appeal. The Court of Appeal of British Columbia has found such a duty to exist.[89]

In *White v Jones* the problem central to the case as expressed by Nicholls LJ, was that, absent a direct duty owed by the solicitors to the intended beneficiaries of their client's will:[90]

> ". . . in considering the liability question it is of the utmost importance to keep in mind that if there is no liability the result, as pointed out by Sir Robert Megarry V-C in *Ross v Caunters*[91] is striking: the only person who has a valid claim against the solicitor has suffered no loss, and the only person who has suffered a loss has no valid claim. . . . It would be a sorry reflection on English law if, indeed, that is the position today".

A similar situation could arise in this field of the law in a case where the legal title to the property lies in a personal trustee who is acting dishonestly in breach of duty. In such a case an action by the trustee against his assister might well be met with the defence of *ex turpi causa non oritur actio*, or contributory negligence,[92] and with the contention that in any event the trustee

[86] *Royal Brunei* [1995] 2 AC 378, 391; *Harmer v Armstrong* [1934] Ch 65; *Field v Firmenich* [1971] 1 All ER 1104.

[87] [1995] 2 AC 378, 392.

[88] [1995] 2 AC 207; *Baden v Société Generale* [1993] 1 WLR 509, 610-612. *Cf* Lionel Smith, "Constructive Fiduciaries?" in P Birks (ed), *Privacy and Loyalty* (OUP, 1997) 268.

[89] *Linsley v Kirstiuk* (1986) 28 DLR (4th) 495, 502–503. The solicitors were held liable under the reliance principle: the beneficiaries were entitle to rely upon the solicitors acting properly, and they negligently failed to fulfil their retainer (by the trustees) to give proper legal advice (in fact they did not advise at all).

[90] *White v Jones* [1995] 2 AC 207, 220; and see further *ibid*, 259, 261, 268, 275.

[91] [1980] Ch 297, 303A.

[92] The defence of *ex turpi causa* will not arise in a case where the fiduciary has misappropriated his principal's property, because the principal is a victim of the agent's breach of duty, and will be not be tainted by the assister's wrongdoing: *Belmont Finance v Williams* [1979] Ch

has suffered no loss, because he has had the benefit of the beneficiaries' property. The fact that the trustee still remains liable to the beneficiaries does not give the trustee a claim for damages. In principle, the beneficiaries, who have suffered the loss, should have a valid claim: but, if they do, it must be on an independent basis.

An example of such a case is *Williams v Williams* in 1881.[93] The solicitor was negligent in believing a husband, who denied that there was a marriage settlement, against his wife, who asserted that there was one. He accepted instructions from the husband to make a will by which trust property which had been the husband's land was sold to pay his debts, and the proceeds of sale passed through the solicitor's hands. The children, beneficiaries of the settlement, failed to recover compensation because the solicitor, although negligent, was not dishonest. Given the developments in the law of negligence since 1881, that does not now appear to be a just result.

While there has been no decision on such a case, it is also notable that Nicholls LJ was prepared to contemplate the possibility of such a duty being owed to intended beneficiaries not yet born, *eg* grandchildren.[94]

It may be argued that, because there is a claim under the rules of equity which depends on proof of dishonesty, therefore there is no need for beneficiaries to have a claim in negligence. But this would be a non-sequitur, and mistakes the relationship between equity and the common law. Equity may be taken to have followed the law, even though the law was not declared until later.[95] So developments in equity should not inhibit similar, or different, developments of the common law.

It is hard to see why persons who are no more than intended beneficiaries should be owed a duty of care by solicitors to the person proposing to make a will, when others who are actual beneficiaries should be owed no duty of care by the solicitors to his executors. As Lord Browne-Wilkinson said:[96]

> "In *Henderson v Merrett Syndicates Ltd*[97] your Lordships recently applied the concept of assumption of liability to cases where the defendants (the managing agents) had pursuant to a contract with a third party (the members' agents) undertaken the management of the underwriting affairs of the plaintiffs. For present purposes the case is important for two reasons. First, it shows (if it was previously in doubt) that the principle of a special relationship arising from the

250, 260–261; *PCW Syndicates v PCW Reinsurers* [1996] 1 WLR 1136, 1143–1144; *Brink's Mat v Noye* [1991] 1 Bank LR 68, 73. If the beneficiary has a cause of action against both the trustee a fiduciary and the assister, then liability can be apportioned between them: *K v P* [1993] Ch 140; C Mitchell, "The Civil Liability (Contribution) Act 1978" [1997] RLR 27, 49.

[93] (1881) 17 Ch D 437.

[94] [1995] 2 AC 207, 226.

[95] *Trustee of the Property of FC Jones & Sons v Jones* [1997] Ch 159, 169G.

[96] *White v Jones* [1995] 2 AC 207, 274.

[97] [1995] 2 AC 145.

assumption of responsibility is as applicable to a case of negligent acts giving rise to pure economic loss as it is to negligent statement. Second, it demonstrates that the fact that the defendant assumed to act in the plaintiffs' affairs pursuant to a contract with a third party is not necessarily incompatible with the finding that, by so acting, the defendant also entered into a special relationship with the plaintiff with whom he had no contract".

It appears that it may be sufficient for the assister to owe a duty of care to the beneficiary, provided, first, that "the defendant assumed to act in the plaintiffs' affairs", and, second, that, if there were no duty the only person who has a valid claim against the solicitor would have suffered no loss, and the only person who has suffered a loss would have no valid claim.[98]

MONEY LAUNDERING AS A CRIME

It is an offence, known as money laundering, for a person to be concerned in an arrangement whereby the retention by another of his proceeds of criminal conduct is facilitated, if the person so concerned knows or suspects that the other person is or has been engaged in criminal conduct or has benefitted from criminal conduct.[99] The defendant may be guilty even if he did not know the identity of the criminal or the nature of the criminal conduct concerned, so long as he knew or suspected that the arrangement he entered into was one which related to "any person's proceeds of criminal conduct".[100] The defence is "that he did not know or suspect that the arrangement related to any person's proceeds of criminal conduct".[101] It does not appear to suffice for that defence that the defendant was ignorant of the particular offence, if he so much as suspected that the arrangement related to the proceeds of some criminal conduct. "Proceeds of criminal conduct" include any pecuniary advantage derived in connection with the commission of an offence.[102] It seems that these words are wide enough to include the benefits of tax evasion.

Of course, there are obvious reasons why not all conduct which is criminal should give rise to civil liability. But if a victim of a fraud, which is both a civil wrong and a crime, is unable to find the proceeds of the fraud as a result of a

[98] Assumption of responsibility is a reason why the solicitors of one party may owe a duty to the other party, even in hostile litigation: *Al Kandari v JR Brown & Co* [1988] 1 QB 665, 672, 676.

[99] Criminal Justice Act 1988, s 93A, as amended by the Criminal Justice Act 1993, s 29. There is a similar provision in the Drug Trafficking Act 1994, s 50. For the offence of concealing of transferring the proceeds of crime, see the Criminal Justice Act 1988, s 93C(2), as amended by the Criminal Justice Act 1993, s 31. For drug trafficking, see the Drug Trafficking Act 1994 s 49(2).

[100] Criminal Justice Act 1988, s 93A(2) and (4).

[101] Criminal Justice Act 1988, s 93A(4)(a).

[102] Criminal Justice Act 1988, ss 71(4)–(5) and 102.

further offence of money laundering, it seems reasonable that the victim should be able to recover compensation from the money launderer under the civil law.[103] If a victim has no cause of action in tort or under the rules of equity, it may be appropriate to consider whether the statutes creating the offences of money laundering can give rise to civil liability.

CONCLUSION

As mentioned above, Lord Nicholls pointed out that in some cases the assister will be liable at common law to make good the beneficiaries' loss if his fault was no more than one of negligence. So it is clear that *Royal Brunei* was not intended to be a statement that a person assisting in a breach of a fiduciary's duty should never be liable merely on the basis of negligence. Powerful arguments have been put forward as to why in equity a test less onerous than dishonesty should be sufficient.[104]

A review of the causes of action available at common law appears to show that liability may arise without dishonesty, whatever may be the requirements of the rules of equity. If plaintiffs had based their claims on common law causes of action wherever that was possible, there would have been less need to debate the difficulties in the rules of equity relating to assisters.

If *Royal Brunei* does not represent an assimilation of the requirements of knowledge for liability under the rules of equity with the requirements now existing for criminal liability, then such an assimilation, both in equity and in the common law ought to be made in the future.

If the rules of equity have made that development, but the common law has not, there may cases where only the rules of equity provide a cause of action, in particular where the fiduciary is a trustee in whom the legal title to the misappropriated property was vested. One example may be where the assister admits that he believed that the transaction was dishonest, but he did not know that it involved a breach of fiduciary duty. Another may be where the trustee's own dishonesty prevents him from making a claim against the assister for the benefit of the trust. In many commercial cases the victim will be a company which can claim against the assister either as a joint tortfeasor with the company's director or agent who has acted in breach of duty, or for breach of the professional duties in contract and tort owed directly by the assister to the company.

[103] For the powers of the criminal court to make compensation and confiscation orders see the Powers of the Criminal Courts Act 1973, s 35; Criminal Justice Act 1988, s 71–72. These may not be suitable powers for the resolution of the issues which can arise in claims against those who have assisted in dishonest schemes.

[104] Gardner (1996) 112 LQR 65.

There is scope for considerable further inquiry into this area of the law. No attempt has been made in this paper to consider whether the remedies available to a plaintiff who establishes dishonesty on the part of the assister are, or should be, more extensive than if he merely establishes negligence, or whether a plaintiff who pleads his case in dishonesty may benefit from other advantages, such as immunity from a plea of contributory negligence.[105]

[105] I am indebted for these observations to the helpful suggestions of those who attended when this paper was delivered.

10

Recovering Misdirected Money from Banks: Ministerial Receipt at Law and in Equity

MICHAEL BRYAN*

A. INTRODUCTION

In 1917 one MS Taylor, a Canadian serving as an officer in the Royal Naval Air Service, provided the necessary authority for his pay of £20 a month to be paid directly into his current account held at the High Holborn branch of the National Provincial Bank. In March 1918 he transferred to the newly formed Royal Air Force and was killed in July 1918. After his transfer he received his full pay as an RAF officer until his death. By mistake his transfer and death were both overlooked by the RNAS, which continued to credit his account monthly with £20. Over £400 was accumulated in this way. The mistake was not discovered until 1920 when the Admiralty Commissioners, acting on behalf of the RNAS, sought recovery of the entire amount paid since Taylor's transfer to the RAF. Meanwhile, Taylor's father had taken out letters of administration in Saskatchewan, but the letters had not been sealed in England. In a short unreserved judgment, in *Admiralty Commissioners v National Provincial and Union Bank*,[1] Sargant J held that it was unnecessary for Taylor's father to be joined to the proceedings as a party, and that the bank was liable to repay the mistaken payments to the Admiralty Commissioners. The bank's argument, that "the money, having once been credited to the customer's account, the bank became liable to pay it to the customer," was disposed of in the following words:[2]

* Senior Lecturer in Law, University of Melbourne. In preparing this paper I have benefited from many conversations with my colleague, Dr Robert Chambers. He is of course not responsible for any errors.

[1] (1922) 127 LT 452.

[2] *Ibid*, 453.

> "In my opinion, any contract by which a bank agrees to honour cheques of the customer on his current account does not extend to amounts standing to the credit of that account in so far as they are swollen by inadvertent payments made in mistake of fact. As a result of an order for repayment of the amount claimed, the customer's current account will be deflated by that amount. Any subsequent action by the customer's legal representative to recover that amount from the bank would have no reasonable chance of success."

This tale of the death of a pioneer air force pilot followed by bureaucratic muddle contains within its brief compass the issues discussed in this paper, although the judgment touches only lightly upon some of them. If A's money has been wrongly paid into the B bank to be credited to C's account, in what circumstances can A obtain restitution from the B bank? Can B defeat the claim by arguing that restitution can only be obtained from C? The payment may be wrongful because it has been paid under a mistake, or because fraud or forgery has been committed of which A is the victim. In the interests of simplicity of exposition it will be assumed that payment has been made by a money transfer order but the relevant principles are, unless otherwise indicated, equally applicable to cheque payments. A's right of restitution has been held on some authorities to depend on the state of C's account at the time of receipt, so the alternatives of an account in credit and an overdrawn account both need to be considered.

The questions posed might seem to belong to the footnotes of a restitution text than to mainstream theory. In fact they raise issues of both practical and theoretical significance. Banks are "natural defendants" in the law of restitution; they are usually solvent and amenable to the jurisdiction of the court. Failure to obtain restitution from the bank, for whatever reason, compels the plaintiff to redirect his or her claim against the customer, who may be elusive or of doubtful solvency. At the theoretical level, exploration of these issues may contribute to a better understanding of how enrichment-based defences operate.

Claims against banks in restitution can be brought at common law or in equity. It is sometimes argued that the meaning of receipt in equity differs from its common law signification. The common law, it is said, "defines receipt too widely"[3] in imposing liability to make restitution, subject to defences, upon any recipient of a wrongful payment. In equity, on the other hand, a recipient will be accountable only if he or she has received property for personal use and benefit.[4] Legal authority on the meaning of receipt is actually very slight. It has to be pieced together by drawing inferences from the princi-

[3] Sir Peter Millett, "Tracing the Proceeds of Fraud" (1991) 107 LQR 71, 79.
[4] *Ibid*, 83. *Agip (Africa) Ltd v Jackson* [1990] 1 Ch 265, 292, *per* Millett J.

pal restitutionary causes of action as well as from defences, such as change of position and ministerial receipt,[5] which extinguish or qualify liability.

A conclusion of this paper is that no distinction can, or should, be drawn between receipt at common law and in equity. It is a truism of banking law and practice that a bank receives money for its own purposes, to mix, lend or invest as it thinks fit. A customer whose account is in credit is a creditor of the bank, entitled to be repaid the amount lent, together with interest if the terms of the loan so provide, upon demand in accordance with the conditions of banking. There is no room for a concept of beneficial receipt on the conventional analysis of the banking relationship. It will be suggested that recent decisions on overdraft reductions and currency transfers have overlooked this axiom of banking law.

The argument being put forward is essentially a restatement and defence of the common law conception of receipt, which has been criticised for its excessive width. If it is too wide then a bank's interest in security of receipts must be protected by the application of the appropriate restitutionary defences such as change of position, good faith exchange and ministerial receipt.[6] The equitable requirement, if such it is, that a receipt-based constructive trust can only be imposed upon a recipient with knowledge of the prior breach of fiduciary duty also protects the recipient's interest in transactional security, although it will be argued that an extension of ministerial receipt as a defence to equitable claims is a more coherent method of safeguarding this interest.

Of these defences ministerial receipt requires particularly close attention. This is partly because a bank's agency status is a natural shield against claims in restitution, and partly because a special attraction of the defence for banks and others is that detriment or prejudice is said to be an ingredient of change of position, but not of ministerial receipt.[7] The existence of the defence of

[5] It is convenient to describe ministerial receipt as defence even though its function is to redirect rather than to extinguish liability. See *infra*, text at fn 25, and Andrew Burrows, *The Law of Restitution* (Butterworths, London, 1993), 485.

[6] No systematic attempt will be made to explore the rationale of these defences, for example, whether ministerial receipt is a species of change of position. Implicit in the text is an assumption that, even if ministerial receipt is not the same species as change of position, it belongs to the same genus. See William Swadling, "The Nature of Ministerial Receipt", in P Birks (ed), *Laundering and Tracing* (Clarendon Press, Oxford, 1995), 253–259, and Peter Birks, "Overview: Tracing, Claiming and Defences", also in *Laundering and Tracing*, 341–347. See also Burrows, *The Law of Restitution*, 484–486.

[7] Burrows, *The Law of Restitution*, 485. Compare Peter Birks, "Overview: Tracing, Claiming and Defences", *Laundering and Tracing*, 344–346. *Australia and New Zealand Banking Group Ltd v Westpac Banking Corp* (1988) 164 CLR 662, 681–684. In Australia the defence of change of position has been lamed, temporarily it is to be hoped, by the decision of the New South Wales Court of Appeal in *State Bank of New South Wales v Swiss Bank Corporation* (1996) 37 NSW LR 294 that in assessing good faith only evidence derived from the payor can be considered. See Robert Chambers, "Change of Position on the Faith of the Receipt" [1996] *Restitution Law Review* 103.

ministerial receipt is not in doubt but its scope is extraordinarily hard to determine, in spite of many decisions of high authority. Two models of ministerial receipt will be examined. The first, more favourable to plaintiffs, only permits a bank to plead its agency status as a defence when a banking transaction is irreversible: in other words, when a bank cannot make restitution to the plaintiff by debiting its customer's account. The rationale for this version is that security of receipts is not threatened if a bank can reverse a transaction without incurring legal liability to its own customer. The second model, which places greater emphasis on the bank's interest in finality of transaction, recognises ministerial receipt whenever the bank has credited the customer's account or paid the money to the order of the customer. Neither model has been unequivocally accepted by English law. More authorities can be marshalled in favour of the first version, but the second is easier to apply. The choice between the models depends ultimately upon a legal system's structure of restitution, and in particular how it balances the plaintiff's interest in recovery against the bank's interests in transactional security and, where cheques or other instruments are presented, negotiability.

These arguments are not new; they repeat or build on previous published analysis.[8] Taken together, their aim is to provide more direct and practical answers to what has become an overconceptualised area of restitution. The meaning of receipt should be kept as simple as possible. In this area banking legislation points the way forward. Section 4 (1) of the Cheques Act 1957 provides a defence to an action in conversion for a bank which in good faith and without negligence receives payment of a cheque for a customer. A cheque is received for the purposes of this provision when it is handed to the collecting bank.[9] The alternative, that a bank receives money only when it is credited to the account of the customer of the collecting bank, has been rejected. Of course, the matter cannot be quite so simple when what is received is not corporeal property, such as a cheque, but a chose in action, in the form of money received by electronic transfer. Nevertheless, the law of restitution should, as far as possible, follow the pragmatic example of banking law in construing the word "receipt".

The next section briefly examines the legal character of the banker-customer relationship. The relevant principles are neither complex nor controversial, but failure to appreciate them underlies the different treatment of

[8] In addition to material listed *supra* n 4, other important sources are Simon Gleeson, "The Involuntary Launderer: the Banker's Liability for Deposits of the Proceeds of Crime", in *Laundering and Tracing*, EP Ellinger and Eva Lomnicka, *Modern Banking Law*, 2nd ed (Clarendon Press, Oxford, 1994), especially chs 4 and 11, and CEF Rickett, "Banks and the Recovery of Mistaken Payments" (1994) 16 *NZULR* 105.

[9] *Savory v Co v Lloyds Bank Ltd* [1933] AC 201. Ellinger & Lomnicka, *Modern Banking Law*, 515.

receipt at common law and in equity. Later sections attempt to apply these principles to the question posed at the beginning of this paper.

B. THE RELATIONSHIP BETWEEN BANK AND CUSTOMER AT COMMON LAW

Since the landmark House of Lords decision in *Foley v Hill*[10] the legal relationship of a bank to its customer has been accepted as being in essence a relationship of debtor and creditor. If the customer's account is in credit the money deposited belongs to the bank, which can apply it in any lawful way for its own commercial purposes. In the words of Lord Cottenham LC: "The money placed in the custody of a banker is, to all intents and purposes, the money of the banker, to do with as he pleases."[11] In return the customer has a contractual chose in action entitling him or her to repayment of a sum equal to the amount deposited, together with an agreed amount of interest where the money has been placed in an interest-bearing account. The one departure from the debtor-creditor model is that the debtor is not required to seek out the creditor to repay the debt. A term is implied in the banking contract that the money is repayable to the customer only upon demand.[12]

If the customer's account is overdrawn, whether by agreement or by the bank's acquiescence in the customer withdrawing funds in excess of the balance, the roles of the parties are reversed and the customer becomes the bank's debtor. The bank is treated as having lent the customer money from its pool of funds available for investment. An overdraft does not, however, alter the basic debtor-creditor characterisation of the relationship.

In *Foley v Hill* the House of Lords expressly rejected the argument that a bank is accountable to its customer as a fiduciary. This is not because of any necessary inconsistency between banking and fiduciary obligations. A bank may, for example, find itself labelled as a fiduciary in respect of investment advice given to the customer. Advice-giving is not inherently fiduciary, but equitable obligations will be imposed where the bank can reasonably be considered to have undertaken to act in the best interests of its customer in giving the advice.[13] The core activities of crediting and debiting accounts are not,

[10] (1848) 11 HLC 28, 9 ER 1002.

[11] 11 HLC at 36. The fact that a bank enjoys full beneficial ownership of money received does not mean that it has separate legal and equitable title to the money. This needs to be stressed in view of statements in constructive trust cases, considered *infra* E, to the effect that banks "beneficially" receive some of their funds. See Robert Chambers, *Resulting Trusts* (Clarendon Press, Oxford, 1997), 52–55.

[12] *Joachimson v Swiss Bank Corp* [1921] 3KB 110.

[13] *Woods v Martins Bank Ltd* [1959] 1 QB 55; *Commonwealth Bank of Australia v Smith* (1991) 102 ALR 453.

however, fiduciary. Trust accounts are not an exception to this proposition since it is the account holder, not the bank, who owes fiduciary obligations to the nominated beneficiary.[14]

It is not completely accurate to explain the banking relationship in terms of debt, since a "superadded obligation"[15] of agency is engrafted onto the basic relationship. A bank acts as its customer's agent in executing payment orders and crediting the customer's account. Agency, however, supplements but does not supplant the principle of *Foley v Hill.* Money paid to a customer's order is the bank's own money. A bank can rely on its own title to money in claiming restitution of an unauthorised withdrawal from a customer's account.[16] It used to be thought that the logic of *Foley v Hill* dictated that any action for restitution of money unlawfully taken from a customer's account must be instituted by the bank. *Agip (Africa) Ltd v Jackson*[17] and *Lipkin Gorman v Karpnale Ltd*[18] have established that the customer can sue independently of the bank. It is not the purpose of this paper to add to the debate on the juridical nature of the customer's title to sue.[19] One analysis, suggested by Dr Lionel Smith and drawing support from the Court of Appeal decision in *Agip*, is that the customer can sue because in these cases he or she cannot insist, as against the bank, on a recrediting of the account with the amount of the payment wrongly withdrawn. The terms of the banking contract, or the law of the country where the misdirection occurred, may preclude recrediting. "The reality is a payment by the customer, at any rate where the customer has no right to require a recrediting of his account."[20] A customer who cannot obtain repayment from his or her own bank is entitled to institute proceedings against the recipient bank or its customer. This analysis has the merit of establishing a symmetry between the plaintiff customer's title to sue, based on the customer's inability to claim a recrediting of a misdirected payment from his or her own bank, and the defendant bank's liability to be sued, which, at least on one version of ministerial receipt to be considered in this paper, is based on that bank's own contractual authority to redebit the payee's account. Whatever the true explanation, however, the relaxation of *Foley v*

[14] *Re Kayford Ltd* [1975] 1 WLR 279. A bank may be liable for knowingly assisting a breach of fiduciary duty by the account trustee: *Rowlandson v National Westminster Bank Ltd* [1978] 1 WLR 798.

[15] *Joachimson v Swiss Bank Corp.* [1921] 3 KB 110, 127, *per* Atkin LJ.

[16] *Colonial Bank v Exchange Bank of Yarmouth* (1885) 11 App Cas 84; *Australia and New Zealand Banking Group Ltd v Westpac Banking Corp.* (1988) 164 CLR 662.

[17] [1990] Ch 265, affd [1991] Ch 547.

[18] [1991] AC 548.

[19] Lionel D Smith, "Three-Party Restitution: A Critique of Birks's Theory of Interceptive Subtraction" (1991) 11 *OJLS* 481, 500–502. Peter Birks, "Mixing and Tracing: Property and Restitution" (1992) 45 CLP 69.

[20] *Agip (Africa) Ltd v Jackson* [1991] Ch 547, 561, *per* Fox LJ. Lionel Smith (1991) 11 OJLS 481, 502.

Hill on this point has been welcomed on the ground that it "accords with the general understanding of the business world."[21]

A bank acts as its customer's agent not only in paying out money but also in receiving it and crediting it to the customer's account. It is in this context that the defence of ministerial receipt comes into its own. The bank can resist a claim for restitution by proving that it received the wrongful payment in its capacity as agent, and that the proper defendant is the customer. The existence of the defence is not in doubt but its precise application to banks remains unanalysed and obscure. On one view, ministerial receipt should be limited to cases where one party holds property to the order of another, without authority to mix or derive any profit from the property.[22] This approach would almost never allow banks to shelter behind their agency status. The suggestion has the virtue of consistency with the principle of *Foley v Hill*: if banks receive money, including wrongful payments, in their own right and can invest the money as they please, they should in return be expected to make restitution in their own right. But, for all its logical attractiveness, this approach is hard to reconcile with the bank's contract with its customer, which requires it to pay the customer an equivalent sum to the amount it has received. If B bank makes restitution to A by debiting C's account when it turns out that C has a defence to the claim, B will find itself compelled to pay C the amount it has just paid to A. Ministerial receipt is intended to solve this kind of agent's dilemma, although, as the next section shows, lack of clear agreement as to the essentials of the defence has meant that the protection it confers on agents is not always adequate.

C. THE BANK AS MINISTERIAL RECIPIENT[23]

Ministerial receipt has a pedigree worthy of any reputable, long established restitutionary defence: a classic analysis by Lord Mansfield,[24] and at least two House of Lords decisions in which the application of the defence was the central point in issue.[25] Analyses of the defence by lower courts in England and appellate courts in other common law jurisdictions are not hard to find. For all that it enjoys a respectable body of case law, however, most academic

[21] Ellinger & Lomnicka, *Modern Banking Law*, 393.

[22] Simon Gleeson, *supra* n 8, at 127.

[23] For more general discussions of ministerial receipt see Swadling, "The Nature of Ministerial Receipt", *supra* n 6, and Burrows, *The Law of Restitution*, 480–486.

[24] *Buller v Harrison* (1777) 2 Cowp 565; 98 ER 1243.

[25] *Kleinwort Sons & Co v Dunlop Rubber Co* (1907) 97 LT 263; *Kerrison v Glyn, Mills Currie & Co* (1911) 81 LJKB 465. In *Rahimtoola v Nizam of Hyderabad* [1958] AC 379 the Court of Appeal's discussion of ministerial receipt ([1957] Ch 185) was overshadowed in the House of Lords by the defendant's successful assertion of sovereign immunity.

discussion assumes that the defence is still in an embryonic stage of its development. The ingredients of the defence, and the policies it is intended to serve, are still unsettled questions.

A threshhold question is whether ministerial receipt should be characterised as a defence at all. It is clearly a defence in the sense of being a judicially recognised reason for denying restitution from a specific defendant. It fulfills a more positive role, however, in identifying the enriched party against whom any claims for restitution must be brought. Ministerial receipt resembles change of position in being an "enrichment-based" defence but, in contrast to that defence, it does not erase enrichment but redirects it from the agent to the principal. Successful reliance on the agency defence deflects, but does not defeat, a claim to restitution.

Looked at from the agent's point of view, ministerial receipt avoids the dilemma of being unable to escape liability for its handling of a misdirected payment. If B bank receives a payment from A, to the account of C, which A later alleges was paid by mistake, B bank may, in the absence of the defence of ministerial receipt, find itself liable to A if it credits the payment to its customer, C, or to C if the money is returned to A and not credited to C. Ministerial receipt resolves the agent's dilemma in favour of payment to the principal provided that the conditions of the defence are satisfied. The agent's dilemma has shaped the evolution of the defence even if its policy significance has not always been appreciated. An agent who is not on the horns of this particular dilemma should arguably not be entitled to the defence. On one model of ministerial receipt to be considered, B bank should be compelled to make restitution to A if it can do so without incurring liability to C. The decision in *Admiralty Commissioners v National Provincial and Union Bank* was decided on this basis: the bank had to repay the mistaken payment to the Admiralty Commissioners since any claim by Taylor's father, as personal representative, had "no reasonable chance of success."

An agent will be entitled to the benefit of the defence if three requirements are satisfied. Two are uncontroversial. The third, payment over, receives a section to itself since the existence of this requirement has been doubted, and its application to banking transactions highlights some ambiguities as to what is meant by a payment over.

(a) The recipient must have received the money as an agent and not in the capacity of principal. Banks are the agents for their customers for the collection of cheques and for the debiting of accounts, but they act as principal in many other banking transactions.[26] For example, where a bank advances

[26] *Baylis v Bishop of London* [1913] 1 Ch 127; *Kleinwort Sons & Co v Dunlop Rubber Co* (1907) 97 LT 263, where a jury finding that the bank had acted as principal was upheld by the House of Lords.

money to a seller of goods in return for an assignment of the right to receive the purchase price from the purchaser, the bank will, by virtue of the assignment, receive the purchase price as principal and not as the seller's agent.[27]

(b) The agent must have acted in good faith and without notice of the true owner's claim to the money. This is also a requirement of change of position, and arguments from consistency suggest that "good faith" and "notice" should be construed in identical fashion for the purposes of both defences. Agents operate, however, within a different legal framework from other recipients. They are required by the terms of the agency to account to the principal for money received. Their contractual obligations will be a powerful inducement to pay money to the principal even where doubts might be entertained as to whether the principal was entitled to the payment. Complying with the terms of the agency agreement enables the agent to stand aside from the restitution claim and leave the plaintiff and the principal to sort it out between themselves. The agent's contractual mandate is not an argument for a more lenient test of good faith and absence of notice, but it does argue for some sympathy for the agent's dilemma should he or she resolve the dilemma by paying the money to the principal rather than undertaking a detailed investigation of the merits of the plaintiff's claim to restitution.

The burden of showing good faith and absence of notice of the plaintiff's claim rests, like the onus of establishing restitutionary defences generally, on the defendant. The application of the normal rule has, however, been doubted where the proceedings have been brought by the payer's bank against the payee's bank. It may be commercially more realistic to require the former to show that it gave timely notice of its claim for restitution before the latter accounted to the payee. In *Australia and New Zealand Banking Group Ltd v Westpac Corp*[28] the defendant bank conceded that it bore the onus of establishing ministerial receipt. The High Court of Australia expressed some reservations as to whether the concession had been rightly made, and considered, albeit tentatively, that in inter-bank transactions it was for the claimant bank to show that no defence of ministerial receipt was available.[29] The High Court's reservations may be more a counsel of prudence for banks seeking restitution than an exception carved out specifically for inter-bank litigation. Where the plaintiff is not a bank there is no obvious policy reason for displacing the usual rule that it is for the defendant to establish the ingredients of a defence.

[27] *Continental Caoutchoc & Gutta Percha Co v Kleinwort Sons & Co* (1904) 9 Com Cas 240; 90 LT 474.

[28] (1988) 164 CLR 662.

[29] *Ibid*, 675. See also *Agip (Africa) Ltd v Jackson* [1990] 1 Ch 265, 288.

D. PAYMENT OVER BY A BANK

The final condition to be satisfied is that the agent must have paid over the money received to the principal. Both theoretically and in practice, this is the most problematic aspect of the ministerial receipt defence.

A preliminary question is whether the agent need pay money over to the principal at all. Some decisions of respectable antiquity have recognised ministerial receipt without any apparent payment over to the principal.[30] The acceptance of the defence of change of position has also been put forward as a reason for reassessing the necessity for a payment over.[31]

The early cases on ministerial receipt shed only faint light on the justification for the payment over requirement. Payment over has been linked to the question of title to money received, so that an agent who has not paid over has been said to retain title to the misdirected payment and is therefore the party from whom restitution should be sought.[32] In the leading decision of *Buller v Harrison*,[33] where it was found that the agent had not paid over, Lord Mansfield was much exercised by the practical difficulties involved in suing a principal outside the jurisdiction of the court and barely known to the insurer who had negotiated the insurance policy through an English agent:

> "The defendant [agent] has trusted Ludlow & Co [principal] and given them credit. He trafficks to the country where they live, and has agents there who know how to get the money back. The plaintiff is a stranger to them and never heard of their names."[34]

To modern ears there is a ring of risk allocation about this argument. More relevantly to a restitution lawyer, Lord Mansfield characterised payment over as a species of what would now be termed change of position:

> "In this case there was no new credit, no acceptance of new bills, no fresh goods bought or money advanced. In short, no alterations in the situation which the defendant and his principals stood in towards each other on the 20th April [when the plaintiff settled the defendant agent's claim under the insurance policy.]"[35]

This is a justification of the agency defence framed in terms of change of position, with the difference, previously noted, that a payment over does not extinguish the enrichment but transmits it to the principal.

[30] *Sadler v Evans* (1766) 4 Burr 1984; 98 ER 34; *Duke of Norfolk v Worthy* (1808) 1 Camp 337; 170 ER 977; *Ellis v Goulton* [1893] 1 QB 350.

[31] Peter Birks, "Overview: Tracing, Claiming and Defences", *supra* n 6, 344–347.

[32] *Cary v Webster* (1721) 1 Str 480; 93 ER 647.

[33] (1777) 2 Cowp 565; 98 ER 1243.

[34] (1777) 2 Cowp 565, 568.

[35] *Ibid.*

Decisions involving banks have little to offer to the debate about the purpose of the payment over requirement. This is because all money received by a bank *as agent* is in fact credited to a customer's account or paid at the customer's direction. The critical case for testing the necessity for a payment over is that of A paying money to B as agent for C, which B, at the time of action, has not accounted to C. Opponents of a payment over requirement would allow B the benefit of the ministerial receipt defence; proponents would deny the availability of the defence. But such cases do not feature in banking litigation, where typically B, the bank, credits C, the customer, with the money received. There is abundant authority exploring the meaning of payment over, as it applies to banks as receivers of misdirected payments, but none of it challenges the assumption that some sort of payment over is required.

The application of payment over, even to standard banking transactions, has given rise to immense difficulties. For example, does the simple act of crediting a customer's account constitute a payment over? One would have thought that this elementary question would long ago have been authoritatively answered, but remarkably this is not the case. Two versions of payment over can be deduced from the cases. English law has not made an irrevocable commitment to either of these versions, and it is suggested that the choice should depend on how satisfactorily each model solves the problem of the agent's dilemma. The two models of payment over to be examined have been designated the reversibility model and the mandate model. The labelling is my own and is a response to unsettled judicial terminology, although it carries the risk of imposing a false uniformity on a highly disordered area of law.

1. The reversibility model

A textbook example of a payment over is that of a tenant who pays £50 rent owing, in notes, to a landlord's agent. After the agent hands over the notes to the landlord the tenant discovers that the rent was not due. The landlord's agent can resist a claim to restitution by showing that the money has passed to the landlord. The agent is, in the hallowed judicial cliché, "a mere conduit pipe" for the collection and accounting for the rent to the landlord.

In the commercially more significant case of a transmission of a chose in action the courts have developed and refined the concept of "constructive payment over." An important line of authority concerns the repudiation of marine insurance policies, usually for non-disclosure, where the insurer has previously paid out on the policy to the insured's agent. An agent sued for restitution of the money paid out under the policy will often try to show that it has been paid over to the insured, or "constructively paid over" as part of the continuing business relationship between the agent and the insured.[36] Constructive payment over occurs when the agent has settled his or her account with the insured by crediting the money received from the insurer on behalf of the insured against debts the insured has contracted with the agent. The account then becomes a settled account "and the transaction is in effect the same as though the agent had paid over the whole amount to the principal and had received back the amount of his claim."[37] It is otherwise where there is no settled account between the agent and insured but the agent simply claims the right to set off the payment received from the insurer against debts owed by the insured. In such a case "the mere passing of money in account where there is no settled account is not such a payment by an agent as will excuse him from paying money which his principal is not entitled to retain."[38] There can be no payment over without a final settlement of accounts between agent and principal.

To stretch the insurance concepts of "constructive payment over" and "final settlement of account" on the procrustean bed of the banker/customer relationship would be a particularly egregious example of mechanical jurisprudence. A bank usually pays money into the active, continuing account of its customer and not in final settlement of their respective mutual claims. The reversibility model can nevertheless be considered an adaptation of the concept of final settlement to banking practice. According to this version, a bank cannot plead its agency status in defence where it can lawfully reverse the credit to the customer's account and debit the account by the amount of the wrongful payment. Restitution should be ordered against an agent who is entitled to recover a misdirected payment from the principal and repay it to the plaintiff. On the other hand, a bank can avail itself of the defence of ministerial receipt if the transaction turns out for any reason to be irreversible. The justification for the reversibility model is that an agent should make restitution where it can do so without incurring either liability to the principal or detriment to itself.

A bank cannot establish ministerial receipt on this model of the defence simply by crediting the customer's account with the amount of the wrongful payment. This proposition has a sound basis in authority. In *Colonial Bank v Exchange Bank of Yarmouth*[39] one Rogers requested agents in Antigua to pay the proceeds of goods sold there to the plaintiff bank's branch in Antigua, which was then to remit them to the Halifax branch of the Bank of British

[36] *Buller v Harrison* (1777) 2 Cowp 565; 98 ER 1243; *Holland v Russell* (1861) 1 B & S 424; 121 ER 773; *Scottish Metropolitan Assurance Co Ltd v P. Samuel & Co Ltd* [1923] 1 KB 348.

[37] *Holland v Russell* (1861) 1 B & S 424, 435, *per* Cockburn CJ.

[38] *Scottish Metropolitan Assurance Co Ltd v P Samuel & Co Ltd* [1923] 1 KB 348, 354, *per* Bailhache J.

[39] (1885) 11 App Cas 84.

North America. The proceeds were remitted by mistake to the defendant bank, to whom Rogers owed money. The defendant used the money received to reduce Rogers's overdraft. The Privy Council held that the defendant had not paid over the money to its principal, Rogers, and was therefore liable to make restitution. In the words of Sir John Hobhouse, "it was not true that the sum had been used and could not be recalled. The defendants had only got to run a pen through some private entries in their own books and the matter would then have stood in precisely the same position as it stood before the mistake was made."[40]

To the same effect is the decision of the House of Lords in *Kerrison v Glyn, Mills, Currie and Co.*[41] A firm of New York bankers, Kessler and Co, agreed to pay cheques drawn on the Bote Mining Co, a silver mining company in Mexico, provided that the plaintiff, the company's managing partner in England, put the defendant bank, Kessler's correspondent bank in England, in credit. The plaintiff paid £500 to the credit of Kessler at the defendant bank even though at the time of the payment Kessler, "if not commercially dead, . . . were at least in a state of suspended animation, utterly incapable of carrying on business, making advances, or of doing the very things he lodged this money to their credit to enable them to accomplish."[42] The House of Lords held that the defendant had been enriched at the expense of the plaintiff, and that crediting Kessler's account did not constitute a payment over to Kessler.

The banks in these cases could correct the mistake without risk of legal action by its own customer and without having to satisfy the plaintiff's claim from their own resources. But in other cases money paid to a customer's account cannot so easily be recalled. A banking transaction may be irreversible for one of two reasons:

(a) *The terms of the bank's mandate*

Suppose that A by mistake pays B bank £500 to the credit of C. Can A's right of restitution from B be barred by the term of a contract between B and C which prohibits B from repaying A? An instinctive response is that a private agreement between B and C should not affect A's right under general law to restitution from B. A, after all, is not a party to the agreement. Lord Atkinson was of this opinion in *Kerrison v Glyn, Mills and Currie and Co*:[43]

40 *Ibid*, 89.

41 (1911) 81 LJKB 465.

42 *Ibid*, *per* Lord Atkinson.

43 (1911) 81 LJKB 465, 470. The example may not be well chosen as the payee's death will usually terminate an agency relationship.

> "It is admitted, as I understand, that if money be sent direct by one person to another in payment in advance for some service to be rendered by that other, in the belief that the latter is alive when, in fact, he is dead, it could be recovered by the sender from the person, whether agent or legal representative of the deceased, into whose hands it came. The fact that the deceased was largely indebted to such an agent, and the latter would, as between himself and the legal representative of the deceased, be entitled to set off pro tanto the money received as against the debt due to him, could not possibly prejudice the rights of the person transmitting the money. He would obviously have the same rights as against the agent to whom nothing was owed. And this would be so even though the deceased authorised the agent to apply the money, when received, to the discharge pro tanto of the sum due to him."

But, accepting the correctness of this dictum, there is a material distinction to be drawn in this context between a contract between B and C under which B owes money to C, which cannot affect A's right to restitution from B, and a term in a contract between B and C which prevents B from paying A. B should be entitled to set up such a term as the basis of a payment over, leaving A to seek restitution from C. The justification for applying the defence of ministerial receipt here is that, if the defence were not available, B could be trapped in the agent's dilemma. If a bank cannot show ministerial receipt when it is contractually precluded from debiting its customer's account in order to make restitution to the plaintiff, it could never act lawfully: it would be liable to the plaintiff if it did not make restitution in respect of the wrongful payment, and liable to its principal in contract if it did make restitution by debiting the principal's account. Ministerial receipt facilitates escape from the dilemma.

Some support for this argument can be found in the judgment of the High Court of Australia in *Australia and New Zealand Banking Group Ltd v Westpac Banking Corp*,[44] where the Court stated that it was "led to speculate about what [the recipient bank's] position vis-à-vis [its customer] would have been if it had, of its own initiative, dishonoured those cheques and reversed those entries and provisional credits. Certainly, its position would have been a difficult one if it had subsequently turned out that [the plaintiff's] claim could be met by a good defence on the part of [its customer]."[45] Ministerial receipt prevents a bank from being placed in the impossible situation alluded to by the High Court: caught between its duty to make restitution to the plaintiff and its contractual obligations to its customer.

[44] (1988) 164 CLR 662.

[45] *Ibid*, 678. Concessions made by Westpac, the recipient bank, in the course of argument prevented the High Court from exploring the contractual position further.

(b) *Withdrawal of the misdirected payment from the account*

As well as contractual proscription, a bank may be unable to reverse a misdirected payment where the customer has withdrawn the payment from his or her bank account. It would clearly be wrong to compel a bank to make restitution where the customer had closed the account and withdrawn the funds immediately after the misdirected payment had in good faith been credited to the account.

A more unusual problem, which confronted the Court of Appeal in *Gowers v Lloyds and National Provincial Foreign Bank Ltd*,[46] concerned withdrawals from an account by an unascertained principal. The plaintiffs, who were responsible for paying pensions to retired colonial civil servants, paid a pension to the defendant bank for the account of Gibson, a pensioner who lived in France. Unknown to the bank, Gibson died in 1929. Relying on a forged signature, the bank continued to receive the pension money and to forward payments in good faith to the person purporting to be Gibson. The fraud was not discovered until after the death of Mrs Gibson in 1935. The bank was held to be a ministerial recipient of the money and therefore not liable to make restitution to the plaintiffs. Sir Wilfred Greene MR declared that the bank was the agent of "a person, whose identity has not been ascertained, and who purported to be Mr Gibson,"[47] to whom the pension money had been paid away. All the money had been withdrawn from the account, and there was no possibility of recovery from the undetected perpetrator of the fraud. The decision seems right in view of the bank's good faith. Praying in aid the fiction of the "unascertained principal" to defeat the plaintiff's claim is, however, questionable. The artifice could now be avoided by applying the defence of change of position.

The application of the principle of reversibility to active bank accounts raises complex and little explored issues of identifying money withdrawn from an account. Suppose that A mistakenly pays money into B bank for the credit of C and, subsequent to the payment, C withdraws funds but also pays other money into the account. Can B argue that C has withdrawn the mistaken payment, thereby rendering the transaction irreversible? One solution is to apply the rule in *Clayton's Case*,[48] whereby the first payment into an active bank account is appropriated to the first payment out of the account. By setting off withdrawals from the account against credits it can be determined whether the mistaken payment has been withdrawn by the principal,

[46] [1938] 1 All ER 766.
[47] *Ibid*, 773.
[48] *Devaynes v Noble*; *Clayton's Case* (1816) 1 Mer 529, 35 ER 767.

or to his or her order. The rule is being applied here in its strict sense as a rule of appropriation between banker and customer, and not in its more capricious and objectionable sense to determine priority between the claims of two or more beneficiaries to money mixed in a fiduciary's bank account.[49] Application of the rule enabled the High Court of Australia in *Australia and New Zealand Banking Group Ltd v Westpac Banking Corporation* to conclude that a mistaken payment paid into the account of a Westpac customer had been entirely spent in discharging its customer's liabilities.[50]

An alternative argument, put forward by the authors of *Modern Banking Law*, would deny the bank the benefit of the ministerial receipt defence where, in spite of withdrawals, the balance in the account is sufficient to repay the plaintiff. In their words, "The bank is a reservoir of money, and the accrued balance is a debt owed by it to the customer. Moreover, it holds the funds as an agent. As the money is still available to the customer – who benefited from the windfall – why should it not be reclaimable from the bank – the customer's agent and debtor?"[51] The argument has a strong moral appeal but it runs counter to recent decisions on tracing which suggest that a bank is not to be regarded as an undifferentiated "reservoir of money," at least for the purpose of identifying wealth in customer accounts.[52]

The final issue, in this protracted examination of the reversibility version of payment over, is whether a bank can establish ministerial receipt where the customer has withdrawn money from the account, leaving insufficient funds from which restitution can be made. The bank should not be required in this situation to make restitution of more than the balance standing to the customer's credit. This will be the outcome, in any event, of applying the rule in *Clayton's Case*, as suggested above. Even if *Clayton's Case* is inapplicable, the bank should not have to pay the plaintiff more than the amount standing to the credit of the customer, always assuming that it acted in good faith and without notice of the plaintiff's claim in crediting the account. An insufficiency of funds in the customer's account from which repayment can be made is a clear example of irreversibility. To permit restitution in full against the bank would be to compel it to pay the plaintiff from its general funds. The plaintiff's recourse in such a case must be against the customer.[53]

[49] *Barlow Clowes International Ltd v Vaughan* [1992] 4 All ER 22; DA McConville, "Tracing and the Rule in Clayton's Case" (1963) 79 LQR 388.

[50] (1988) 164 CLR 662, 676-680. The application was made subject to several concessions made by Westpac.

[51] Ellinger and Lomnicka, *Modern Banking Law*, 410 (footnotes omitted).

[52] *Re Goldcorp Exchange Ltd* [1995] 1 AC 74, 109-110; *Bishopsgate Investment Management Ltd v Homan* [1995] Ch 211.

[53] An important question is whether a customer's insolvency should also be treated as an irreversible payment. Suppose that in *Chase Manhattan Bank NA v Israel-British Bank (London) Ltd* [1981] Ch 105 the plaintiff had sought restitution from Mellon Bank International, who received

2. The mandate model

The reversibility model of payment over enjoys strong support in the case law. A secondary line of authority, however, favours a broader approach to payment over, conferring correspondingly greater immunity on banks. On the mandate model of the defence money is paid over by a bank whenever it is applied in accordance with the mandate, or authority, of the payer. A bank paying a wrongful payment into an account in credit, or applying the money to the discharge or reduction of an overdraft, has in both cases paid over the money to the customer, from whom restitution must be sought.

The mandate model has most frequently been invoked when the wrongful payment has been used by the bank to reduce the customer's overdraft. On the reversibility model a bank using a wrongful payment to reduce the amount by which the account is overdrawn cannot establish payment over; it is always open to the bank to reverse the transaction, increase the overdraft to the previously agreed, or at least permitted, level and make restitution to the plaintiff. On the mandate version, however, a bank is as much entitled to apply a wrongful payment for this purpose (assuming the other requirements of ministerial receipt are satisfied, and that the application is authorised by the terms of the banking contract) as any other money received on behalf of the customer. So long as the money is applied in an authorised manner the bank is entitled to the benefit of the defence. As the discussion of the legal character of the banking relationship has demonstrated, overdrawn accounts are not fundamentally different in law from accounts in credit. Nevertheless, the payment of a wrongful payment into an overdrawn account throws into sharp relief the differences between the two models of payment over.

An early endorsement of the mandate model, as it applies to overdrawn bank accounts, can be found in a dictum of Collins MR in *Caoutchouc and Gutta Percha Co v Kleinwort Sons & Co.*[54] Construing the use of a mistaken payment to reduce an overdraft as a payment over, he stated:

> "[The agent] has no doubt benefited by getting his debt paid, but he has done so in discharging his primary duty of passing the money on to his principal. He has constructively sent it on and received it back, and has done nothing incompatible with his position as a conduit-pipe or intermediary. He was entitled to be paid

the mistaken payment for Israel-British Bank. The latter bank then went into insolvent liquidation. Could Mellon Bank establish ministerial receipt on the basis that debiting Israel-British Bank's account is now impossible? Although a bank in the position of Mellon Bank might argue that the customer's insolvency has in effect created an insufficiency of funds, it is submitted that the general principle that supervening insolvency does not alter private law entitlements should apply here and that the bank remains liable to make restitution.

[54] (1904) 9 Com Cas 240, 248–249; 90 LT 474, 476.

and has been paid by his debtor, who was no doubt put in funds to do so by the receipt of the money, and who therefore, and not the intermediary, has had the benefit of the windfall. Hence the care with which the courts have considered whether the sum has been effectually passed out of the hands of the agent into those of the principal, no entry by the agent in his books sufficing until the assent of the principal has completed the transaction."

The argument is laboured and somewhat unconvincing. It has been pointed out[55] that the principal's assent is not required where money is used to reduce an existing overdraft; the assent is given when the overdraft account is opened. Moreover, the dictum does not explain why using money to reduce an overdraft amounts to a payment over when crediting an account which enjoys a healthy balance does not. A bank compelled to make restitution of a mistaken payment which it has applied in reducing its customer's overdraft suffers no overall detriment since it retains its own remedies against the customer under the overdraft agreement. In *Kleinwort, Sons & Co v Dunlop Rubber Co* Lord Loreburn LC doubted whether the application of a mistaken payment to reduce an overdraft amounted to payment over.[56]

A more categorical authority for holding that the application of a wrongful payment to the reduction of an overdraft constitutes ministerial receipt is the decision of the High Court of Australia in *Australia and New Zealand Banking Group Ltd v Westpac Banking Corp.*[57] As a result of a clerical error the ANZ Bank telegraphically transferred $114,158.20 to Westpac for the credit of Westpac's customer, Jakes Meat Pty Ltd In fact the ANZ Bank had been instructed to transfer only $14,158.20. The Jakes account was $67,700.96 overdrawn. Jakes acknowledged the mistake but had only repaid a small part of the overpayment before it was placed in liquidation. The High Court held that Westpac had paid over the mistaken payment to Jakes and was therefore not liable to make restitution. On the basis of concessions made by both parties it was found by the court that the money had been withdrawn by Jakes and used to repay various business debts. This analysis is consistent with the reversibility model of payment over discussed in the previous section. However, the High Court went on to consider whether Westpac could show payment over if the greater part of the money had been applied, as appeared to have happened if the concessions were ignored, to the discharge of Jakes's overdrawn account with Westpac. The court's judgment challenged the essential premise of reversibility theory by stating that Westpac was not *obliged* to reverse the transaction and repay ANZ Bank, even if it had power to do so.

55 Ellinger and Lomnicka, *Modern Banking Law*, 409.
56 (1907) 97 LT 263, 264. It should be noted, however, that this dictum was based on a jury finding that the bank had received the payment as principal.
57 (1988) 164 CLR 662.

To repay ANZ might expose Westpac to legal action by Jakes if it turned out that Jakes had a defence to the claim for restitution.[58] The principle applied was stated as follows:[59]

> "[I]f money is paid to an agent on behalf of a principal and the agent receives it in his capacity as such and, without notice of any mistake or irregularity in the payment, applies the money for the purpose for which it was paid to him, he has applied it in accordance with the mandate of the payer who must look to the principal for recovery."

Authority for the mandate theory in English law is slight. On the other hand, no decision, even at House of Lords level, can be said to have rejected it. The critical question, assuming the retention of a payment over requirement, is one of policy: should an agent be entitled to the defence of ministerial receipt upon proof that money received has been applied at the direction of the principal, even if it can be recalled?

The answer to this question should not depend on the state of the recipient's account at the time of receipt. It is true that the reversibility model is more often applied usually to deny the bank the benefit of the defence of ministerial receipt, when the account is in credit at the time the wrongful payment is made. The mandate model, in contrast, has been favoured when the account is overdrawn at the time of payment. It would, however, be wrong to construct a legal rule on the basis of this distinction. A bank that can lawfully reverse a credit in order to make restitution to the plaintiff should reasonably be expected to restore its customer's overdraft to the level, presumably tolerated it not actually authorised, at which it stood immediately prior to the receipt of the wrongful payment. A plaintiff's right to restitution from the bank should not turn on the fortuitous fact that the account happened to be in credit *at the time of receipt*, although, on the reversibility model of the defence, the *subsequent* pattern of withdrawals will certainly be relevant to determining the application of the defence.

In choosing between the two models the focus should not, in my opinion, be on the state of the customer's account but on the position of the bank or other agent. From this perspective the significant advantage enjoyed by the

[58] *Ibid*, 677.

[59] (1988) 164 CLR 662, 677-682. The authorities cited in support of the wider principle adumbrated by the High Court are not compelling. *Holland v Russell* (1861) 1 B&S 424, as already noted in the text to n 35, recognised ministerial receipt only where there had been a settlement of accounts. In *Fitzpatrick v M'Glone* [1897] 2 IR 542 a recipient of money from executors was held not liable for applying money in accordance with the terms of the will for charitable purposes before receiving notice that the will was invalid. There is a statement of the principle of ministerial receipt by Palles CB at 551 in very general terms. As a secondary ground for not holding the defendant liable, the recipient was held to be the agent of the executors in administering the will. The case is of interest as a precursor of *Re Diplock* [1948] Ch 465.

mandate model over its rival is that it resolves convincingly the problem of the agent's dilemma. Banks, in a world made more frenetic by the pace of technological change, have very little time to make more than a tentative assessment of a claim for restitution. Even if the terms of the contract with the customer permit the debiting of a wrongful payment, there seems no good reason for placing on the bank the responsibility for assessing the merits of the plaintiff's claim. That task should be left to the principal. In *Admiralty Commissioners v National Provincial Union Bank*[60] Sargant J considered that any defence to restitution advanced by Taylor's personal representative would have "no reasonable chance of success." The merits of the plaintiff's case will not always be so overwhelming. And, even if they are, the bank will not always initially appreciate the strength of that case and should not be called to account for failing to do so. The mandate model saves the agent from the predicament of having to balance the duty to make restitution against the obligation to account to the principal. It authorises escape from the agent's dilemma provided that the agent acts strictly in accordance with the principal's instructions.

E. BANKS AND THE RECEIPT-BASED CONSTRUCTIVE TRUST

Claims for restitution against banks are not confined to common law claims in respect of mistake, fraud or forgery. A bank may be liable in equity where a fiduciary has misapplied money (hereinafter "the trust money") to which the beneficiary is entitled in equity, and paid it into a personal or nominee bank account. The beneficiary can of course sue the fiduciary directly for breach of obligation. Tracing claims can also be made to identify and recover assets acquired with the money. But if the fiduciary is insolvent, or has absconded with the assets beyond the jurisdiction of the court, a more realistic alternative is to bring an action against the bank to hold it liable as constructive trustee for having received the money in breach of obligation. The constructive trust is here a formula for the imposition of a personal liability to account. It is not proposed to reopen the debate as to whether the recipient is strictly liable to account, or whether the plaintiff must show that the recipient possessed knowledge, in some sense, of the breach of fiduciary obligation.[61] Nevertheless, the arguments of this section – that equitable liability

[60] (1922) 127 LT 452, 453.

[61] Peter Birks, "Misdirected Funds: Restitution from the Recipient" [1989] LMCLQ 296; Peter Birks, "Persistent Problems in Misdirected Money: a Quintet" [1993] LMCLQ 218. It is too early to be sure whether the "conscience" analysis of Lord Browne-Wilkinson in *Westdeutsche Bank v Islington London Borough Council* [1996] AC 669, 705–706, will significantly influence the outcome of this debate.

as a constructive trustee should not be premised on the recipient's beneficial receipt, and that ministerial receipt is as good a defence to equitable restitutionary claims as to those at common law – reinforce the logic of holding the recipient strictly accountable for the benefit received, subject to the application of restitutionary defences.

A bank will only be liable as constructive trustee under the first limb of *Barnes v Addy*[62] if it has received money which belongs in equity to the beneficiary.[63] It has been held that receipt for this purpose means beneficial receipt. In *Agip (Africa) Ltd v Jackson*[64] Millett J stated:

> "The essential feature of [knowing receipt liability] is that the recipient must have received the property for his own use and benefit. This is why neither the paying nor the collecting bank can normally be brought within it. In paying or collecting money for a customer the bank acts only as his agent. It is otherwise, however, if the collecting bank uses the money to reduce or discharge the customer's overdraft. In doing so it receives the money for its own benefit."

In the *Agip* case one of the defendants, Bowers, was a partner in Jackson & Co, which had received the proceeds of the fraud committed by the plaintiffs's accountant, and had passed them through the partnership's own bank account before paying the money out to other parties. Millett J held that Bowers was not accountable as constructive trustee by virtue of his status as partner of the firm through whose account the money had passed.

The *Agip* case is the best known, but not the only, case to confine the receipt-based constructive trust to recipients who have not acted as agents. The distinction between beneficial and agency receipt has also become well established in antipodean and Canadian jurisprudence.[65] The beneficial receipt requirement has an obvious appeal to judges, as well as to banks whose participation in fiduciary wrongdoing has been limited to acting as a temporary depository of funds. As the law now stands, proof that funds have not been beneficially received avoids complex and costly inquiries into the knowledge possessed by the relevant officers of the bank at the time of receipt.

In spite of these attractions, it is suggested that restricting constructive trusteeship to beneficial receipt is wrong in principle, and that *any* recipient

[62] (1874) LR 9 Ch App 244.

[63] A bank not in receipt of money from the fiduciary may nonetheless be liable for having assisted in a breach of fiduciary obligation, but this requires proof of dishonesty: *Royal Brunei Airlines v Tan* [1995] 2 AC 378.

[64] [1990] 1 Ch 265, 292. See also Sir Peter Millett, "Tracing the Proceeds of Fraud" (1991) 107 LQR 71, 83.

[65] *Adams v Bank of New South Wales* [1984] 1 NSWLR 285; *Stephens Travel Services International v Qantas Airways* (1988) 13 NSWLR 33; *Lankshear v ANZ Banking Group (New Zealand) Ltd* [1993] 1 NZLR 481; *Nimmo v Westpac Banking Corp.* [1993] 3 NZLR 218. For Canadian law see *Gold v Rosenberg* (1997) 152 DLR (4th) 385 (SCC) and *Citadel General Assurance Co v Lloyd's Bank Canada* (1997) *ibid* 411 (SCC); Rotherham [1998] RLR.

should, subject to defences, be accountable in equity for the value of the benefit received. The restriction is flawed, as Simon Gleeson has pointed out, because it is inconsistent with the principle of *Foley v Hill* that a bank is entitled to do anything it pleases with money it has received to the credit of a customer provided that it pays the customer an equivalent sum upon demand.[66] The principle applies to trust money as to any other, unless it has been received upon the (highly unusual) terms that it is neither to be mixed with the bank's other money nor invested for profit. Banks are in the business of making all money, irrespective of source, work for them, with a view to yielding profit for the institution, as well as interest for the customer. They receive beneficially all money deposited. To distinguish between "beneficially" and "non-beneficially" received money is to draw a distinction that reflects neither the law nor the practice of banking.

The unfortunate consequences of ignoring the legal framework of banking are only too apparent in recent cases on the receipt-based constructive trust. "Beneficial receipt" has been applied as the essential criterion for determining whether a bank is to be held liable as constructive trustee for having received trust money in consequence of a breach of fiduciary duty, or for having assisted in the breach. The distinction between receipt and assistance is crucial since an assister, but not a recipient, must be shown to have acted dishonestly.[67] The outcome of applying the touchstone of "beneficial receipt" to distinguish receipt from assistance is that actions brought against banks have been randomly assigned to the "receipt" or "assistance" categories according to judicial perception as to whether the bank has beneficially received the money in question, and in total disregard of the principle that banks receive all money beneficially.

The treatment of currency exchanges in *Polly Peck International v Nadir (No 2)*[68] illustrates the confusion that results from ignoring the basic precepts of banking law. Following an alleged fraud, the Central Bank of Northern Cyprus exchanged £45 million received from another bank, IBK, for an equivalent sum of Turkish lire. At the same time nine sterling transfers were credited to IBK's account held at the Central Bank. At first instance Millett J refused to characterise either transaction as a beneficial receipt by the Central Bank. The Court of Appeal, on the other hand, while agreeing that the nine sterling transfers had not been beneficially received by the Central Bank, held that the Bank's exchange of sterling for Turkish lire constituted a beneficial receipt. Scott LJ distinguished the transactions as follows:[69]

66 Simon Gleeson, "The Involuntary Launderer", *supra* n 8, at 126–127.
67 *Royal Brunei Airlines v Tan* [1995] 2AC 378.
68 [1992] 4 All ER 769.
69 *Ibid*, 777.

> "In respect of the nine sterling transfers I think that [the judgment of Millett J] is right. The Central Bank received the funds transferred not in its own right but as a banker, and as a banker credited the funds to IBK in Northern Cyprus. But in respect of the bulk of the transfers the case is, in my opinion, one of 'receipt' rather than assistance. The Central Bank was exchanging Turkish lire for sterling and became entitled to the sterling not as banker for IBK but in its own right. IBK became entitled to the Turkish lire."

The legal significance of distinguishing between the two transactions is that crediting IBK's account rendered the Central Bank liable, if at all, as an assister, and the currency exchange exposed the Bank to liability as a receiver of trust money. This in turn is significant because strict (or at least stricter) restitutionary liability is imposed on recipients than the fault-based liability imposed on accessories. The distinction drawn by the Court of Appeal is, however, a false one. The Central Bank received all money from IBK for its own commercial purposes. It was liable, as debtor, to pay IBK an equivalent sum upon demand. Whether the payment is made in sterling or Turkish lire was a simple matter of customer preference. Any liability imposed on the Central Bank should have been under the first limb of *Barnes v Addy*, and the precise mechanics of the banking transactions should have been disregarded. In *Nimmo v Westpac Banking Corp*,[70] Blanchard J, reviewing this aspect of the *Polly Peck* decision, confessed that he did not "pretend to understand the point of distinction." The failure to comprehend is entirely understandable since the distinction has no point.

Another, more deeply entrenched, misconception is that the application of trust money to reduce the fiduciary's overdraft constitutes a beneficial receipt, whereas a bank paying the fiduciary's money into an account which is in credit acts solely as an agent, and therefore cannot be accountable in equity for having received the money. This distinction, drawn in *Agip v Jackson*,[71] was applied in the New Zealand decision of *Lankshear v ANZ Banking Group Ltd*,[72] where $80,000 was paid by a partner, acting in breach of a partnership agreement, into an account which immediately prior to payment was overdrawn by $53,117.60. The $80,000 was applied in discharging the overdraft, leaving a surplus on the account of $26,882.40. The amount applied in discharging the overdraft was characterised by Wallace J as a beneficial receipt, whereas the bank had never "received" the surplus and could only be

[70] [1993] 3 NZLR 218, 225–226. See also Ellinger & Lomnicka, *Modern Banking Law*, 212–213.

[71] [1990 1 Ch 265, 292. But note Sir Peter Millett, "Tracing the Proceeds of Fraud" (1991) 107 LQR 71, 83, n 46, for the qualification that the mere continuation of a running account in overdraft, without some conscious appropriation of the sum paid into the account to reduce the overdraft, should not constitute beneficial receipt.

[72] [1993] 1 NZLR 481.

accountable as constructive trustee on the basis of knowing assistance. It is not obvious why a bank's liability to make restitution under a receipt-based constructive trust, as opposed to its obligation to pay compensation as an accessory, should be determined by the amount by which the trust money credited to the fiduciary's account exceeds the previous overdraft. The arbitrary line drawn between receipt-based and accessory liability in these cases is in fact a symptom and not the cause of the deeper problem of what is meant by receipt.

Where *Agip*, and the cases following *Agip* on this point, have fallen into error is in assuming that a bank "benefits" from the reduction of an overdraft but not from crediting money to an account that is already in credit. Paradoxically perhaps, reducing a customer's overdraft is no more (or less) a benefit to the bank than any other application of the money it has received. Indeed, as the High Court of Australia observed in *Australia and New Zealand Banking Group Ltd v Westpac Banking Corp*:[73]

> ". . . The proposition that a financial institution which makes profits by lending money at interest is better off whenever a corporate customer, which is not known to be insolvent, reduces its use of an overdraft facility which has been made available on commercial terms sounds somewhat strangely in modern ears."

The use of trust money to reduce the fiduciary's overdraft is simply a decision taken by the bank to apply its own money in this way rather than for other lending or investment purposes. To reiterate, all money received by a bank has at the moment of receipt been beneficially received; its subsequent application to reduce a debt owed to the bank by the fiduciary no more alters this characterisation than a crediting of the fiduciary's account which increases the debt owed by the bank to the customer.

The basis of the beneficial receipt requirement in authority prior to *Agip* is slight.[74] A failing of much of the case law on this subject has been a tendency to elide the issue of receipt with the knowledge, or notice, possessed by the bank of the breach of fiduciary obligation. For understandable reasons courts do not want to visit banks and other agents with equitable sanctions when they have done no more than act at the direction of their principals. The traditional approach has been to hold accountable only those agents who have knowledge of the breach of fiduciary duty and who, in the terminology of the older cases, are therefore privy to the breach.

An important line of nineteenth century authority concerns the liability of banks as constructive trustees where the bank has accepted a cheque drawn

[73] (1988) 164 CLR 662, 681.

[74] Charles Harpum, "The Stranger as Constructive Trustee" (1986) 102 LQR 114, 148–150.

on a trust account and credited the fiduciary's personal account with money from the trust account.[75] The critical question was whether, in the words of Lord Cairns LC in *Gray v Johnston*,[76] "there is proof that the bankers are privy to the intent to make this misapplication of the trust funds." So, when in *Coleman v Bucks and Oxon Union Bank*[77] a bank received money to pay into the trust account of James Gurney which it credited, pending instructions, to Gurney's overdrawn personal account, the bank was held not liable to account as a receipt-based constructive trustee upon Gurney's bankruptcy three years later. The bank had no knowledge of a breach of trust committed by Gurney in obtaining the money "notwithstanding the fact that in point of law the money must have been regarded as having been applied at the moment in reduction of the overdraft."[78]

The decision of Fry J in *Foxton v Manchester and Liverpool District Banking Co*[79] falls on the other side of the line. An account for the administration of a will trust was opened at a branch of the defendant bank. One of the trustees held his personal account at the same branch. The trustee arranged for trust money to be transferred from the trust account to reduce an overdraft on his personal account. The bank was held liable to make good the deficiency as constructive trustee as it could not show that "the payment was a legitimate and proper one, having reference to the terms of the trust."[80] The distinction between these cases is not to be found in any notion of beneficial receipt. Rather in *Coleman* the bank had no knowledge of Gurney's breach of trust, whereas in *Foxton* the bank was aware of the breach of trust. Both accounts were held at the same branch, and the account from which the money was drawn was known to be a trust account.[81]

Some older authorities would almost certainly have been decided differently if beneficial receipt had been a prerequisite of receipt-based constructive trusteeship. One example is *Williams v Williams*,[82] where a solicitor sold a

[75] *Gray v Johnston* (1868) LR 3 HL1; *Foxton v Manchester and Liverpool District Banking Co* (1881) 44 LT 406; *JR Thomson v Clydesdale Bank Ltd* [1893] AC 282; *Coleman v Bucks and Oxon Union Bank* [1897] 2 Ch 243.

[76] (1868) LR 3 HL 1,11.

[77] [1897] 2 Ch 243.

[78] Ibid, 254, *per* Byrne J.

[79] (1881) 44 LT 406.

[80] *Ibid*, 408. The onus was placed on the bank to justify its own role in the transfer of the money.

[81] *Cf Stephens Travel Services International v Qantas Airways* (1988) 13 NSWLR 33, where a bank which kept a travel agent's account under close review and was aware that the proceeds of sale of airline tickets were held on trust for the airline until paid over was held accountable for receipt of the proceeds.

[82] (1881) 17 Ch D 437; Simon Gleeson, "The Involuntary Launderer", *supra* n 8, 126–127. Ellinger & Lomnicka, *Modern Banking Law* identifies *Carl Zeiss Stiftung v Herbert Smith & Co* [1969] 2 Ch 276 as another decision where the status of the recipient as agent was ignored for the purposes of determining liability under the first limb of *Barnes v Addy* (1874) LR 9 Ch App

client's land which was, unknown to the solicitor, subject to a marriage settlement, and applied the purchase money in payment of the client's debts. Kay J held that the solicitor was not accountable as a receipt-based constructive trustee for the purchase money which passed through his hands. The decision was argued and determined on the basis of the solicitor's notice and fault. There is no hint of a suggestion that he might have escaped liability as a non-beneficial recipient.

The basis for the beneficial receipt requirement in legal principle and authority is therefore fragile. The policy justification for the requirement is, however, a great deal stronger. As Millett J makes clear in *Agip*, the purpose of limiting accountability under a receipt-based constructive trust to beneficial recipients is to prevent agents, especially banks, from being exposed to the agent's dilemma: banks can of necessity make only limited inquiries in discharging their paying and collecting responsibilities. Previous discussion has shown that the dilemma is an acute one for banks, as decisions taken in the clearing process require commercial judgment of a high order and still rest to a large extent on the good faith and trust of the parties involved. Restricting liability to beneficial recipients is, however, not an efficient method of conferring immunity on banks whose only involvement in a fraud has been to act as the proverbial "conduit pipe" for funds transmitted to the fiduciary's personal account.

A preferable approach, and one consonant with the principles of banking law, is to abandon the specific requirement of beneficial receipt and to substitute the proposition enunciated in *Foley v Hill* that all money deposited with a bank belongs to the bank, without separation of legal and equitable title. Overdraft reduction is not some particularly self-serving activity by the bank, attracting the moral opprobrium of equity. It simply constitutes one application of money received for its own use. If trust money is applied for this purpose, the bank will be accountable in equity as constructive trustee as a recipient. But this form of restitutionary liability will also extend to payment of trust money into an account enjoying a healthy balance. In either event, the bank should be entitled to the defence of ministerial receipt, to be made available in precisely the same circumstances in equity as it already is at common law. A choice must perforce be made between the reversibility and mandate models of payment over, but the preferred model should apply to receipt-based constructive trust claims as well as to those brought at common law.

A possible objection to this proposal is that little would be gained from the reconceptualisation of receipt-based liability. In legal analysis, as in the social sciences generally, new ways of saying old things are often mistaken for new

244. But see *Adams v Bank of New South Wales* [1984] 1 NSWLR 285, 292, *per* Moffitt P, where *Carl Zeiss* is analysed as an example of "true" or "beneficial" receipt.

things being said. The replacement of the concept of beneficial receipt by an extension of ministerial receipt into equity is scarcely a momentous change. Few cases would be decided differently. There is no point in reorganising the conceptual furniture of restitution if the room looks much as it did before. However, the scheme proposed is, I believe, more than an exercise in arid doctrinal rationalisation. One important consequence will be that, whenever trust money is misappropriated and paid into a bank account, the bank's liability, if any, will always be receipt-based. Cases will not be siphoned off into the knowing assistance category of constructive trusteeship on the ground that the bank did not benefit from the receipt. Or, to express the same point differently, equitable liability will not depend on the fortuity of whether the misappropriated money reduces an overdraft (receipt-based liability) or augments a healthy bank balance (when liability will only be imposed upon a bank which can be characterised as a dishonest assister). Currency exchanges will not be distinguished from other banking activities. Another difference relates to the placing of the burden of proof. Once the plaintiff has shown that the bank has received trust money the onus shifts to the bank to establish ministerial receipt. This is not unreasonable as the evidence required to substantiate the defence will usually be found in the bank's own records. Finally, the scheme restores congruity between restitution and banking law. It recognises the dual role of banks as risk takers with money deposited, as well as agents for their customers in crediting and debiting customer accounts.

F. CONCLUSION

This paper is premised on the principles laid down in *Foley v Hill*,[83] namely that the banker-customer relationship is one of debtor-creditor and that, subject to special customer arrangements, the bank is entitled to use money deposited for its own purposes.

A bank in receipt of a misdirected payment must make restitution to the party at whose expense the payment was made. The bank may, however, establish a restitutionary defence, including the defence that it received the money in a ministerial capacity as agent for its customer. To make out the defence it must show that (i) acting in the capacity of agent, and (ii) in good faith and without notice of the plaintiff's claim, (iii) it paid over the money to its customer.

Two models of payment over have been analysed. The first emphasises the reversibility of banking transactions. A bank that can lawfully debit the

[83] (1848) 11 HLC 28.

customer's account in order to repay the plaintiff should be required to do so. A transaction may be irreversible, however, either because of the existence of contractual restrictions prohibiting the debiting of the customer's account, or because the money has been withdrawn from the account. The second model of payment over, the mandate theory, affords the bank a defence provided that the bank pays money received to, or at the direction of, its customer. Properly understood, neither theory distinguishes between payments into accounts in credit and payments into overdrawn accounts.

In spite of several House of Lords decisions where the defence was explicitly considered, neither model is firmly established in English law. The first model is more sensitive to the plaintiff's interest in restitution; the second safeguards the bank's interest in security of receipt more effectively. The second model, however, succeeds in avoiding the agent's dilemma of being liable to the principal if restitution is made to the plaintiff, and of being liable to the plaintiff if it pays the money received to, or at the direction of, the principal.

A bank may also be liable to account in equity as a receipt-based constructive trustee for money received in breach of fiduciary obligation. Accountability has been held to depend on whether the bank beneficially received the money. The concept of beneficial receipt is inconsistent with the principle that a bank can deal with money it receives as its own, and should be discarded. Banks are the beneficial recipients of all money they receive, unless otherwise specified in the contract governing the deposit. They should be entitled to the defence of ministerial receipt in equity as well as at law. The model of payment over adopted at common law should also apply in equity.

These proposals will promote consistency between the law of restitution, in its application to banks as recipients of wealth, and banking law. They will also eradicate a number of anomalies, such as the analysis of currency exchanges and overdraft reduction in equity. Finally, eliminating the requirement of beneficial receipt from the receipt-based constructive trust will promote functional consistency in the resolution of common law and equitable restitutionary claims brought against banks and other agents.

11

The Burden on the Bank

PETER BIRKS*

The law merchant developed from the practice and needs of merchants. The same close interaction is still observable today. We have become more sensitive to the balance which has to be struck between the legitimate expectations of those trying to make money and the protection of those from whom the money is likely to be made. Nevertheless, in the commercial and financial sector the law, while keeping one eye on that balance, is constantly adjusting to the reasonable needs of those engaged in these activities. It is only to be expected that banks and finance houses should follow the development of the law of restitution of unjust enrichment with a certain amount of apprehension. They have a legitimate interest in not being exposed to excessive restitutionary liabilities. They are after all routinely in the business of receiving money and other valuable assets and, at the same time, the most attractive of defendants. This chapter is a selective overview of what has been said in the previous ten, and its theme is the question whether, in the light of all that has been said in the earlier chapters, banks have reason for anxiety. Do they have just cause to be worried by either the present state of the law of unjust enrichment or the likely trajectory of its future development?

It is not always a matter of liability. Banks sometimes need to rely on their own restitutionary rights. Towards the end of the chapter, the discussion will turn to some aspects of their position as plaintiffs seeking restitution. As Robert Goff J pointed out in *Barclays Bank Ltd v WJ Simms Son & Cooke Ltd*,[1] the new technology has not reduced the incidence of mistaken payments. The strength of the banks' entitlement to restitution will to some extent determine the nature of their precautions in-house. Obstructed access to the law of restitution might mean more care taken, but more care means in turn more expense and slower response.[2]

* QC DCL FBA, Regius Professor of Civil Law in the University of Oxford and Fellow of All Souls College, Oxford. Abbreviated footnote references are to previous chapters.

1 [1980] QB 677, 682.

2 An equation which is a theme of J Beatson and W Bishop, "Mistaken Payments in the Law of Restitution"(1986) 36 U Toronto LJ 149.

No pretence is made of making a comprehensive review. The coverage will necessarily be topical, and it will have to rely heavily for detail on what has been said in the previous chapters. The emphasis will be on potential liabilities. In broad terms the answer will be that, properly understood, the law of unjust enrichment poses no unreasonable threat. This answer is given subject to the qualification that doctrinal uncertainty is always dangerous and wasteful, and that doctrinal uncertainty must therefore be cleared up.

The division between liabilities and rights is to some extent artificial. A doctrine which goes to a bank's liability in one case will often define its right to restitution in another. Dr Smith's chapter will be considered at the end, because it cannot, even artificially, be assigned to right or liability but belongs equally to both. It is about the process of tracing and, in particular, about claims which, not being contingent on successful tracing, can escape the complexities which he alone completely understands.

I. THE BANK'S RESTITUTIONARY LIABILITIES

Although they are not always easy to keep completely separate, there are two principal areas of anxiety. One is the taking of security and the other is the constant risk, inherent in the banker's business, of receiving misdirected or imperfectly intended payments.

A. Taking security

Does the law of restitution of unjust enrichment threaten to undermine or unsettle the business of taking security for money lent? In one particular area it has undoubtedly being doing so. However, the problems there are problems of a protective purpose undergoing rapid doctrinal adjustment, not of excessive liability. We will come to that below. We turn first to an important case the implications of which might on some interpretations seem to have set the cat more generally amongst the pigeons. But the fears will turn out to have been illusory.

Macmillan v Bishopsgate Investment Trust Plc (No 3)[3]

The facts are set out in full above.[4] The defendant finance houses had taken shares as security for large loans at a time when the equitable beneficial inter-

[3] [1995] 1 WLR 978; affd [1996] 1 WLR 387 (CA). The appeal may proceed, since only the issue of the applicable law has so far been heard.

[4] Moss and Toube, 90; Segal, 100–103.

est was outstanding in a third party, the now plaintiffs, Macmillan. They hoped to obtain priority over Macmillan's equitable ownership by relying on the defence of bona fide purchase for value. But for the complex issues in the conflict of laws, and the particular way in which Macmillan sought to resolve those issues, nobody would have thought that the case had anything to do with the restitution of unjust enrichment. Subject to what will be said below, the defence of bona fide purchase has nothing particular to do with the law of unjust enrichment. Its primary role is a part of the compromise made in English law between the sanctity of ownership and the security of transactions. The defence, when it operates, allows a bona fide purchaser from X to defeat a proprietary interest outstanding in Y, however that interest may have arisen. Occasionally it may happen that the proprietary interest outstanding in Y is an interest which was itself generated by unjust enrichment. But this was not that rare case. The interest of Macmillan was perhaps initially referable to a resulting trust arising from a gratuitous transfer, but there followed almost immediately an express declaration of trust by the transferee.

How did restitution of unjust enrichment creep into the picture? It suited Macmillan to argue that English law should apply.[5] The attraction of English law was that it could be argued to take a strict and narrow view of what it meant to be a bona fide purchaser. The easiest path to the application of English law seemed to Macmillan to be through unjust enrichment. They argued that the claim to recover their shares should be analysed as a claim to restitution of unjust enrichment and should therefore be subject to the law of the place where the enrichment had been received, namely London.

This argument failed. The courts appear to have accepted that Macmillan's claim was a claim in restitution.[6] They nevertheless escaped the conclusion that English law applied. But they never quite nailed the fallacy on which the argument was based, namely that, even if the claim was indeed a claim to restitution, it was not, as pleaded and presented, a claim in unjust enrichment. As one who has argued that restitution and unjust enrichment form a perfect square, the effect (restitution) quadrating with its cause (unjust enrichment), I confess my own share of responsibility for the error.[7] However, it is an error nonetheless. The quadration of unjust enrichment and restitution is and

[5] The conflicts issues will not be addressed here: see Moss and Toube, 89, *passim*.

[6] [1996] 1 WLR 387, 398 (Staughton LJ), 407 (Auld LJ), 417 (Aldous LJ); [1995] 1 WLR 978, 988–990 (Millett J).

[7] P Birks, *Introduction to the Law of Restitution*, revised ed (Clarendon Press, Oxford, 1989), 26, where the square is already false in that it is made to include restitution arising from wrongs as such, as well as restitution arising from unjust enrichment independently of wrongs. My paper "Misnomer" in *Restitution: Past, Present and Future* (Hart Publications, Oxford, 1998, forthcoming) is devoted to the problematic nomenclature.

always was artificial. There are natural instances of restitution which are not triggered by unjust enrichment. And this is one of them.

It is necessary to distinguish two elements of Macmillan's contention. The first is that which the Romans would have recognized as a *vindicatio* and more specifically the distinctive *intentio* of that kind of action: "Those shares are ours!" The common law recognises no such claim, but equity does.[8] The essence of the *vindicatio* is the direct assertion of a proprietary right. The second element derives from the inert nature of any pure proprietary claim. Differently from a judicial declaration of any obligation ("The defendant ought to pay the plaintiff £100") a declaration of a proprietary right implies no imperative ("The shares belong to Macmillan"). Something more has to be tacked on. What, if anything, will the court make the defendant do? In equity, provided that the plaintiff asks for something more than a declaration, a successful *vindicatio* will end in an order for specific transfer to the plaintiff. The successfully vindicating plaintiff therefore evidently has a personal right that the defendant transfer the thing. That right, with its correlative obligation to transfer, is distinct from the inert proprietary interest.

That personal right does not arise from unjust enrichment. The event from which it arises is simply the receipt and retention of something which belongs to another in equity. The language of restitution applies, because the effect is that the one party must give back something to the other. But the natural application of "restitution" does not indicate an origin in unjust enrichment. If we were to maintain the contrary we would encounter an insuperable difficulty. The subsidiary obligation would become subject to the defence of change of position. It would mean that, simply because their inert nature requires to be enlivened by the ancillary obligation to deliver, all equitable property rights, even those not born of unjust enrichment, would at one stage removed be subjected to the characteristic and essential weakness of rights which are born of unjust enrichment.

If and so long as "restitution" and "unjust enrichment" are taken, artificially, to quadrate and are therefore to be treated as synonyms, albeit from different perspectives, the answer to Nick Segal's question whether pure proprietary claims are part of the law of restitution[9] is unequivocal. They are not. Neither the right vindicated nor the enlivening obligation to deliver up can be referred back to the causative event which, generically stated, is unjust enrichment at the plaintiff's expense. There are qualifications to be made in relation to the language used. They may indeed be called part of the law of restitution, if restitution is taken to include all instances of yielding up a benefit, but the natural scope of the word "restitution" is not indicative of an

[8] *Cf* Smith, 124.
[9] Segal, 107–111.

origin in unjust enrichment. And it is necessary to be wary of the word "pure", lest it be taken to indicate that there is no such thing as a vindication of a proprietary right which has been created by unjust enrichment.[10] "Pure", on analysis, means "generated by an event other than unjust enrichment" and, if the word is justified at all, it indicates that, not having that origin, they are not infected by that weakness of all rights which do arise from unjust enrichment, namely vulnerability to change of position.

The complication, and the potential cause of anxiety, arises from the possibility of alternative analysis.[11] Had it pleaded the matter more carefully, Macmillan could have elected to argue for a restitutionary obligation arising from unjust enrichment. Every recipient from a trustee in breach of trust stands in danger of concurrent claims of different kinds. While he has the *res*, he is exposed to the *vindicatio*. Whether he has it or not, he is exposed to personal claims traditionally expressed in the language of accountability as a constructive trustee. It is, to put the matter at the lowest, arguable that one alternative possibility is a personal claim in unjust enrichment. Macmillan never disentangled its options. It made a pure proprietary claim, a *vindicatio,* but attempted to characterise it as a claim in restitution capable of attracting rules applicable to unjust enrichment. That claim asserted an anterior proprietary right which did not arise from the unjust enrichment of the defendants at Macmillan's expense. And, had it succeeded, it would have been activated by a restitutionary obligation arising, not from unjust enrichment, but simply from the defendant's receipt of Macmillan's shares.

We need not at this point ask what the fate of an election for an alternative analysis founded in unjust enrichment would have been.[12] Our question here is only whether this shadow behind the *Macmillan* case poses any threat to the taking of security. Could the alternative claim based on unjust enrichment be a more powerful weapon? We can test that by supposing, for the moment merely hypothetically, that the alternative claim might mirror exactly the structure of the strict personal claim in unjust enrichment pursued at law in *Lipkin Gorman v Karpnale Ltd.*[13] That would mean that the finance houses would have been strictly liable to make restitution of the enrichment received, subject to defences. On the face of things, that is a threatening possibility.

[10] Virgo has perceived and described the non-quadration of restitution and unjust enrichment: G Virgo, "Reconstructing the Law of Restitution" (1996) 10 TLI 116, where, however, he does occasionally allow himself to imply that a direct vindication of a property right can never be a claim founded on unjust enrichment. *Chase Manhattan Bank v Israel-British Bank* [1981] Ch 105 was such a case. *Cf* Birks [1997] NZLRev 623.

[11] This is a familiar phenomenon: facts which obviously disclose a breach of contract can sometimes be re-analysed to disclose a tort, and vice versa (*Henderson v Merrett Syndicates* [1995] 2 AC 145) and facts which disclose a tort can re-analysed to disclose an unjust enrichment; *cf* Birks (*supra*, n 7), 314–315.

[12] Further discussion, *infra*, text from n 45.

[13] [1991] 2 AC 548.

This brings us to the crucial question. Would this strict claim in unjust enrichment escape the defence of bona fide purchase? We noticed above that that defence has nothing particular to do with the law of unjust enrichment. It is part of the compromise made by the law as a whole between sanctity of ownership and security of transactions. In this it differs from change of position. Change of position is a defence specifically to claims which arise in unjust enrichment. However, even personal claims in unjust enrichment have to give way to the defence of bona fide purchase in any situation in which, if they were allowed, they would in substance subvert the operation of that defence as an exception to *nemo dat quod non habet*. Even at law, title to money passes to one who bona fide gives value for it. It would make nonsense of that rule if the law of unjust enrichment could ever impose an obligation on such a purchaser nonetheless to make restitution of the value of the money which had become his. In *Lipkin Gorman v Karpnale* itself the only reason why the defence of bona fide purchase did not apply was that in the eye of the law there had been no transaction at all between the casino and the third party from whom it received the money. Had gambling contracts not been void, the casino would clearly have been able to plead the defence, notwithstanding that it was defending a personal claim arising in unjust enrichment. That kind of claim could not have been allowed to subvert the proprietary consequences of bona fide purchase. To this extent if no more, the law of restitution must admit the defence of bona fide purchase.[14]

It follows that, even if the finance houses in the *Macmillan* case could have been attacked in the law of unjust enrichment, and even if that attack took the strong form analogous to the common law claim in *Lipkin Gorman v Karpnale*, the defence of bona fide purchase would still have applied, and the security interests would have been as safe as the defence of bona fide purchase could make them. There is therefore no special threat in the offing from the law of unjust enrichment.

In this sector, therefore, if there is any question of an excessive exposure to liability, it can only come from outside the law of unjust enrichment and, in particular, from an unsatisfactory definition of what it is to be a bona fide purchaser. The remedy for that will be constantly to recall that the very narrow view of the defence which has been worked out in the context of conveyancing reflects what is reasonable to expect in that context. It is true that a certain pressure has historically been exerted to intensify the degree of diligence required in that context, for the courts of equity had no interest in undermining the robustness of equitable proprietary interests. Nevertheless, under the formula "constructive notice" always lay the standard of reason-

[14] Segal, 112.

ableness. This, as Nick Segal says, is the key.[15] If that standard is allowed to take the strain, it will not be necessary to say that constructive notice has no place in commercial transactions outside the conveyancing context but only that different contexts require the reasonable purchaser to make different inquiries. Lindley LJ's famous remarks on the evils of importing constructive notice into commerce[16] are to be understood, not of the underlying standard, but only of its particular yield in the conveyancing context.

Barclays Bank Plc v O'Brien[17]

The doctrine surrounding the restitution made available by *Barclays Bank Plc v O'Brien* has unsettled a good many securities taken in good faith. But it is the uncertainty and artificiality of the doctrine which is causing the trouble, not its upshot. The upshot is that the taking of a particular kind of security has been regulated, much as though a code of conduct had been imposed upon it by legislation. When the competitive world of commerce goes cap in hand to the non-competitive world of the family and the family home, it is entirely reasonable to insist on certain precautions. Janet O'Sullivan distinguishes between the juristic interest in explanation and the banker's interest in knowing what has to be done.[18] We might think that banks now more or less know what has to be done. But the volume of wasteful litigation shows that the world of finance also has an interest in sound doctrine and the certainty which it assures. It should never be thought that the work of jurists, certainly academic in the best sense, in that it seeks to get to the bottom of things and make them fully understood, lacks immediate practical importance.

The emergent proposition needs fine tuning, but in outline it must run on these lines: where security is taken by a lender for the indebtedness of another, and the party giving the security stands in a non-commercial relationship to the principal debtor, the security will be set aside unless the lender took adequate precautions to ensure that the party giving security understood the risks. There are numerous examples of transactions which are considered to be too sensitive to be left to the self-regulation implicit in freedom of contract and which are therefore regulated *ab extra*, whether by statute or judge-made law. Mortgages are the oldest case. Without such intervention we would not now have the equity of redemption.

[15] Segal, 114.

[16] *Manchester Trust v Furness* [1895] 2 QB 539, 545.

[17] [1994] 1 AC 200. The digest section of the *Restitution Law Review* shows that few cases have stimulated more literature: see [1994] RLR 3 (Cretney); [1995] RLR §175 (A Arora), §176 (G Battersby); [1996] RLR §151 (A Lawson), §154 (J Mee); [1997] RLR §97 (M Chen-Wishart), §100 (B Fehlberg), §107 (E O'Dell), §109 (M Richardson).

[18] O'Sullivan, 42.

The difficulties arise from the attempt to evolve this protective regime from the general law of undue influence and misrepresentation. This has given rise to a string of artificialities. Typically, the facts are that a wife gives real or personal security to a bank to support the business borrowing of her husband. Things go badly. The bank seeks to enforce the security, and the wife seeks to rescind it. Formally, her relief depends on the bank's having notice of undue influence upon or misrepresentation to the wife. As Morritt LJ said in *Barclays Bank Plc v Thomson*:[19]

> "It arises from the principle that the right to set aside a transaction for undue influence or misrepresentation is exercisable against a third party who has notice of such invalidating tendency. The third party may have notice of such invalidating tendency if he is put on inquiry as to the circumstances in which the person seeking to set aside the transaction gave his or her consent."

The artificialities start with the super-constructive nature of the notice which is deemed to be sufficient. Constructive notice in this context has detached itself from the standard of reasonableness on which it properly depends. Janet O'Sullivan rightly says that terminology which is first borrowed and then stretched is likely to cause trouble.[20] As Lord Jauncey said in *Smith v Bank of Scotland*,[21] a bank has no real reason to suspect that the husband has misrepresented matters to his wife. In *Banco Exterior v Thomas*,[22] Sir Richard Scott V-C went further: "A bank has no business inquiring into the personal relationship between those with whom it has business dealings or as to their personal motives for wanting to help one another." Another aspect of the artificiality of constructive notice is that a bank can shake it off by taking certain mechanical steps – the steps required to satisfy the code of conduct – even when those steps could not reasonably be said to have released it from any reasonable suspicion of impairment and may even have aggravated the suspicion.[23]

The artificialities do not end with a constructive notice which looks more like a rule of law. Undue influence, which used to be rather difficult to prove, is now recited more or less as a matter of course. And a switch in the onus of proof in *Barclays Bank Plc v Boulter*[24] now makes the recitations resemble the dead words of the old forms of action. Moreover, this last case exposes the greatest difficulty of all, namely the problem of explaining how the requirement of notice was to be integrated into the general law.

[19] [1997] 4 All ER 816, 828d-e.

[20] O'Sullivan, 44; *cf*, at 45: "there is nothing fundamentally wrong with *O'Brien*, just its terminology."

[21] 1997 SCLR 765, 769. *Cf* O'Sullivan, 48.

[22] [1997] 1 All ER 46 (CA), 55j–56a.

[23] O'Sullivan, 59–64.

[24] [1997] 2 All ER 1002 (CA).

The mortgage had been executed by both Mr and Mrs Boulter. The debtor was Mr Boulter. Upon his default, the bank brought proceedings for possession. Mrs Boulter resisted and counterclaimed for a declaration that she held her half share free of the legal charge. Her pleading alleged, *inter alia*, that Mr Boulter had procured her signature by misrepresentation and that he had been the bank's agent to obtain her signature. It did not allege that the bank had constructive notice of the misrepresentation. The bank therefore maintained that she had confined herself to the agency point and could not attempt to bring herself within the *O'Brien* relief. The judge upheld that objection. Mrs Boulter could have amended her pleading. She did not want to, since if she won only on the pleadings as amended she would face an order for all prior costs. She appealed instead. Her appeal succeeded. It was not incumbent on her to plead and prove that the bank had notice of the misrepresentation. This conclusion switches the onus of proof.

If what the law is really moving towards is a rule of law invariably requiring a lending bank to take certain special precautions in this kind of sensitive transaction, it is sensible to put the onus on the bank to show that those steps have been taken. But can that sensible result be coaxed out of the law of undue influence and other similarly operating unjust factors? The Court of Appeal did it by rooting the requirement of notice in the defence of bona fide purchase. In the crucial passage, Mummery LJ, with whom Sir Brian Neill and Leggatt LJ agreed, said this:[25]

> "The relevant substantive law confirms this conclusion. On the authority of Lord Browne-Wilkinson's speech in *O'Brien's* case and on well-established equitable principles, the burden is not on Mrs Boulter to plead and prove that the bank had constructive notice: it is on the bank to plead and prove that it did *not* have constructive notice. . . .
>
> It is well established at this level of decision that the doctrine of bona fide purchaser for value without actual or constructive notice is a defence which can be raised to defeat a claim of an equitable right or interest and that the burden is on the person raising that defence to plead and prove *all* its elements: it is a 'single defence'."

[25] [1997] 2 All ER 1002, 1007. This passage is supported by full reference to classical authority on the nature of this defence, of two kinds: first, passages from F W Maitland, *Lectures on Equity* ed Brunyate, 2nd ed (Cambridge, 1936, repr 1969), 119 and R Meagher, W Gummow and J Lehane, *Equity: Doctrines and Remedies*, 3rd ed (Sydney, 1992), 257–259; and, secondly, to well-known quotations from the leading cases: *Pilcher v Rawlins* (1872) LR 7 Ch App 259, 268–269 (James LJ); *A-G v Biphosphated Guano Co* (1878) 11 Ch D 327, 337 (Thesiger LJ); *Re Nisbet and Potts Contract* [1905] 1 Ch 351, 402 (Farwell J), [1906] 1 Ch 386 (CA), 403, 404, 409, 410; *Wilkes v Spooner* [1911] 2 KB 473, 486. The same position had been taken very shortly before by E O'Dell, "Restitution, Coercion by a Third Party, and the Proper Role of Notice" [1997] CLJ 71.

The judgment is thus squarely based on the defence of bona fide purchase. However, one sentence reveals a doubt:[26]

> "The speech of Lord Browne-Wilkinson in *O'Brien's* case supports the view that the same approach to pleading and proof of constructive notice applies in *O'Brien* as in the standard case of the bona fide purchaser for value of the legal estate without notice of an equitable estate or interest."

We must infer from this that the *O'Brien* facts are admitted to be atypical. They are not quite "the standard case". It is very difficult to see how this kind of explanation can work. The arguments advanced by Kit Barker in this volume must be right,[27] although in one respect it may be that his approach requires modification.

As we have said above, the general defence of bona fide purchase has no part to play except in the case in which a claimant stands on *nemo dat quod non habet*: "That thing was mine and I never transferred it to you!" The defence is advanced in the hope of trumping *nemo dat*: "But I received in good faith and for value from a third party; and in these circumstances the law gives me a good title!" In our situation, the wife is not standing on *nemo dat*. She did transfer and she had a good title. She wants to say that the transfer was vitiated and must be undone. A wife sells her jewels to a jeweller. He innocently misrepresents their nature and value. She wants the jewels back. This has nothing to do with *nemo dat*. Bona fide purchase is irrelevant. It is not the right configuration of facts even to begin to think whether the defence might apply. The question will be whether he did or did not misrepresent. Suppose the misrepresentation came, not from the jeweller, but from another person, perhaps her husband. That would weaken her case, but it still would not make relevant the defence of bona fide purchase.

The truth appears to be, so long as we insist on tying the *O'Brien* restitution into undue influence and misrepresentation, that notice can only be a fact which the wife must prove. How does it then work? Does it make the bank a wrongdoer? This kind of constructive notice is a tenuous basis for saying that it does so. The difficulty is made all the greater now that *Royal Brunei Airlines v Tan*[28] has made it plain that a participatory liability must depend on dishonesty. Moreover, misrepresentation and undue influence are not wrongs, though they may become wrongs when mixed with more than the minimum matter.

It is true that Lord Browne-Wilkinson repeatedly refers to them as wrongs in his speech in *Barclays Bank Plc v O'Brien*:[29]

[26] [1997] 2 All ER 1002, 1008.
[27] Barker, 79, 80–87.
[28] [1995] 2 AC 378 (PC).
[29] [1994] AC 180, 191.

> "But in surety cases the decisive question is whether the claimant wife can set aside the transaction, not against the wrongdoing husband, but against the creditor bank. Of course, if the wrongdoing husband is acting as agent for the creditor bank in obtaining the security from the wife, the creditor will be fixed with the wrongdoing of its own agent and the surety contract can be set aside as against the creditor . . ."

Again:[30]

> "there is a substantial risk in transactions of that kind that, in procuring the wife to act as surety, the husband has committed a legal or equitable wrong that entitles the wife to set aside the transaction."

And:[31]

> "the surety obligation will be valid and enforceable by the creditor unless the suretyship was procured by the undue influence, misrepresentation or other legal wrong of the principal debtor; . . ."

The old orthodoxy has been that it is not in the character of a wrong that a misrepresentation gives rise to the setting aside of contracts. A misrepresentation may or may not be a wrong. When the facts admit of alternative analysis, the misrepresentee will be able to bring an action for damages without rescinding the contract, in some cases for deceit and in others for negligence.[32] But this kind of alternative analysis is not invariably possible. Some misrepresentations are not wrongs but simply unjust factors entitling the representee to rescind. In much the same way, non-disclosure of material facts in relation to a contract of utmost good faith operates as a factor entitling the other to rescission but cannot be presented as a wrong for the purpose of seeking damages for consequential loss.[33]

In the same way undue influence is a factor entitling the party whose autonomy is impaired to obtain rescission and restitution. There may again be facts on which more than one analysis is possible, but, just as with misrepresentation, it does not need to be characterized as a wrong to justify rescission, and it is not in that character that it entitles the impaired person to rescind.[34] A presumed wrong is anyhow a monster. In *Allcard v Skinner*[35] the defendant

[30] *Ibid*, 196.

[31] *Ibid*, 198.

[32] Sir Guenter Treitel, *The Law of Contract*, 9th edition (Sweet & Maxwell, London, 1995), 318–338, esp 337, noting the difficulty of explaining the damages for wholly innocent misrepresentation under the Misrepresentation Act 1967, s 2(2).

[33] *Banque Keyser Ullmann v Skandia (UK) Insurance* [1990] 1 QB 665 (CA), seemingly approved on this point when affirmed [1991] 2 AC 249, 288.

[34] This is the theme of P Birks and NY Chin, "On the Nature of Undue Influence", ch 3 of J Beatson and D Friedmann, *Good Faith and Fault in Contract Law* (OUP, Oxford, 1995, pbk 1997), 57–98.

[35] (1887) 36 Ch D 135.

was a nun of unimpeachable rectitude. Even in *Williams v Bayley,*[36] in which a father had paid off the defendants, the victim of his son's dishonesty, to save his son from prosecution, Lord Westbury leaned over backwards to insist that the rescission implied no slur on them:[37]

> "I do not mean for one single moment, by anything I have said, to cast any imputation on the character of these gentlemen. I am only dealing with abstract principles of law. They might, perhaps, fairly have thought that they were doing the best for the family of Mr William Bayley and for the father. I beg particularly that it may not be understood that I mean to convey, by any words that I have used, any reproach on their character."

An explanation based on wrongdoing will not work.[38] Some cases may fit within the doctrine which relieves against unconscionable exploitation of the specially vulnerable. But, unless the bank has more than the super-constructive notice which is taken to trigger these results, it will not fall within the terms of that doctrine. The only solution capable of keeping the law in touch with undue influence and misrepresentation seems to be one which sees notice as an additional requirement designed to cut down the incidence of relief for these factors as against strangers to the relationship within which they arose. We have to say that, in the interest of maintaining the efficacy of the bargaining process, the law does not begin to allow these unjust factors to be relied on outside the relationship in which they arise without the proof of an extra fact, namely that the stranger to the relationship had notice of them. It has to be admitted, however, that super-constructive notice does not play well in this role either, for in truth one wants to say, more simply, "unless the stranger knew of them."

There are shades of difference between this explanation and that of Kit Barker. For one thing he does not free his explanation from the notion that the husband has committed a wrong, so that the requirement of notice is necessary in order to involve the bank in that wrong.[39] Secondly, whereas this

[36] (1866) LR 1 HL 200.

[37] *Ibid*, 221–222.

[38] Professor Rickett has recently introduced a new approach to the explanation through wrongdoing. Basing himself, rather awkwardly, on *Smith v Bank of Scotland* 1997 SCLR 765, he proposes that, having reasonable ground for suspicion, the bank comes under a duty of care to the wife or other surety, and in this way he finds a basis for the bank's committing a primary wrong if it falls into breach. This "tort" is evidently an unusual one in giving rise to rescission, but presumably he would accept the attendant logic of a remedy in damages. His evidence, it should be noted, would equally support the inference favoured in this chapter, namely that the law simply takes this kind of transaction and imposes on it a protective regime, rendering it voidable unless the necessary steps are taken: CEF Rickett, "The Financier's Duty of Care" (1998) 114 LQR 17.

[39] Barker, 85. *Cf* O'Sullivan, 45, 46, 47, the inverted commas revealing uneasiness with the notion of the husband as a wrongdoer.

explanation says that notice is required to protect the efficacy of the bargaining process, he says, more absolutely, that what matters is simply that there is prima facie a valid contract for good consideration between the bank and the wife.[40] Without the wrongdoing point, which has to be put aside, that does not in itself explain why notice is required in the three-party situation while in a simple two-party situation a contract can be set aside for totally innocent misrepresentation, or totally innocent undue influence, without any fuss about reconciling total innocence with a requirement of notice. The law simply takes the view that in the two-party situation the bargaining process is not impeded by relieving a party of the risk of induced mistakes and autonomy impaired by undue influence. In the three-party situation the bargaining process would be seriously impaired if each party had always to be on the look-out for mistakes induced *ab extra* or impaired autonomy arising *ab extra*. If that is the general proposition, the irony remains that in our protective context that anxiety is evidently overridden by the protective policy itself, the proof being that the requirement of notice is allowed to be satisfied by lip service only – that is, by super-constructive notice.

The next great case must rest the desirable *O'Brien* results on a new foundation. If the law is not working with the general doctrine of undue influence and misrepresentation but is merely building up rules for controlling one kind of sensitive transaction, the precautions which the cases now insist upon can be regarded as in themselves entirely reasonable, and there is no reason why that regime should not put the onus on the lender to demonstrate compliance.

B. *Money received*

The sub-title speaks of money, and the discussion will be conducted in terms of that common case. But the principles apply to all enrichments received. There are two situations to be considered. One is where the bank D receives

[40] Barker, 84. He says, at 85, that I argue that security of transactions is always best dealt with by defences. Security of receipts is in general so protected, notably by change of position but also by bona fide purchase. But the efficacy of the bargaining process is protected in the definition of the cause of action. Relief for mistake, *in a bargaining situation*, is heavily restricted by the requirement that the mistake be such as to render the contract void or voidable, or, in other words, by the requirement that the mistake, whether by its nature or by virtue of its origin in misrepresentation or, sometimes, non-disclosure, be such as to lie outside the risks inherent in the contract. In that context, to relieve automatically for any causative mistake would undermine the whole institution of bargaining. In a bargaining context there is no restitution unless we are sure that restitution is wholly compatible with the risky nature of the activity; the mistake must not be within those risks. When it is not, we say that first the contract goes and then restitution follows, but in fact we have merely defined the cause of action for restitution in the way in which it has to be modified for the bargaining context.

money from X which belongs to P, in circumstances in which P gives no consent to the transfer, typically because he knows nothing about it. The other is where the bank receives money from P to whom it belongs but who pays by mistake or because his intention to pay is impaired by some other factor. Discussion will be confined at this stage to personal claims or, in other words, to restitutionary obligations arising from unjust enrichment. The question whether banks face an excessive liability depends largely on the operation of defences available to them against restitutionary claims, but that question cannot be discussed without first stabilising the view of the nature of their prima facie liability in unjust enrichment. At the moment their protection clearly consists in part in the view taken that at least in some cases that liability is fault-based. However, to put the matter at the lowest, that view is precarious.

1. Liability for assistance

Liability for assisting the misdirection of money is a liability in the law of wrongs, not in the law of unjust enrichment. Nevertheless, although factually and conceptually distinct, it is contextually relevant. Whenever restitutionary liability for money received is in question, there lurks in the wings the possibility that the recipient bank may also have made itself liable, whether by its receipt or its subsequent payment out or both, for assisting a misdirection initiated by others and intended to accrue to the advantage of others.

Michael Tugendhat's chapter ventures into a minefield which others usually skirt. *Bank Tejarat v Hong Kong and Shanghai Banking Corp (CI) Ltd and Hong Kong and Shanghai Bank Trustee (Jersey) Ltd*[41] illustrates the common evasion. A fraud by third parties induced Bank Tejarat to make a mistaken payment of millions of Deutschmarks for the credit of an account held in Jersey, from which the money was paid away to Paris and lost. One question was whether the defendant banks were liable for assisting the fraud. They had done many acts which objectively assisted it. The judge went to great lengths to show that the money paid by mistake was money which had become impressed with a trust. Having thus made it possible to invoke the law of knowingly assisting a breach of trust, he finally answered the question negatively on the ground that the defendant banks had not been dishonest.

The reason for that detour is the certainty that there is a liability for dishonestly assisting a misapplication of trust money. The minefield to be avoided is the question whether the same result follows in the case of a simple

[41] [1995] 1 Lloyd's Rep 239 (QBD, Commercial Court: Tuckey J).

commercial fraud with no hint of trust about it.[42] We know that it should apply. We know that, if from nothing else, from the willingness to stretch the notion of a trust in order to reach the equitable wrong of assisting its breach.[43]

Tugendhat courageously explores the different ways in which the common law can make liable a party who assists a misdirection. In his view that liability might in some cases be more extensive than the equitable liability for dishonest assistance as purified by *Royal Brunei Airlines v Tan,*[44] on which assumption even those who assist breaches by fiduciaries might escape from the equitable frying pan only to fall into a common law fire fuelled by something less than dishonesty. However, for the purposes of the present theme, it is enough to say that, so far as any claim is based on dishonesty or on any other species of *dolus malus*, no question arises of any excessive liability. The same applies to liability for the tort of negligence, though not for the same reason. Liability in negligence is threatening, but the tort has its in-built control mechanism in the form of the inquiry into the existence and scope of the duty of care. Provided that mechanism is not evaded (as, for instance, by imposing the liability in language which conceals its relevance), the assumption must be that the courts will nip any excessive liability in the bud.

2. The basis of the bank's restitutionary liability in unjust enrichment

The model of liability in unjust enrichment at common law is strict, mitigated by defences. Before the recognition of the defence of change of position, the severity of the strict liability was quite obvious. A mistaken payment was recoverable from a totally innocent payee even when the enrichment had been lost or used up in reliance on secure entitlement to it.[45] It is clear that the same strict personal liability attaches at law where a recipient D receives from X money legal title to which is in P. P, ignorant of the transfer of his money to D, may in some circumstances have other recourses, but he can certainly make a personal claim, in the nature of the old action for money had and received, against the recipient D. In more modern language, he has a personal action in unjust enrichment for restitution from D.

[42] P Sales, "The Tort of Conspiracy and Civil Secondary Liability" [1990] 49 CLJ 491; Birks, "Civil Wrongs, A New World": *Butterworth Lectures 1990-1991* (London, 1992) 55, 99–101; *cf* Sir L Hoffman, "The Redundancy of Knowing Assistance", ch 2 of P Birks (ed), *The Frontiers of Liability*, vol 1 (1994).

[43] The same detour can be seen in *Agip (Africa) Ltd.* v. *Jackson* [1990] Ch 265, affd [1991] Ch 547. However, it is there made more plausible in that the primary fraudster could reasonably be described as a fiduciary.

[44] [1995] 2 AC 378 (PC).

[45] *Kelly v Solari* (1841) 9 M&W 54.

In *Lipkin Gorman v Karpnale Ltd*[46] the facts were more complex. If we think of the casino as D, the gambling solicitor as X, and the firm seeking restitution as P, the complication was that, at the moment X paid D, legal title was technically in X. It was only by the exercise of rights contingent on common law tracing that it was possible for P to make out his claim. But it is perfectly clear that our facts, in which there is no doubt that X pays over P's money, would have been regarded by their Lordships as the simpler case. The same strict personal liability would have been imposed. The case is exactly the same as that in which P loses his money and D picks it up, except only that in our case it is deflected to D by the intervention of the third party X. In the simple two-party loss and finding the old action for money had and received lay.[47] In both the two-party situation and the three-party situation P's money, remaining his, passes to D without his knowledge and a fortiori without his consent. The law allows it to be reclaimed as a debt generated by unjust enrichment.

This same result is confirmed by the decision at common law in *Jones (FC) & Sons (a firm) (Trustee of the property of) v Jones*,[48] in which X, being D's husband, transferred some of P's money to her. D, the wife, who was never said to be a wrongdoer, invested it successfully. It was held by the Court of Appeal that she owed to P not only the initial sum but also all that she made from it. There was a complication in that case in that the entire sum had been traced to her bank, and the bank had then interpleaded, leaving it to the court to decide as between P and D. There is no need at this point to chase that complication. Had P sued D just for the sum initially received, there is not a shadow of doubt that she would have been strictly liable.

The common law on this matter cannot be better put than in a crucial passage from Lord Goff's speech in *Lipkin Gorman* v *Karpnale Ltd*, in which he sets out the basis on which a claimant can sometimes leapfrog an immediate recipient and sue a third party who has in turn received from him. Such a claimant, he says:[49]

> "has to establish a basis on which he is entitled to the money. This (at least as a general rule) he does by showing that the money is his legal property, as appears from Lord Mansfield's judgment in *Clarke v Shee and Johnson* (1774) 1 Cowp 197. If he can do so, he may be entitled to succeed in a claim against the third party for money had and received to his use, though not if the third party has

[46] [1991] 2 AC 548. The House declined the invitation to depart from Privy Council cases which laid down that on these facts title to the money taken from the bank passed to the gambling solicitor, an authorised signatory to withdraw, albeit not for the purpose of gambling: 682.

[47] *Holiday v Sigil* (1826) 2 Car & P 177; *Moffatt v Kazana* [1969] 2 QB 152.

[48] [1997] Ch 159 (CA); pet diss [1997] 1 WLR 51 (HL); noted R Davern [1997] *Restitution LR* 92; Birks (1997) 11 TLI 2.

[49] [1991] 2 AC 548, 572.

received the money in good faith and for a valuable consideration. . . . Furthermore, it appears that in these cases the action for money had and received is not usually founded upon any wrong by the third party, such as conversion; nor is it said to be a case of waiver of tort. It is founded simply on the fact that, as Lord Mansfield said, the third party cannot in conscience keep the money – or, as we would say nowadays, for the third party to retain the money would result in an unjust enrichment of the third party at the expense of the owner of the money."

In equity the still dominant view is that the strict claim in unjust enrichment is only available in respect of assets misdirected in the administration of a deceased's estate: the *Diplock* personal claim.[50] Outside that context a plaintiff entitled in equity can on this view either vindicate his asset from a defendant who still has it or advance a fault-based personal claim, arguably founded on a wrong. This produces an indefensible asymmetry between equity and the common law. A variation of *Lipkin Gorman* illustrates. There the solicitor-plaintiffs were able to maintain a strict claim in unjust enrichment at common law, subject to defences and, in particular, to the defence of change of position. What would have been the position had they had to rely on equity? They would have failed. They could not have proved that the defendant still traceably held the money received, for the purpose of the *vindicatio*. They could not have proved guilty knowledge necessary to sustain a fault-based claim for knowing receipt. Finally, although they would have been seeking to recover misdirected funds, they would not have been able to take advantage of the personal claim in unjust enrichment recognised in *Re Diplock*, because in their case the funds had not been misdirected from the estate of deceased person.

These problems of the present law make it likely that, when the opportunity arises, it will be held that equity does fully recognise a liability in unjust enrichment which is in principle not fault-based but strict, subject to defences.[51] Lionel Smith mounts an argument defending the proposition that "knowing receipt" in equity is and should be a fault-based equitable wrong, essentially the wrong of misappropriation. He says that it should not be reinterpreted as a claim in unjust enrichment.[52] He may be right that I have been

[50] *Re Diplock* [1948] Ch 465 (CA), affd *Ministry of Health v Simpson* [1951] AC 251.

[51] On the necessity of this development, see C Harpum, "Knowing Receipt and Knowing Assistance: the Basis of Equitable Liability", in Birks (ed), *Frontiers of Liability*, vol 1 (OUP, Oxford, 1994) 9, 24–25, where he vividly conveys the clash between historical truth and analytical necessity. It is impossible now to defend the historical truth, except as history. But some remain sceptical or hostile. Sceptical: S Gardner, "Knowing Assistance and Knowing Receipt: Taking Stock" (1996) 112 LQR 56; hostile: PD Finn, "The Liability of Third Parties for Knowing Receipt or Assistance", in DWM Waters (ed), *Equity, Fiduciaries and Trusts* (Carswell, Toronto, 1993), 195.

[52] Smith, 124; *cf* LD Smith, *The Law of Tracing* (OUP, Oxford, 1997), 373–375. See also Segal, 111–112.

in error in trying to force it into that mould. But the answer is that we should not argue in terms of inherited formulae but analytically in terms of causes of action in wrongs and in unjust enrichment. It may be that the continuing confusions surrounding "knowing receipt" are best seen as arising, not because what is in truth an unjust enrichment is being treated as though it were a wrong, but rather because in the one formulaic phrase "knowing receipt" both unjust enrichment and wrongdoing have been contending together beneath the insufficiently analysed surface. It may be that the equitable *vindicatio* is indeed backed up by a personal claim based on a wrong of misappropriation, and it may be that we could now assign the label "knowing receipt" to that wrong, but the analytical question remains whether, after that assignment, the equitable *vindicatio* is also backed up by an alternative personal claim in unjust enrichment.

The common law has no *vindicatio*. It therefore moves two kinds of personal claim into the front line, the one for the wrong of conversion, the other for unjust enrichment, formerly mediated through the action for money had and received. Equity might be said clearly to allow the same two personal claims, with the curious restriction that it is currently understood to restrict its personal claim to cases of misdirection from a deceased person's estate. The model of the personal claims at common law and the indefensible nature of the restriction of the equitable claim in unjust enrichment together make the strongest case for generalising the *Diplock* claim, subject to the ameliorating defences applicable to all claims in unjust enrichment. The ambiguity of "knowing receipt" before its unequivocal assignment to wrongs provides a further argument. These things combine to found a prediction that a strict obligation in unjust enrichment, subject to defences, will be fully recognised in equity. It is on that assumption that the discussion now turns to the bank's defences.

3. Defences

Strict liability is prima facie alarming. Yet the practical difference between the two approaches, the one fault-based and the other strict but subject to defences, must not be exaggerated. Where liability is prima facie strict, fault filters back into the discussion in relation to the defences, because fault can disqualify a recipient from pleading a defence and thus in effect enlarge his liability. Provided that the degree of that disqualifying fault is not too slight, nobody need fear that enlargement of prima facie liability. It is unnecessary, and indeed demonstrably wrong, to leap to the conclusion that only a fault-based liability will be tolerable.[53] The paragraphs which follow seek to show that the fault-based model, despite its protective attractions, has the bad effect of insulating from restitutionary liability some recipients of whom all reasonable people would agree that they ought to make restitution. The discussion assumes that, whatever the hesitations in the early stages,[54] the defence of change of position will in due course turn out to be a liberal defence from which, in the absence of special circumstances, only the dishonest will be disqualified.

(a) Change of position: liability limited to surviving enrichment

The defence of change of position, once it has settled down, will be shown to have the effect of ensuring that the recipient of an enrichment can never be liable beyond the extent to which he remains enriched at the time from which he is disqualified from the defence. The defence protects the security of receipts. Unless and until disqualified, the recipient may safely regard himself as able to dispose of all the wealth which appears to be at his disposition. He need have no fear of having to repay wealth which he has consumed. And he ought not to be disqualified until he knows that the wealth in question is in fact not at his disposition or, in other words, until his state of knowledge renders further reliance on the enrichment dishonest.

Although the liability to make restitution is prima facie strict, yet, putting the liability and the defence together, the honest defendant can only be compelled to give up the surviving enhancement of his wealth. This has nothing to do with tracing. The question is not what traceably survives but the extent to which his assets remain swollen. Suppose D still has in his pocket the £20 note just mistakenly paid to him by P. P immediately explains to him what has happened. Let us suppose that P is a shopkeeper who miscalculated the amount of change due to D, momentarily believing that D had given him £20 more than was in fact the case. It is no answer in law or morality for D to say that he was not at fault in receiving that money. Suppose that P's explanation comes the next day. D has meanwhile used that £20 to buy a bottle of champagne, and D and his friends drank the champagne before dinner in the evening. D was going to buy that bottle anyhow. It was the next item on his

53 This error, which underlies much of *Westdeutsche Landesbank Girozentrale v Islington LBC* [1996] AC 669, is present in an extreme form in *Citadel General Assurance v Lloyds Bank* (1997) 152 DLR (4th) 411, to be taken with *Gold v Rosenberg* (1997) 152 DLR (4th) 385.

54 *South Tyneside BC v Svenska International Plc* contains a dictum indicating that not only the dishonest may be disqualified: [1995] 1 All ER 545, 569. More ominous, in Australia, is *Swiss Bank v State Bank of NSW* (1995) 39 NSWLR 350, noted R Chambers, "Change of Position on the Faith of the Receipt" [1996] *Restitution LR* 100.

shopping list. It happens that he used the £20 which he received from P. The money is no longer traceable, but D's assets are still swollen. In short, D has not changed his position. D is no stronger than before, when he still had the very note. Neither in morality nor in law does he have any plausible answer to P's demand for repayment. Innocent though he was, the strict liability which the law imposes is entirely justified. It does not cease to be justified unless and until D is asked, not to yield up the surviving enrichment, but to put his hand in his pocket to make good P's loss.

Let us suppose instead that D had no intention of buying the champagne but, looking in his purse and finding that he had more money than he thought, made up his mind to splash out. On these facts, the champagne once drunk, the enhancement of his wealth would have been eliminated. The question would be whether he or P should bear the loss: should he be made worse off than he was at the beginning of the story? That question does turn on fault. If he was honest, he can plead the defence of change of position, and P will bear the loss. If he was dishonest, he will be barred from the defence, and he will bear the loss. A system which has a properly working defence of change of position in effect imposes a strict liability in respect of surviving enrichment, a fault-based liability in respect of enrichment which no longer survives. A system which opts for a liability which is fault-based *ab initio* will, without good reason, let off some recipients who are still sitting on swollen assets.

(b) Ministerial receipt

Michael Bryan's excellent chapter explores the application of the defence which an agent recipient has long been known to have, the defence of ministerial receipt. He shows that that defence is in urgent need of review. It has many loose ends. At common law an agent recipient can be sued but is said to have a special defence once he has paid over to, or in accordance with the orders of, his principal. Even then his liability may endure if at the time of payment over his good faith was impaired by knowledge of the payer's entitlement to restitution. A bank which receives for the credit of its customer is squarely within the scope of the defence thus outlined, if indeed the defence is analytically distinct from change of position. Professor Watts has recently asserted that it is.[55] Mr Swadling thinks that it is distinct from change of position but should be regarded as turning on a species of estoppel.[56]

[55] Peter Watts, "Restitution – a Property Principle and a Services Principle" [1995] *Restitution LR* 49, 69.

[56] W J Swadling, "The Nature of Ministerial Receipt" in Birks (ed), *Laundering and Tracing* (OUP, Oxford, 1995), 243.

Goff & Jones,[57] from the beginning sternly critical of the earlier failure of English law to recognise the defence of change of position, treated the agent's defence as the bridgehead from which the battle for its introduction might be fought. Now that the battle has been won, it is not clear that the bridgehead is not simply absorbed by the advance made on the wider front. *Goff & Jones* still deals with it under the general heading of change of position and estoppel but accept that there are some particularities.[58] A sensible plan for the review which must come when a suitable case presents itself will be to ask first what the defence of change of position can do and only then to put the crucial question whether the defence of ministerial receipt can or ought to do more. This approach will be good for both defences, if indeed there be two. Change of position is itself still not fully formed and cannot be finally stabilised until its role in reconciling the central tension between the demand for restitution and the interest in security of receipts is fully understood. But a review of ministerial receipt in the light of the now undoubted existence of the change of position will help to stabilise both.

A strong defence of ministerial receipt: the model of the German law

Ministerial receipt would certainly remain a separate defence if it worked as it does in German law. This is a model which English equity appears to be trying to emulate. The German rule, in close accord with the fundamental English conception of agency as applied in most other contexts, is that, in the case of receipt by an agent, the agent simply drops out and the action has to be brought against the principal. That still leaves room for the agent to be sued as a wrongdoer. The German law on this has been outlined by Heinrich Dörner in this way:[59]

> "If an agent acts on behalf of the recipient and makes it known that he is acting in such a capacity, the performance will be one made not to the agent but directly to the principal. . . . Take, for example, *Australia and New Zealand Banking Corp Group v Westpac Banking Corp* . . . Similar

[57] R Goff and G Jones, *The Law of Restitution*, 1st ed (Sweet and Maxwell, London, 1966), 486–487.

[58] G Jones (ed), Lord Goff of Chieveley and G Jones, *The Law of Restitution*, 4th ed (Sweet and Maxwell, London, 1993), 751.

[59] Heinrich Dörner, "Change of Position and *Wegfall der Bereicherung*" in W J Swadling (ed), *The Limits of Restitutionary Claims: A Comparative Analysis* (London, 1997) 64, 65–66. The German rule entails the conclusion that the plaintiff can immediately sue the principal, even before the agent pays over. On general principles that ought to be the English rule too, despite the continuing liability of the agent till payment over. But in *Barclays Bank v Simms* [1980] QB 677, 702, Robert Goff J hesitated to enter judgment against a principal who had not yet received and wanted to hear argument on the point. The report records only that, after a discussion with counsel and, semble on the basis of the resulting agreement of both sides, he did enter judgment against the principal.

> cases have also come before the German courts, cases which all involved a ten-fold amount being credited to the recipient. In each case it was simply taken for granted that the action should be brought against the holder of the account . . . and not the receiving bank . . . . From the German standpoint, the credit to [the customer's] account only increases *his* wealth by £100,000."

One would expect a similar result to follow from the dominant principles of English agency. But at common law it certainly does not. However, there is some evidence of equity inclining to that position. In *Agip (Africa) Ltd v Jackson*[60] the defendant was held liable for knowing assistance but was said to be immune as an agent recipient to the receipt-based equitable claim. In his chapter, Bryan reviews the thin authority for that immunity and finds it wanting.[61] He is quite right. He also attacks it as being unsound in principle as applied to cases in which the immediate recipient receives on terms that he may use the money for his own purposes, as a bank may, subject only to personal accountability to a principal. It is not so clear that it is vulnerable to that criticism. An agent does not cease to be an agent be being only personally accountable for his receipts.

Equity's position remains to be settled. The resolution cannot precede the re-examination of the relation in equity between wrong-based liability and liability based on unjust enrichment. If the agent has committed a wrong he will be liable for it. The question is as to the operation of the *Diplock*[62] style of liability, at present assumed to be confined to money misdirected from the estate of a deceased person. That question has not been faced. However, its shallow roots are against this manifestation of a strong immunity, and the common law has never been so stated. It would not do to harden another asymmetry. Moreover, given the availability of the defence of change of position, there is no pressing need for any separate defence of ministerial receipt. On balance, therefore, it would seem best to repress the new equitable doctrine, however sensible and principled it might have seemed *re integra*.

The illusory advantages of ministerial receipt

Applying the method suggested above, what results would the application of the defence of change of position yield? Would there, without the radical

[60] [1990] Ch D 265 (Millett J); affd [1991] Ch D 547 (CA).

[61] Bryan, 180–85. Though he is right to say that banks receive beneficially in all cases in which their obligation is merely to extend credit in a like sum, it does not follow from that truth that their role as agents should not confer a special immunity to claims in respect of money received for the credit of their principals. It is therefore not on that ground that I agree with his conclusion. Though they receive in one sense beneficially, it would not be impossible to describe the receipt as non-enriching.

[62] [1948] Ch 465. *Cf* the discussion *supra*, text to n 48.

departure contemplated above, be any work left for a special defence of ministerial receipt? From the standpoint of the defence of change of position the fundamental proposition would have to be that a bank which receives money for the credit of its customer ought to be protected by that defence if it honestly eliminates the enrichment received from the payer. The relevant question should not be expressed in terms of payment over but rather of reliance. The right test in terms of the defence of change of position is whether the bank, once it has credited the payment to the customer in reliance on the receipt, is bound to let the credit stand. It must be correct that there will be no disenriching change of position, so long as the relevant entry in the customer's account can be unilaterally reversed.

The bank may be bound to let the credit stand even though it has never made any cash or other payment to the customer in reliance on the money received from the payer. For it is possible for the bank in some circumstances to be estopped from rectifying the account in favour of a customer who has acted in reliance on it.[63] There is in addition an unexplored possibility of the bank's being found to have attorned to the customer and therefore being caught by *Shamia v Joory*.[64] If, for one reason or another, the bank is bound to let the credit stand, it will have lost any enrichment which it received even before it pays out in reliance on that receipt.

On the other hand, there may be cases in which the bank makes actual payments out in reliance on the payment in without fully erasing its enrichment. This depends on how the law handles any viable claim to recover the sum so paid. Authoritative dicta assert that a mistaken payee who donates one half of the money to charity has pro tanto an immediate defence.[65] Since the money is paid under a mistake and he therefore has an action to recover it, a strict view might be that the change of position should be measured by the difference between the value of the donation and the value of the action for restitution, much as though, if the money were spent on a car, the defence would bite only the difference between the money received and the value of the car.[66]

[63] *United Overseas Bank v Jiwani* [1976] 1 WLR 964. An account can also become binding as an account stated. But a bank statement or a bank pass book does not in any ordinary case become an account stated: *Kepitgalla Rubber Estates Ltd v National Bank of India Ltd* [1909] 2 KB 1010.

[64] [1958] 1 QB 448.

[65] *Lipkin Gorman v Karpnale Ltd* [1991] 2 AC 548, 579.

[66] It might be said that this problem does not arise in the case of the bank, because the bank, unlike the donor to charity, pays under a valid contract with its customer, but in *Admiralty Commissioners v National Provincial and Union Bank* (1922) 127 LT 452, 453 [see Bryan, 161–162] Sargant J held to the contrary: "In my opinion, any contract by which the bank agrees to honour cheques of the customer on his current account does not extend to amounts standing to the credit of the account in so far as they are swollen by inadvertent payments made by mistake of fact. As a result of an order for repayment of the amount claimed, the customer's account will be deflated by that amount. Any subsequent action by the customer's legal representative to recover that amount from the bank would have no reasonable chance of success."

However, the dicta in relation to donations to charity suppose a more lenient analysis, which would allow the defence to operate immediately so as to reduce the plaintiff payer's claim by one half, probably at the same time subrogating the payer to the restitutionary claim against the charity.[67]

Against that sketch of the perspective of the defence of change of position, we can look for advantages to the agent of having a distinct defence of his own. We must note that there might be disadvantages in being an agent. That is, an agent who had changed his position might be shut out of the defence because he was an agent. That theoretical possibility may be optimistically discounted.[68] As for possible advantages, there seem to be three small possibilities, but each is on closer examination based on hypotheses as to the development of the law which would be either incorrect or undesirable.

(i) Notice. If even a careless defendant were disqualified from change of position – the wrong choice – and if only dishonesty disqualified the agent from relying on ministerial receipt, it would be true that the careless agent would have a fall-back position. However, it is unlikely that the requirements as to knowledge will be driven apart.

(ii) Payment over. The requirements might be stated differently. Suppose the agent had only to show that the money received was paid over and that this was a mechanical question, looking to the very money received and asking whether that specific input had gone out. Recourse to *Clayton's Case*[69] in relation to a running account might seem to suggest that that is the right approach in the case of the agent.[70] It is certainly not the right approach in relation to change of position. The change of position inquiry generally looks for reliance expenditure, a payment out in reliance on the payment in, not a payment out *of* a payment in. Change of position has nothing to do with tracing. It looks to see whether the swelling of the assets has been eliminated. This touches on Dr Smith's paper, to which we will come below. The defendant who pleads change of position is not trying to tell the court what happened to any specific subject-matter or to other assets which were substituted for it. His case is only that a given inflow of wealth by which his assets were swollen was eliminated by a given outflow, the connection between inflow and outflow in nine cases out of ten being reliance on the former in the making of the other.

[67] On the action against the person enriched by the disenrichment, see *infra*, text to n 117.

[68] Yet *US v Seele* (1959) 175 F Supp 24 was decided against a defendant whose agency was undisclosed long after the American recognition of the defence of change of position. An undisclosed agent, barred from the agent's defence for want of disclosing the agency, was held to have no defence at all by virtue of having accounted to his principal. The "unjust decision" is heavily criticised by Palmer: G E Palmer, *The Law of Restitution* (Little Brown, Boston, 1978, with supps) vol 3, 519–522.

[69] (1817) 1 Mer 572. *Cf* Bryan, 176.

[70] *ANZ v Westpac* (1988) 164 CLR 662, 676–680.

But Michael Bryan rightly emphasises that in relation to the agent *Clayton's Case* is used in its original role, which was to identify which of two or more debts a debtor who had not expressly appropriated the payment to any of them should be regarded as having paid. Reliance is just as much the proper test for the agent as it is for the general defence. An agent is often not bound to keep the agency money separate from his own. The question whether the agent has honoured his obligation to pay over to the principal turns on whether in making a later payment, or entry in an account which later became binding, the agent acted because of the payment in. It is a causal question, and the index of causation is intentional reliance. The agent who credited an account will be able to show that he relied by pointing to the entry made in the account. But then the question will be whether the matter went any further. Was that entry ever paid out? At this stage the evidential impasse can be resolved by the application of "first in, first out". But that is not a particularity of the agent's defence. At that stage the general defence of change of position would resolve the impasse in the same way. In relation to both, therefore, *Clayton's Case* merely provides the solution to a sub-issue which arises when the reliance in question first takes the form of an entry in an account.

But there could still be a difference. It might be that the agent who has honoured the obligation by paying the relevant sum is once and for all entitled to his defence, while the plaintiff relying on change of position is not yet home and dry. *Goff & Jones* picks up the High Court of Australia' s statement in *ANZ v Westpac* that the agent may be allowed to leave out of account any right that he might have to recover back his payment out.[71] It might be that the defence of change of position would lead to a different conclusion. This depends on how the law of change of position will turn out to handle any viable claim to recover the outlay on which the defence is founded. We have already said that the more lenient view is more likely right.[72] On that assumption this difference between the two defences disappears.

(iii) Detriment. If it were true that change of position required something called detriment, and the agent's defence did not, there would be a reason for an agent to prefer the special defence. Though this came up in *ANZ v Westpac* the High Court did not uphold any such proposition. It only said, cautiously, that either detriment was unnecessary or:[73]

> "If the matter needs to be expressed in terms of detriment or change of position, the payment by the agent to the principal of the money which he has received on the principal's behalf, of itself constitutes the relevant detriment or change of position."

[71] *Goff & Jones, supra* n 57, 758.
[72] *Supra*, text from n 65.
[73] (1988) 164 CLR 662, 682.

This tells us something about the agent's defence, without actually excluding a stronger requirement of detriment in other cases. But, if the general defence of change of position appears to require detrimental reliance, that is only because it requires disenrichment. There is no point in playing with the word "detriment" if it is disenrichment which really matters. This important sentence thus applies to all instances. If the matter has to be put in terms of detriment, the detriment is the disenrichment.

On balance, therefore, these three differences appear illusory. Caution is necessary, especially since illiberal interpretation of change of position, however undesirable, could reveal real advantages in the agent's special defence. That danger apart, the conditions for the special defence seem always to satisfy the requirements of the more general defence. If there is insufficient room to develop a full-scale immunity of the agent, obliging the plaintiff in unjust enrichment to sue the principal as the true payee, it becomes very difficult to see a good reason for maintaining the separate existence of the agent's defence. The broader the defence of change of position, the less the need, or possibility, of keeping ministerial receipt as a separate defence. If, however, change of position were narrowed, some differences might appear. The narrowing of the defence of change of position would impair the structural strategy which is based upon it, and the law would be the worse for that. More generally, the multiplication of subtly different entities is not to be encouraged, certainly not where there is no pressing need. If the law has in effect decided not to immunise the agent from claims in unjust enrichment, the defence of change of position probably can and should do the rest of the work.

(c) Bona fide purchase

This discussion cannot entirely omit the bank's problematic entitlement to this defence. It is clear that, in *Lipkin Gorman v Karpnale*, had the gambler been addicted to champagne and caviar, and had the defendant casino been instead the Ritz Hotel, a different result would have been reached. There would have been no void contract, and the Ritz would have had the defence of bona fide purchase, even to a personal claim in unjust enrichment. Even at law the giving of value in good faith destroys earlier interests which might otherwise subsist in the money. A personal claim for the value of the money would utterly subvert that useful proprietary rule. In order to prevent that, the personal claim also encounters the defence. All that is straightforward.

However, the case throws a shadow which falls across banks. Lord Goff expressly assumed, in the course of reasoning directed to another point, that it was obviously incorrect to say that "a bank with which money was deposited by an innocent donee from a thief could claim to be a bona fide purchaser simply by virtue of the fact of the deposit."[74] It can be seen from the context that he meant that the contractual undertaking to repay could not possibly be value given for the money received. In the same way Lord Templeman says that a building society which takes a deposit from a thief has no defence against the victim of the theft unless it has actually repaid the debt so created.[75] This fits with the fact that in relation to the classical defence of bona fide purchase a contractual obligation to pay money counts for nothing: all the money must be paid, and it is at that moment of full payment that the payer who has obtained the legal estate must be acting without notice of the adverse interests.[76]

Banks give all sorts of other services, often without charge and therefore for no other consideration than the making of deposits. Nevertheless, it seems that in relation to deposits made by a non-owner or an encumbered owner the banking contract cannot in itself support the defence of bona fide purchaser for value. In this respect a business which sells the banking services which go with a current or other account is worse off than a business which sells food and drink. It is different when a bank sells foreign currency to someone who buys it with another's money or, rather more controversially, bona fide accepts such third party money in discharge of a customer's existing debt. A bank which accepts third party money as a deposit into an account which is in credit has not yet given value for it. A bank which accepts the same deposit for the credit of an overdrawn account has already paid for the repayment in the making of the earlier advance.[77]

II. THE BANK AS PLAINTIFF

The common case, and the only one addressed in this book, is a mistaken payment by the bank. The starting point is that the general law applies. If a bank pays money by mistake, in the sense that the mistake causes the payment, then the bank is prima facie entitled to restitution. The law was reviewed and restated in that liberal form in the brilliant judgment of Robert Goff J, as he then was, in *Barclays Bank Plc v WJ Simms, Son & Cooke (Southern) Ltd.*[78]

[74] [1991] 2 AC 548, 577.
[75] [1991] 2 AC 548, 562.
[76] *Story v Windsor* (1743) 2 Atk 630; *Wigg v Wigg* (1739) 1 Atk 382.
[77] L D Smith, *The Law of Tracing* (OUP, Oxford, 1997), 389–391, where Dr Smith goes further, arguing that the *Lipkin* dicta denying the defence of bona fide purchaser should be reconsidered. Bryan, 183–185, criticises distinctions taken in the cases between overdrawn and other accounts, but this distinction is good in relation to this defence.
[78] [1980] QB 677.

The bank there paid a cheque which had been stopped. The bank's customer owed money to the defendants for building work which they had done. The customer sent the defendants a cheque for the amount due. Before the cheque was presented, the customer countermanded the bank's authority to pay. Overlooking the countermand, the bank nevertheless paid. The bank thus paid outside the terms of its mandate, without any authority from its customer. Robert Goff J held that it was entitled to restitution.

This is not the only great case to have been applauded for its creative mastery of the relevant principles, only to be doubted by some in the application of those principles to the facts.[79] In this volume Justice van Zyl mounts a spirited defence of the reasoning and result of *Barclays Bank v Simms* in the face of its rejection in the Appellate Division of the Supreme Court of South Africa in *B & H Engineering v First National Bank of SA Ltd.*[80] Justice van Zyl would go one step further even than is warranted by *Barclays Bank v Simms* itself.[81] He would give the bank an alternative remedy against the countermanding customer to the extent, not of the amount of the payment, but of the customer's enrichment. The customer's enrichment might well be less, for it might be that, as things have turned out, the creditor whom the bank paid off could not have recovered the full amount of his claim.

However, despite Justice van Zyl's arguments, a shadow of doubt lingers, cast from the United States, where the Uniform Commercial Code (§4-407) also takes a contrary position. Professor Andrew Kull, criticising the result in *Barclays Bank v Simms*, has recently summed up the position in the United States thus:[82]

> "The fact that the bank made a mistake in paying the check is not grounds, in and of itself, to recover the payment. The Uniform Commercial Code denies a direct recovery by the bank against a payee who took the check in good faith and for value, a condition satisfied by any creditor not engaged in fraud. In other words the UCC applies the rule in *Price v Neal* (1962) 3 Burr 1355 to the case of a check paid over a stop order. The bank may, in fact, recover some or all of its mistaken payment, but not necessarily from the payee of the check, and only to the extent that the bank can demonstrate the unjust enrichment of some party on the facts of the transaction as a whole. The Code solution, in effect, is to subrogate the bank to whatever valid claims its mistaken payment may happen to have discharged. Depending on the circumstances, these will include claims against the drawer/ buyer (asserted by the seller under the sales contract or by a holder

[79] *Cf* the comments of Eyre CJ on *Moses v Macferlan* (1760) 2 Burr 1005 in *Phillips v Hunter* (1795) 2 H Bl 402, 416.

[80] 1995 (2) SA 279 (A); van Zyl, 21–24.

[81] Van Zyl, 25–26.

[82] A Kull, "Rationalizing Restitution" (1995) 83 Calif L Rev 1191, 2015. The last lines of this quotation are based on an example earlier introduced, in which a disappointed buyer stops the cheque with which he paid the price of a car.

in due course of the check), as well as claims against the payee/seller (asserted by the buyer under the seller's warranties)."

Justice van Zyl's enrichment action against its customer, the debtor-drawer of the cheque, is here conceded by way of subrogation. The bank takes over the position of the creditor-payee, with all its weaknesses, whatever they may be. In that way it obtains restitution of whatever benefit its payment actually conferred on its customer. However, it is not conceded by way of an alternative recourse. Under the regime of the UCC there is no recourse against the payee of the cheque who has received the bank's money, except in the rare case in which that party is a donee or dishonest. The English solution is more circuitous, and it does not require the bank to shoulder any weaknesses which there may have been in the creditor's position. The bank gets back its money from the creditor-payee and, except that the action on the cheque itself has now gone, the other two parties are left to face each other just as they did before.

Scylla and Charybdis

The crucial question for the English solution, too deep to be properly investigated here, is whether it is possible satisfactorily to explain why the action by the bank against the creditor-payee is not barred by either *Aiken v Short*[83] or *Price v Neal*[84].

Aiken v Short was a case in which the bank had, with the authority of its debtor, paid off a prior charge on the debtor's property, intending to increase its own exposure to the debtor while advancing its own security. It then discovered that the debtor had no title to the property and it therefore had no charge. The bank was denied restitution from the first chargee, whom it had paid off. Robert Goff J explained that result by formulating an exception to the basic rule covering the case in which a plaintiff who had made a causative mistake would nevertheless not recover from the payee:[85]

> "the payment is made for good consideration, in particular if the money is paid to discharge, and does discharge, a debt owed to the payee . . . by the payer or by a third party by whom he is authorised to discharge the debt . . ."

A few lines later the exception is then itself qualified:

> "However, even if the payee has given consideration for the payment, for example by accepting the payment in discharge of a debt owed to him by a third party

83 (1856) 1 H & N 210; 25 LJ Ex 321.
84 (1762) 3 Burr 1354.
85 [1980] QB 677, 695.

on whose behalf the payer is authorised to discharge it, that transaction may itself be set aside if the payer's mistake was induced by the payee, or possibly where the payee, being aware of the payer's mistake, did not receive in good faith."

The situation of Barclays was then quite different from that of the plaintiff in *Aiken v Short*. The bank did pay to discharge a debt but it was not authorised to do so and its payment did not discharge the debt owed by its customer to the defendants. Barclays fell within the exception.

The difficulty arises from the fact that this explanation of *Aiken v Short* is open to objection and that there is at least one other which, if it were right, would make it much more difficult to steer safely past. The objection is that there is no general proposition to the effect that the receipt of good consideration in exchange for a payment bars restitution. If there were, there would be little restitution for misrepresentation and undue influence. That is why Robert Goff J qualified his exception to try to allow for cases in which the transaction for good consideration would itself be set aside. But the qualification is itself doubtful. Except in the case of payment made under a valid contract as opposed to a bare payment, it is hard to say why mistake should be treated differently from factors such as these.[86] The usual way of dealing with an exchange of that kind nowadays is, unless the plaintiff can be held to be immune to this requirement,[87] to insist on counter-restitution and then to allow for changes of position. It is important to notice that in *Aiken v Short* itself that was not perceived to be a problem. Bramwell B expressly said that, if the plaintiff could make out his claim, "there would be no difficulty in the way of the defendant suing Carter".[88] The point was not that the plaintiff had a prima facie claim which encountered a defence, but that on the facts there was no claim at all.

The other explanations of *Aiken v Short* are more difficult to negotiate. One which has a secure root in the case itself is the proposition that, at least in some circumstances, *suum recepit* (he received his due) is a good answer. In particular, the defendant has a good defence to a restitutionary claim if he can

[86] The fundamental principle is that in a bargaining situation restitution must be compatible with respect for the process of bargaining; when there is no bargain that interest is not in play, *cf supra* n 40. Since relief for mistake is compatible with the interest in bargaining if the mistake is as to a matter essential to the contract but outside the risks inherent in it, one way to avoid the difficulty of deciding whether a "transaction" does or does not require to be treated as putting the bargaining interest in play is to suppose that it does and then to ask directly whether the mistake was of that kind, right outside the risks, if any, inherent in that particular "transaction". It might be thought that that inquiry would favour *Aiken*, a conclusion which would require the result to be upheld in another way, or not at all. In support of that conclusion might be adduced, in equity, *Magee v Pennine Insurance Co Ltd* [1969] 2 QB 607 and, at law, *Associated Japanese Bank v Crédit du Nord SA* [1988] 1 WLR 255.

[87] As in *David Securities Pty Ltd v Commonwealth Bank* (1992) 175 CLR 353.

[88] (1856) 1 H&N 210, 216.

show that, mistake or no mistake, that which he received was due to him from a person in whose name it appeared to be paid.[89] The rationale of such a proposition would not be very satisfying, merely that by a fluke the recipient received his due and is not to be deprived of his good luck. If that were the right answer it would obviously reach *Barclays v Simms*. Again, another and *prima facie* more convincing explanation is that the defendant was not the plaintiff's true payee. The observable fact of a payment from A to B is not conclusive of the proposition that A is the true payee, since A may be paying on the credit of C. In *Aiken v Short* the plaintiff bank mistakenly intended to enlarge its exposure to its debtor.[90] Had it made the payment through him, it would have been obvious that only under certain narrow (and even now ill-understood) conditions could it leapfrog him and sue the remoter recipient.

If this last explanation were right, it is difficult to deny that in *Barclays v Simms* the bank also mistakenly intended to pay on the credit of its customer. It paid because it intended to debit the account. The customer was the true payee and the proper defendant. There is a crucial difference in that there was no legal objection to Aiken suing the debtor rather than leapfrogging him and suing the first chargee. In the case of a countermanded cheque there is such an obstacle. If the customer were liable for the amount paid out without authority, there would be no such thing as a countermand. Or a countermand would be no more than precatory. But that brings us back to Justice van Zyl's *actio negotiorum gestorum utilis*, the cousin of the old action for managing another's affairs. That claim would allow the bank to recover from the customer, not the bank's outlay, but the customer's enrichment.

The United States solution, as described in the extract from Professor Kull above, in the different language of subrogation achieves precisely the same result.[91] The bank recovers the enrichment of the countermanding customer.

[89] This seems to be the true basis of the defence recognised in the *Restatement of Restitution* §44 [1]: "a creditor of another or one having a lien on another's property who has received from a third person any benefit in discharge of the debt or lien is under no duty to make restitution therefor, although the discharge was given by mistake of the transferor as to his interests or duties, if the transferee made no misrepresentation and did not have notice of the transferor's mistake." This *Aiken v Short* defence, if one may so call it, was recently applied by the New York Court of Appeals to a countermanded electronic funds transfer: *Bank Worms v Bankamerica International* (1991) 77 NY 2d 362, 570 NE 2d 189.

[90] (1856) 1 H&N 210, 214, where Pollock CB concludes by affirming that the bank paid on behalf of its customer: "The money was, in fact, paid by the bank as agent of Carter." *Cf* Robert Goff J in *Barclays v Simms* [1980] QB 677, 700, to the effect that, if the bank pays on a *valid* cheque but under the mistaken belief that its customer has sufficient funds or overdraft facilities, despite its mistake, its only recourse is against its customer.

[91] In this country it is still necessary, certainly at a procedural level, to distinguish between subrogation as used of debts which are discharged (reviving subrogation) and as used of debts which are not discharged (simple subrogation): Charles Mitchell, *The Law of Subrogation* (OUP, Oxford, 1994), 4–6. However, the fact that the language covers both is an indication that it is not necessary, or permissible, to draw sharp distinctions at the level of substance according as the debt is or is not extinguished.

This is also in accord with the principle underlying the doctrine in *B Liggett (Liverpool) Ltd v Barclays Bank Ltd*,[92] which is that, where money is advanced to X in the erroneous belief that X is the authorized agent of Y, so that there is no legal relation between the "lender" and Y, Y is nonetheless liable to the extent that the money was actually applied in such a way as to benefit him.

Nevertheless, it may be that the English approach can be defended. The explanation through the "true payee" proves too much. It cannot stand unmodified, since it would otherwise endanger the bank's right to recover from the immediate payee any mistaken payment made in the belief that it was paying on the credit of its customer, even an accidental second payment. The English defence, but not the American defence, will answer to the following rationale. A plaintiff who has a contractual right to be paid or repaid by X may not in general leapfrog X by suing another defendant in unjust enrichment. However badly a bank may be mistaken in paying the defendant a sum due from a third party, yet if it paid out on the credit of the third party (the customer) and has a right under his contract with the third party (the customer) to charge the sum to that customer, the defendant will have a defence and by that defence will remit the bank or other payer to his action against the customer. In other words, the payer takes the risk of his contractual partner's insolvency. There are other examples of this. If my car is smashed up and I take it to a garage to be repaired under my insurance contract, the garage actually contracts with the insurance company. Suppose that the insurance company goes into liquidation before paying. The garage cannot sue me, even though it might say that I requested and accepted the work. It has to make its claim against the insurance company, which means in this case proving in the liquidation.[93] On this view, it does not matter how badly the bank is mistaken, not even if it was so mistaken as to render the transaction with the creditor void, so long as it was not mistaken as to its having its customer's authority to advance the money. It is that authority which preserves the contractual right of the bank against the customer. That is precisely the English position. It leaves intact the possibility of an action against the creditor-payee arising from some new and additional fact arising in the relationship between the bank and that payee, as for example a misrepresentation made by the creditor-payee. The bank bears the risk of its customer's insolvency, but not the risk of a misrepresentation by the outsider.

If *Aiken v Short* is Scylla, *Price v Neal* is Charybdis. The bank's direct restitutionary claim against the recipient of the countermanded payment has to be

[92] [1928] 1 KB 48 (Wright J).

[93] *Brown & Davis v Galbraith* [1972] 1 WLR 997. *Cf Pan Ocean Shipping Co Ltd v Creditcorp Ltd (The Trident Beauty)* [1994] 1 WLR 161 (HL).

steered between the doubts ventilated above and the somewhat uncertain scope of the fierce inhibition imposed by Lord Mansfield on the right to seek restitution of payments made because of mistakes made in deciding to pay or to accept bills of exchange and other negotiable instruments. The defence requires the bank to demand repayment only on the day on which the bill is paid. The payment then becomes final.[94] The facts of *Price v Neal* are set out in Justice van Zyl's text, together with extracts from the judgment.[95] It will be convenient to set out again the most crucial passage from Lord Mansfield's judgment:[96]

> "But it can never be thought unconscientious in the defendant, to retain this money, when he has once received it upon a bill of exchange indorsed to him for a fair and valuable consideration, which he had bona fide paid, without the least privity or suspicion of any forgery.
>
> Here was no fraud: no wrong. It was incumbent upon the plaintiff, to be satisfied that the bill drawn upon him was in the drawer's hand, before he accepted or paid it: but it was not incumbent on the defendant, to inquire into it."

Justice van Zyl favours a strong interpretation of the *Price v Neal* defence,[97] but he thinks that Robert Goff J properly distinguished its sphere of application, so as exclude from it the case of payment of a countermanded cheque.[98] However, this balance is somewhat delicate. Its instability is apparent on the face of Robert Goff J's judgment.

His Lordship says that the gist of the *Price v Neal* defence, as interpreted in later cases, is change of position. In particular, it applied where the failure to repudiate the instrument would prejudice the holder's need to give the drawer and any indorsers the notice of dishonour necessary to preserve their liability. This was enough to put the countermanded cheque outside the range of the defence, since by statute no notice of dishonour was required in such a case.[99] However, it was necessary, following this line of reasoning, to explain away the fact that the defence is absolute and never depends on any inquiry whether the defendant did in fact suffer any prejudice from not being informed of the mistake on the relevant day. Robert Goff J was obliged to say that the

[94] *Cocks v Masterman* (1829) 9 B & C 902, 908.

[95] van Zyl, 4–5.

[96] (1762) 3 Burr 1354, 1357.

[97] He rejects, *supra*, 12, the line taken by Kerr J in *National Westminster Bank Ltd v Barclays Bank International* [1975] 1 QB 654, 666, to the effect that it should be confined to cases of payments on "instruments which are not mere forgeries in toto but contain at least one genuine signature and which have been negotiated to at least one innocent holder . . ." And on the same page (*cf* p 7) he supports the emphasis on the commercial policy of making bills absolutely reliable advocated by Professor Steven Dow, "Restitution of Payments on Cheques with Forged Drawers' Signatures" [1995] *Restitution LR* 27.

[98] van Zyl, 15–16.

[99] Bills of Exchange Act 1882, s 50(2)(c).

defendant was "deemed in law" to have changed his position.[100] However, it will be obvious that a change of position which has to be "deemed in law" is not really a change of position at all.

It is obvious that this special defence will have to be reviewed and its limits redrawn. It has been argued that it should give place to the general defence of change of position, which would mean that the bank could recover in the normal way, until the defendant had incurred genuinely disenriching losses.[101] On the other hand, the American view certainly runs the other way. There is much to be said for the strong defence which Justice van Zyl favours, albeit within a more clearly defined field. However, that will mean breaking the fictitious link with change of position.

Lord Mansfield fairly clearly meant to put negotiable interests as near as might be under the same regime as money. Money is kept in currency by the defence of bona fide purchase. It is clearly with bona fide purchase that he intended to align the special defence. To repeat the crucial words from the quotation given above, the relevant situation arose "when he [the indorsee] has once received it [the money] upon a bill of exchange indorsed to him for a fair and valuable consideration, which he had bona fide paid, without the least privity or suspicion of any forgery." To apply the defence of bona fide purchase just as though such instruments were cash can reasonably be thought to go too far, giving the drawee no chance whatever to repudiate. But what Lord Mansfield intended was a defence of bona fide purchase postponed to the actual payment of the bill. The one-day rule extends the postponement. The defence is generated in the transaction with the third party by the giving of value for the bill in good faith, but it bites later, on the money received when the bill is paid.

Banks and insurers

One rock on which the discussion above is founded is that, when a bank pays out in the mistaken belief that it is doing so with the authority of its customer, it must reinstate the account. It has paid without any mandate to do so. It has paid from its own funds and cannot debit the account. English law provides

100 [1980] QB 677, 700–703.

101 EP Ellinger and E Lomnicka, *Modern Banking Law*, 2nd ed (OUP, Oxford, 1994), 418–419. On one reading, Professor Dow, though speaking in terms of a return to Lord Mansfield, must be understood as arguing for the same conclusion rather than for a return to the strict defence: Dow [1995] *Restitution LR* 27, 53–59. In *Barclays v Simms* Robert Goff J himself looked forward to the possibility that the deemed change of position would, with time and the development of the defence of change of position, shake off its constructive nature and be absorbed into the general defence, so that the bank would be barred only when the recipient of the money had genuinely changed his position: [1980] QB 677, 703.

little protection for the bank even against a careless customer, because of the very limited nature of the customer's duties to the bank.[102] Charles Mitchell's short but brilliant chapter draws attention to the seemingly insoluble problem created by the situation in which the customer is entitled to have his account reinstated but is at the same time insured against losses arising from fraud. Suppose a customer company is insured against fraud by its employees. An employee forges cheques, and the bank pays out. The insurance company must make good the customer's loss, and the bank must reinstate the account. Which should bear the burden, the insurer or the bank?

If the bank's liability to the customer is reduced by the amount paid by the insurer, the insurer clearly bears the loss. If the insurer is entitled to be subrogated to the customer's claim to have the account reinstated, the bank bears the loss. A logical argument can be advanced to the effect that technically there never was a loss to the customer. The bank merely continued to owe a sum which it had wrongly debited or, in the case of an overdrawn account, continued to be entitled to the smaller sum due before the erroneous debit. On this analysis the bank should bear the loss, because the insurer's liability merely appeared to have been triggered while in substance it had not been. The contrary result is reached in the one English case which confronted the issue, albeit somewhat distorted by concessions.[103] There the bank's liability to its customer was reduced by the amount which the customer had recovered under a fidelity insurance. In other words, the insurers bore the loss.

Dr Mitchell shows that the American cases mostly jump the same way. They make the insurer bear the loss and rely on a number of arguments to support the "superior equity" of the bank. Treating the problem as a matter of policy in which reasons have to be weighed, Dr Mitchell reviews the arguments tendered in favour of the bank. One by one he knocks them down. In English law the matter must clearly be regarded as open. But nothing obstructs the nearest thing to a logical argument for one party or the other, namely that the bank, acting without a mandate, at no stage had any authority to inflict a loss upon its customer and, though it attempted to do so in fact, in law it never succeeded, its underlying debt to the customer being untouched by the mistaken entries in the account. This is a substantial argument against the American position to the effect that the bank has the superior equity.

[102] Mitchell, 40, n 42, contrasting the American position and referring to criticism of the English law: EP Ellinger and E Lomnicka, *Modern Banking Law,* 2nd ed (OUP, Oxford, 1994), 172–173. Cranston takes the view that the English position is basically sensible and desirable, noting however the Banking Ombudsman takes into consideration the contributory negligence of customers who fail to check their payments: R Cranston, *Principles of Banking Law* (OUP, Oxford, 1997), 153,175–176.

[103] Mitchell, 36–37, discussing the only partially reported *Wealden Woodlands (Kent) Ltd v National Westminster Bank Ltd* (1993) 133 NLJ 719.

However, the question cannot be finally decided without first stabilising and then taking into consideration the rights of the bank to recover from the outsider whom it has paid. A very strict application of *Price v Neal*[104] on that front ought perhaps not to be combined with a rule which the makes the bank bear the loss in a competition with the insurer of its customer.

III. TO TRACE OR NOT TO TRACE?

The point was taken above that the division between a bank's liability in unjust enrichment and its rights is artificial. Sometimes it is bank against bank and, even if it is not, today's defendant is tomorrow's plaintiff. Lionel Smith's complex chapter cannot be fitted into one or other side of the artificial division. His question is whether and when it is necessary to trace electronic transfers through the clearing system. Given that payments are increasingly often made by electronic transfer, it is obvious that this question must be answered of all claims, whether by or against a bank or both. Dr Smith raises some very deep issues, on some of which the present writer has the misfortune to find himself at odds with the positions taken.[105] This comment will confine itself to what might be described as the core of the matter, in relation to which there is less distance between us. It is essential to know when tracing is and is not necessary. Tracing is complex and the case law intensely difficult. A plaintiff must know which mazes he may avoid. Dr Smith's chapter allows us to identify the cases in which there is no need to trace. If it were impossible to trace through the electronic transfer system, this negative inquiry would be much more important than it is. The tracing exercise is possible.[106] It remains a complexity to be avoided if possible.

1. A cash payment

If I pay £100 in cash to you and later want to claim it back as having been paid under a mistake, it is formally necessary for me to show that the sum – the sum in question, not any specific notes – which I want repaid did indeed pass from me to you. However, this issue will remain unnoticed in a cash payment, at least in the absence of very special facts.[107] For on the face of things it is

[104] (1762) 3 Burr 1354.

[105] Dr Smith's position on knowing receipt is partly addressed (and partly accepted) above, text to n 52. The handling of remote recipients will not be considered here, except tangentially.

[106] L D Smith, *The Law of Tracing* (OUP, Oxford, 1997), 243–262.

[107] For example, in *Equiticorp Industries Group v The Crown*, Judgment No 47, Smellie J was compelled to decide whether a defendant could plead a *ius tertii*: could the defendants argue that

obvious that the money which you received came from me. There is no room for "tracing" because there has been no substitution. There is room for "following", which, in Dr Smith's terms, can be said to begin from the first transfer in a chain of transfers.[108] But I am not actually relying on following, because I am not focusing on any specific thing. I am only saying, abstractly, that you received an enrichment to the value of £100 from me.

2. A payment through a friend

More complex is this case. I am under the mistaken impression that I am late in paying £200 to the proprietor of a bookshop in London. I have forgotten that I paid the bill a month ago. I have a friend who lives near the shop. I ring him up and ask him if he would be so kind as to pay the money on my behalf immediately, reimbursement to follow. He pays. I reimburse. If, discounting the agency, I had to trace, it would actually be a rather difficult question whether there was room for tracing here. The better view is that there is. It is a case of backwards tracing. The bookseller was paid with money made available by my incurring a debt, and I then paid money to discharge the debt. The substitutions are complex.[109] But we need not chase that hare, because in this situation I have no need to trace. My friend was my agent to make the payment. His payment was my payment. You received £100 from me. The agency concludes the question. It would make no difference if I had not yet reimbursed my friend. Once again it is desirable to emphasise, with Dr Smith, that my personal claim to restitution from the bookseller does not here turn on the legal status of any particular thing. I have to show that the bookseller was enriched, and that the enrichment came from me.

3. A payment through a bank

Suppose that the facts remain the same as in the last case, except that I choose to use my bank rather than my friend to make the payment. One way or another I request my bank to pay the bookseller £200. This case is no different in law. The payment is my payment. Moreover, just as in the last case, it would have made no difference if my friend had appointed a sub-agent to

the plaintiffs had paid over money which was not their own? He decided, true to the whole history of personal property law, that relative, possessory title sufficed: [1996] 3 NZLR 586, 602. This report gives only the judge's summary of a judgment which runs to hundreds of pages.

[108] On tracing and following, Smith,121; and LD Smith, *The Law of Tracing* (OUP, Oxford, 1997), 6–10.

[109] Smith, *ibid*, 146–149.

execute my request, so here it is nothing to me, or to the law, how the bank complies with my mandate. If it uses a string of agents to achieve my purpose, the payment to the bookseller is still my payment. The payment came from me. There may formally be a dozen substitutions between the debit to my account and the credit at the other end to the bookseller. But the agency chain makes it unnecessary to engage in any tracing exercise.

So far, if there is any disagreement, it is confined to a matter of emphasis. We have in effect established that, because of the agency, there is no need to trace. In a case of the *Bank Tejerat*[110] kind, where by mistake a bank sends off money through the clearing system, the bank's personal claim to restitution of the recipient's unjust enrichment is not contingent on a successful tracing exercise. There is no need to trace. The matter of emphasis is this. It is not clear that the agency argument, or even an argument in terms of causation, is essential to Dr Smith's approach. He would say that tracing is not required because (a) the recipient is indisputably enriched, (b) the personal claim is made, abstractly, for the value of the enrichment and is not focused on the legal status of any particular thing, and (c) the identification of the plaintiff, by the application of the words "at the expense of" is merely a matter of associating the enrichment sufficiently proximately with a corresponding minus suffered by the plaintiff. However, the difficulty arises with the nebulous (c). To my mind, "at the expense of" has to be more tightly stated. If there is to be no tracing, the object of which would be to create a proprietary nexus between the plaintiff and the defendant and which would therefore focus on the status of a specific thing in order to support the conclusion that the defendant received something in which the plaintiff had, at the moment of the receipt, some proprietary interest, the nexus must be established either through agency or, failing that and more doubtfully, by proof of a close causal link, supporting the conclusion that, but for the plaintiff's output, the defendant would not have received the enrichment. On the facts covered by the example above, the agency argument seems the best substantiation of "at the plaintiff's expense".

4. The bookseller substitutes

On receipt of the £200 the bookseller pays it into his bank. That is a substitution in itself. Later he draws money from his account, another substitution, and buys for £300 some antiquarian books, which turn out to be worth five times what he paid for them. He still has those books. If I am going to make

110 [1995] 1 Lloyds Rep 239, discussed *supra*, text to n 41; *cf* Smith, 131.

some claim in respect of those books, whatever kind of claim it is, I must now trace from the receipt to the purchase of the books. There is no agency to rely upon. Unless I can apply the rules of tracing to show that the value which originally reposed in the £200 was invested in whole or part in the purchase of the books, he can say that he bought them with other funds and that they are therefore nothing to do with me. Any kind of claim by me in respect of the books will be contingent on successful tracing. However, as Dr Smith emphasises, successful tracing, though necessary, will not be sufficient. Successful tracing confers no rights. I might show by tracing that you spent the money I gave you for your birthday on a painting, but the tracing exercise will not give me any rights in the painting. So here, if I trace the whole £200 into the books, I will have achieved nothing. If the money was his money, I am no nearer establishing any connection with the books. I must show that the money was my money.[111]

Assuming that the facts will not yield an interest at common law, nevertheless, if *Chase Manhattan Bank v Israel-British Bank*[112] was right as decided, I can say that the receipt of my mistaken payment turned the bookseller into a trustee for me, and, from that proprietary base, I can say that I am also entitled to an interest in the books which are the traceable product of the trust money. If the *Chase Manhattan* case is right only as recently interpreted,[113] I can say either that the inchoate interest which I had at the time of the receipt has been perfected by bad faith supervening while the subject matter remains traceable; or – a dangerously broad interpretation of the reinterpretation – that, though I had no interest, not even an inchoate one, at the moment of the receipt, equity simply gives me one on the basis of the supervening bad faith. At all events, I still do not need to trace through the clearing system. I have to trace from the receipt to the acquisition of the books, and then I have to show that I had an interest in the money. This is true whether I intend to make a personal claim or a proprietary claim in relation to the books. That is to say, it is true whether I propose to vindicate the books ("Those books are mine in equity") or assert that the defendant is under an obligation to me arising from wrongful misappropriation or from the unjust enrichment consisting in the retention without consent of that which is mine ("The defendant ought to pay me because . . .").[114]

[111] This sentence has to be read subject to the dangerously broad (and surely incorrect) doctrine referred to immediately below.

[112] [1981] Ch 105 (Goulding J).

[113] *Westdeutsche Landesbank Girozentrale v Islington LBC* [1996] AC 669, 714–715.

[114] Discussion above, text from n 8 and from n 48.

5. Remote recipients

(*a*) *The bookseller's donation*

Suppose that the story runs on a little. The bookseller sells the old books for £1,500 and subsequently makes a donation to charity of £1,000. We will assume, for the moment, that he is not entitled to the defence of change of position. It is given that the I can trace on from the books to the £1,000 which he sends to the charity. The £1,000 is sent by electronic transfer and credited to the charity's account at its bank. I want to bring a claim against the charity as the recipient of funds in which I had an equitable proprietary interest. Here we run into difficulties with Dr Smith's teaching on the subject of remote recipients, but we must concentrate on the question whether successful tracing is a necessary precondition of any claim which I might make.

A personal claim in unjust enrichment (whether or not it would fail for other reasons) would not in this situation be contingent on successful tracing at the bookseller-charity stage. I would only be seeking to show that the charity was enriched in a certain measure by subtraction from me. The agency argument shows that the charity was enriched by a payment which was the bookseller's payment. If I trace to the bookseller's input, then, provided that I have a sufficient proprietary interest at that stage,[115] I show that, though it was the bookseller's payment, the enrichment came from me, in the sense of from my wealth.

Suppose that I want to vindicate my interest in the money or assert a personal claim for wrongful misappropriation of it. We may agree that for such claims tracing is necessary. For the one I must trace to assets in the hands of the defendant. For the other I must trace to the moment of the defendant's receipt. With that difference, the reason is that in both cases I need to show that a specific *res* was or became mine. I want to say "That is mine!" or "You misappropriated that which was mine!"

In Dr Smith's view I must successfully trace through the EFT system, by which he must mean through every stage of that system. The premiss is right. Tracing is necessary. But that need not necessarily mean that I have to undertake the complex business of tracing through all the stages of the clearing system. Through agents, the bookseller made a payment to the charity, with the consequence that the rights which I had in the £1,000 as it entered the EFT system attach to the credit which came out of it. What was true above of my direct payment to the bookseller is now true of his payment to the charity. It

[115] There is a question mark over this. It may be that the interest floats over the tracing chain, and it is doubtful whether an uncrystallised interest suffices: *infra*, text to n 118.

is his payment, initiated with my money. It is perfectly possible to say that the tracing exercise may now lean on the agency argument so as to show that the money received is the traceable product of the £1,000 and subject to the same rights. In other words the agency argument can be incorporated in the tracing process. We can test this with another example.

(b) The donee from a thief

A thief sends £10,000 of my money to his wife. The transfer is made through the EFT system. This is factually different from but analytically identical to the last case. The wife is a remote recipient, because the thief is the first recipient. Thus, as the bookseller donated money in which I had an equitable interest, so the thief has managed to send to his wife money which was mine at law. Do I have to conduct a complex tracing exercise through the EFT system in order to be able to say that the £10,000 received by the wife was traceably the product of the stolen money? And suppose the thief simply sent the money to himself. That is, he sent it by electronic transfer to another account in another bank. The answer must surely be that in each of these cases the tracing exercise should simply incorporate the agency argument when a transfer is made through the banking system. Similarly, if the court wants to know whether certain money received by the thief represents the price of stolen goods sold, the only question must be whether a buyer of the goods made the payment. In principle the law should ensure that the fewest possible different consequences depend on the mode of payment which is selected. We know what the position would be if the thief handed the cash to his wife. The modern world offers other modes of transfer. The mode of transfer should make no difference.

(c) The bookseller changes his position

The facts are similar to *Remote Recipient (a)*. The differences are that in this case the bookseller is not disqualified from the defence of change of position, and it is no longer given that the £1,000 which he sends to the charity is traceably the money received from the sale of the books. He makes his donation to charity honestly relying on his entitlement to the money raised from the sale of the books, but not traceably from that money. It seems likely on these facts that, until the charity itself changes its position, I can recover from it that sum in respect of which the bookseller can now bar my claim against him.[116] This

[116] Within narrow limits BGB §816 (I)2 provides such a recourse in German law. See the discussion by C Zülch, "*Lipkin Gorman* in German Law" in WJ Swadling (ed), *The Limits of*

example is given because it provides one illustration of a claim against a remote recipient which is not dependent on tracing but on a causal relationship between the remote recipient's receipt and the plaintiff's payment. The remote defendant is enriched at the plaintiff's expense because he would not have received at all but for the first recipient's enrichment at the plaintiff's expense. There is, of course, on these facts an additional factor, namely the bar to the plaintiff's recovery from the immediate recipient. The bar is created by the disenriching change of position.

(d) *Lipkin Gorman v Karpnale Ltd*[117]

The firm leapfrogged the gambling solicitor, Cass, and obtained restitution from the casino. On the face of things this was a case in which the receipt by the casino was held to have been at the expense of the firm by virtue of a proprietary connection: the casino received money in which the firm had a proprietary interest. But there are difficulties with that explanation arising from a combination of the fact that vested title was in the gambling solicitor and the further fact that it may be necessary to conclude that the firm had no more than a floating interest contingent on successful tracing and that that interest had not been crystallized at the moment of the casino's receipts. There is a real question whether an uncrystallized floating interest can suffice.[118] However, an alternative explanation might again rely on a causal connection, in combination with tracing. The plaintiffs on this view would have traced, not with a view to asserting or relying on any proprietary right, but merely to show what tracing can show, namely that the money used by the gambler was indeed the traceable product of their pilfered account. In other words, it was in this limited sense the relevant money. In this explanation the words "at the expense of the plaintiff" are satisfied, exceptionally, by proof of the fact that but for Cass's having this money from the firm's account the casino would never have received at all. Traceability is no more than an element in the finding of that difficult fact.

Whether this explanation works depends on whether it is thought sufficiently to justify the plaintiffs in leapfrogging Cass and thus evading the consequences of his insolvency. The proprietary nexus between the firm and the casino which the House of Lords actually relied upon, if it can be sus-

Restitutionary Claims (London, 1997) 106, 110–115, 119–135. At least in some cases an English equivalent could be explained as subrogation of the plaintiff to the first recipient's own right of restitution for causative mistake.

117 [1991] 2 AC 548.

118 LD Smith, *The Law of Tracing* (OUP, Oxford, 1997), 358–361, for the view that the floating analysis is wrong and an analysis is preferred terms of election between vested rights.

tained, evades that problem, for the money is then not part of the insolvent's estate. The causal nexus may not do so. Nevertheless, this example is given to show that it may sometimes be possible to reach a remote recipient even in the absence of any proprietary nexus, through factual findings as to causation in which traceability is one fact establishing that the enrichment of the remote recipient would not have happened but for the receipt by the first recipient. It should be noted that, the claim being a personal claim in autonomous unjust enrichment, it did not in principle require any more than that the defendant be enriched from the plaintiff without the plaintiff's consent. It was not as a matter of logic tied to the proprietary status of any particular thing. Dr Smith confines his liberal interpretation of "from" in relation to such claims to cases of direct transfer from plaintiff to defendant. This explanation of the *Lipkin Gorman* result is essentially asserting that the liberal interpretation of "from" is not dogmatically limited by direct transfer at all but, within the limits set by the need for precise and articulate tests of "from", only by the necessity of restricting opportunities for leapfrogging an insolvent first recipient and thus evading the invariably painful consequences of insolvency. If the explanation fails, it fails because it cannot meet the demands of that requirement.

IV CONCLUSION

The dominant figure in this review has been strict liability. Liability to make restitution of unjust enrichment must be regarded as in principle strict. A system which insists on a fault-based liability will allow some recipients to evade restitution even though their assets remain swollen by the enrichment. In such a case the absence of fault provides no real answer to a plaintiff asking them to do no more than give up value which they still have and were never intended or entitled to receive. Strict liability is on the face of things threatening. It seems to impose an intolerable burden. But it does not. The defence of change of position exists to protect the interest in security of receipts. It reduces the measure of liability as and when the enrichment is honestly consumed. The dishonest recipient, disqualified from the defence, will have to put his hand in his pocket to make restitution even when his assets are no longer swollen. The dishonest recipient will indeed end up worse off than he was before the story began. There is no cause for anxiety in that.

Other defences protect other interests which would be endangered even by a restitutionary liability restricted by the defence of change of position. The general interest in the security of transactions has to be protected by exceptions to *nemo dat quod non habet*. The defence of bona fide purchase, as applied to claims in unjust enrichment, ensures that such claims cannot undermine the compromise which those exceptions make between the sanctity of ownership and the security of transactions. Sometimes a countervailing interest requires to be protected, not by a defence, but by a modification of the cause of action itself. Amongst the various modifications that can be made is the addition of a requirement of fault on the part of the recipient. But, where a plaintiff seeking restitution is made to prove fault in that way, the system must take care to identify the interest which dictates that restriction of the liability. Fault need not and must not be used as a blunt instrument to reduce the general incidence of restitutionary liability. The identification of the particular countervailing interest guarantees that it is not being so used.

Without that discipline, fault merely competes with change of position in the protection of the security of receipts. It then adds to the shortcomings of all blunt instruments the additional danger of confusion arising from the concurrent use of two competing strategies for achieving the same objective. The banks and the other institutions in the financial world have a great deal less to fear from strict liability to make restitution of unjust enrichment than they have from that kind of confusion. It is not fashionable to insist on accurate analysis and the doctrinal certainty at which it aims. This review has revealed more than one area in which, rapidly as the law of restitution has developed in the three decades since the first edition of *Goff & Jones*, there is still an enormous amount of work of that kind to be done before its structure can be regarded as stable enough to reduce the wasteful incidence of exploratory or opportunistic litigation.

Bibliography

Books

Atiyah, PS, *Vicarious Liability in the Law of Torts* (1967) 142
Atkin's Encyclodepia of Court Forms in Civil Proceedings, 2nd ed (1996). 87
Baker, JH , *An Introduction to English Legal History*, 3rd ed (1990) 7
Baxter, IGF, *The Law of Banking*, 3rd ed (1981). 7
Birks, P, *An Introduction to the Law of Restitution* (Oxford, 1985, rev'd 1989) . . . 83, 105, 106, 124, 191, 193
Birks, P, *Restitution – The Future* (Sydney, 1993) 85
Bowstead & Reynolds on Agency, 16th ed (1996) 151, 153
Britton, WE, *Handbook on the Law of Bills and Notes*, 2nd ed (1961) 6
Bullen & Leake & Jacob's Precedents of Pleadings, 12th ed (1975) 86
Burrows, A, *The Law of Restitution* (1993) 105, 108, 109, 124, 128, 130, 163
Burrows, A, Mackendrick, E, *Cases and Materials on the Law of Restitution* (OUP 1997). 108
Cane, P, (ed) *Atiyah's Accidents, Compensation and the Law*, 5th ed (1993) 32
Casson, D, *Odgers on High Court Pleading and Practice*, 23rd ed (1991). 86
Chambers, R, *Resulting Trusts* (OUP, 1997) 126, 165
Chitty on Contracts, 27th ed (1994) 84
Clerk & Lindsell on Torts, 17th ed (1995) 39, 139, 148, 150
Collins, H, *The Law of Contract*, 3rd ed (1997). 84
Cranston, R, *Principles of Banking Law* (OUP, 1997). 100, 223
Creswell, P, *et al*, *Encyclopaedia of Banking Law* (1997). 142
Dawson, JP, *Unjust Enrichment: A Comparative Analysis* (1951). 130
Dicey & Morris on the Conflict of Laws, 12th ed (1993). 92, 93
Eisenstein, M, *Cummulative Supplement* to *Palmer's Law of Restitution* (1997) . . . 38
Elias, G, *Explaining Constructive Trusts* (OUP, 1990) 108
Ellinger, EP, Lomnicka, E, *Modern Banking Law*, 2nd ed (1994) . . 40, 164, 176, 178, 183, 185, 222, 223
Glover, J, *Commercial Equity - Fiduciary Relationships* (Butterworths 1995) 135
Goff & Jones, *The Law of Restitution*, 4th ed (1993) 107, 108, 209, 213, 232
Goode, RM, *Commercial Law*, 2nd ed (1995) 123
Hapgood, M, (ed), *Paget's Law of Banking* 11th ed (1996). 16
Hart, HLA, Honoré, AM, *Causation in Law*, 2nd ed (1985) 36
Harvey, *Industrial Relations and Employment Law* (1997). 144, 150
Maddaugh, PD, McCamus, JD, *The Law of Restitution* (1990) 7, 11, 17, 124
Maitland, FW, *Lectures on Equity*, ed Brunyate, 2nd ed (1936, repr 1969) 197
Malan, FR, Pretorius, JT, De Beer, CR, (eds), *Malan on Bills of Exchange, Cheques and Promissory Notes in South African Law*, 2nd ed (1994) 21
Mason, K, and Carter, JW, *Restitution Law in Australia*, (1995) 30, 122

Meagher, RP, Gummow WMC, Lehane JRF, *Equity: Doctrine and Remedies*, 3rd ed (1992) 30, 81, 117, 197
Merkin, R (ed), *Colinvaux's Law of Insurance*, 7th ed (1997) 30
Meyer, U, *Der Bereicherungsausgleich in Dreiecksverhältnissen* (1979) 2
Mitchell, C, *The Law of Subrogation* 219
O'Donovan, J, Phillips, J, *The Modern Contract of Guarantee*, 3rd ed (1966) . . 27, 31
Paget's Law of Banking, 8th ed (1972) 15
Palmer, GE, *The Law of Restitution* (1978), Cum Supp (1997). 38, 212
Pothier, RJ, *A Treatise on the Law of Obligations*, 20
Rogers, AW, (ed), *Falconbridge on Banking and Bills of Exchange*, 7th ed (1969) . . 6
Smith, LD, *The Law of Tracing* (OUP 1997). 109, 121, 122, 123, 125, 129, 131, 133, 192, 205, 215, 224, 225, 230
Smith, RJ, *Property Law* (1996). 117
Snell's Equity, 29th ed (1990) 113, 115
Tettenborn, A, *Law of Restitution in England and Ireland*, 2nd ed (1996). . . . 107, 109
Treitel, Sir G, *The Law of Contract*, 9th ed (1995) 296 . . . . 47, 84, 199
Visser, DP, *Die Rol van Dwaling by die Condictio Indebiti* (diss Leyden 1985) 19
Weaver, GA, Craigie, CR, *The Law Relating to Banker and Customer in Australia* (1975) 16
Wessels, JW, *The Law of Contract in South Africa*, (1937) 20
Worthington, S, *Proprietary Interests in Commercial Transactions* (OUP, 1996) 107
van Zyl, DH, *Die Saakwaarnemingsaksie as Verrykingsaksie in die Suid-Afrikaanse Reg* (diss Leyden 1970) 2
van Zyl, DH, *Negotiorum Gestio in South African Law* (1985) 2, 20, 25

Contributions to Books

Barker, K, "After Change of Position: Good Faith Exchange in the Modern Law of Restitution", in P Birks (ed), *Laundering and Tracing*, (Oxford, 1995) 81, 84, 107, 110, 114
Bird, J, "Choice of Law", ch 3 of FD Rose (ed), *Restitution and the Conflict of Laws* (1995) 93
Birks, P, "Civil Wrongs: A New World" in *The Butterworths Lectures 1990–91* (1992). 135, 136, 203
Birks, P, "Overview: Tracing, Claiming and Defences" in P Birks (ed) *Laundering and Tracing*, (Oxford 1995) 83, 107, 123, 163, 170
Birks, P, "Misnomer" in *Restitution: Past, Present and Future* (Oxford, Hart Publications, 1998) 191
Birks, P, and Chin, NY, "On the Nature of Undue Influence", ch 3 of Beatson and Friedmann (eds), *Good Faith and Fault in Contract Law* (Clarendon Press, Oxford, 1995) 50, 199
Canaris, C-W, "Der Bereicherungsausgleich in Dreipersonenverhältnis", *Festchrift für Karl Larenz* (1973) 799 2

Dawson, JP, "Indirect Enrichment", *Ius Privatum Gentium: Festchrift fur Max Rheinstein* 2 (1976) 789 2
Dörner, H, "Change of Position and *Wegfall der Bereicherung*" in WJ Swadling (ed), *The Limits of Restitutionary Claims: A Comparative Analysis* (London, 1997). 209
Dugdale, T, "The Negligent Professional: Liability for a Fair Share?", ch 4 in Birks, (ed), *Wrongs and Remedies in the Twenty-First Century* (1996) 27
Finn, PD, "The Liability of Third Parties for Knowing Receipt or Assistance" in DWM Waters (ed), *Equity, Fiduciaries and Trusts* (Toronto, Carswell, 1993). 205
Gleeson, S, "The Involuntary Launderer: the Banker's Liability for Deposits of the Proceeds of Crime," in P Birks (ed), *Laundering and Tracing* (Oxford 1995) 164, 167, 182, 185
Goode, RM, "Property and Unjust Enrichment" in A Burrows (ed), *Essays on the Law of Restitution* (1991) 126
Harpum, C, "The Basis of Equitable Liability", in P Birks (ed), *The Frontiers of Liability*, vol 1 (Oxford 1994) 141, 205
Hayton, D, "Equity's Identification Rules", ch 1 in P Birks, (ed) *Laundering and Tracing*, (OUP 1995) 123
Hoffmann, Lord, "The Redundancy of Knowing Assistance" in P Birks (ed), *The Frontiers of Liability*, vol 1 (OUP 1994) 136, 203
Schrage, E, Nicholas, B, "Unjust Enrichment and the Law of Restitution: A Comparison", in E Schrage (ed) *Unjust Enrichment: The Comparative Legal History of the Law of Restitution* (1995) 9–30 3
Smith, LD, "Constructive Fiduciaries?" ch 9 of P Birks (ed), *Privacy and Loyalty* (1997) 133, 145, 155, 156
Swadling, WJ, [1992] All ER Rev. 107
Swadling, WJ, "The Nature of Ministerial Receipt", in P Birks (ed), *Laundering and Tracing* (Oxford 1995) 163, 167, 208
Swadling, WJ, "Property and Unjust Enrichment", in JW Harris (ed), *Property Problems: From Genes to Pension Funds* (1997) 107
Swadling, WJ, "Property, Restitution and the Defence of Bona Fide Purchase", in Swadling (ed), *The Limits of Restitutionary Claims: a Comparative Analysis* (1997) 107, 110
Vowen, DV, and Gering, L, (eds), *Cowne on the Law of Negotiable Instruments in South Africa*, 4th ed (1966). 17
Zülch, C, "*Lipkin Gorman* in German Law" in WJ Swadling (ed), *The Limits of Restitutionary Claims: A Comparative Analysis* (1997) 229–230

Articles and Notes

Aigler, RW, "The Doctrine of Price v Neal" (1926) *Michigan LR* 809. 5
Ames, JB, "The Doctrine of *Price v Neal*" (1891) 4 HLR 297 5
Atiyah, PS, "Collateral Benefits Again" (1996) 32 MLR 397 35

Bant, E, "Ignorance as a Ground of Restitution – Can it Survive?" [1998] LMCLQ 18 127

Barak, A, "The Uniform Commercial Code - Commercial Paper; An Outsider's View" (1968) 3 *Israel LR* 7 6

Barker, K, "Restitution and Third Parties" [1994] LMCLQ 305 2

Battersby, G, "Equitable Fraud Committed by Third Parties" (1995) 15 LS 35

Beatson, J, Birks, P, "Unrequested Payment of Another's Debt" (1976) 92 LQR 188 28

Beatson, J, Bishop, W, "Mistaken Payments in the Law of Restitution" (1986) 36 U Toronto LJ 149 189

Birks, P, "Mixing and Tracing: Property and Restitution" (1992) 45 CLP 69 166

Birks, P, "Persistent Problems in Misdirected Money: A Quintet" [1993] LMCLQ 218 . . . . . . 111, 180

Birks, P, "Establishing a Proprietary Base" [1994] RLR 83 . . . . . . 106, 107, 110

Birks, P, (1995) 9 TLI 91 120

Birks, P, "Equity in the Modern Law: An Exercise in Taxonomy" (1996) UWALR 1 125

Birks, P, "On Taking Seriously the Difference Between Tracing and Claiming" (1997) 11 TLI 2 204

Birks, P, "Unjust Factors and Wrongs: Pecuniary Restitution for Undue Influence" [1997] RLR 72 64

Briggs, A, "From Complexity to Anticlimax: Restitution and Choice of Law" [1996] RLR 88 93

Burrows, A, "Misdirected Money - A Reply" (1990) 106 LQR 20 125

Chambers, R, "Change of Position on the Faith of the Receipt" [1996] RLR 103, ... 207

Cowen, DV, "A Bank's Right to Recover Payments made by Mistake: *Price v Neal* Revisited" (1983) 16 CILSA 1 . . . . . . 17, 22

Davern, R, "Common Law Tracing, Profits and the Doctrine of Relation Back" [1997] RLR 92 204

Dickson, B, "Unjust Enrichment Claims: A Comparative Overview" [1995] CLJ 100 . . . . . . 127, 130

Dixon, M, and Harpum, C, "Fraud, Undue Influence and Mortgages of Registered Land" [1994] Conv 421 44

Dow, SB, Ellis, N, "The Payor Bank's Right to Recover Mistaken Payments: Survival of Common Law Restitution under Proposed Revisions to Uniform Commercial Code Articles 3 and 4" (1990) 65 *Indiana LJ* 799

Dow, SB, "Restitution of Payments on Cheques with Forged Drawer's Signatures: Loss Allocation under English Law" [1995] RLR 27 . . . . . . 7, 11, 12, 221, 222

Farnsworth, EA, "Insurance Against Cheque Forgery" (1960) Col LR 284 38

Gardner, S, "Knowing Assistance and Receipt" (1996) 112 LQR 56 . . . . . . 138, 139, 147, 159, 205

Geva, B, "Reflections on the Need to Revise the Bills of Exchange Act – Some Doctrinal Aspects" (1981-82) 6 Can Bus LJ 269 11

Goode, RM, "The Bank's Right to Recover Money Paid on a Stopped Cheque" (1981) 97 LQR 254 16
Grantham, RB, and Ricketts, CEF, "Restitution, Property, and Ignorance – A Reply to Mr Swadling" [1996] LMCLQ 463 127
Harpum, C, "The Stranger as Constructive Trustee" (1986) 102 LQR 114 184
Hedley, S, "Unjust Enrichement" [1995] CLJ 578. 124
Hllafcsak, JJ, "The Nature and Extent of Subrogation Rights of Fidelity Insurers Against Officers and Directors of Financial Institutions" (1986) 47 U of Pittsburgh LR 727. 38
Honoré, AM, "Condiction and Payment" [1958] *Acta Juridica* 135. 18
Honoré, AM, "Third Party Enrichment" [1960] *Acta Juridica* 236 2
Hooley, R, and O'Sullivan, J, "Undue Influence and Unconscionable Bargains" [1997] LMCLQ 17. 60
Kalevitch, L, "Luck of the Drawee: The Finality of Bank Payments to Holders in Due Course" (1988) 105 *Banking LJ* 416. 6
King, R, "The Receiving Bank's Role in Credit Transfer Transactions" (1982) 45 MLR 369. 132
Kloss, WD, "Mistaken Payments and Restitutionary Principles Under the Uniform Commercial Code" (1987-88) 56 *U of Cincinnati LR* 1075 6
Kull, A, "Rationalising Restitution" (1995) 83 Calif L Rev 1191. 216
Langmaid, S, "Some Recent Subrogation Problems in the Law of Suretyship and Insurance" (1934) 47 Harvard LR 976 38
Lee, RW, "The Roman-Dutch Law in South Africa: The Influence of English Law" (1969) 1 *Colombo LR* 1 2
Lehane, JRF, "Undue Influence, Misrepresentation and Third Parties" [1994] 110 LQR 167 48
Luntz, H, "The Bank's Right to Recover on Cheques Paid by Mistake" (1968) 6 Melb ULR 308. . . . . 1, 6, 16
Malan, FR, "The Rule in *Price v Neal*" (1978) 11 CILSA 276. . . . . 1, 4,6, 17, 18
Malan, FR, "Price v Neal Revisited" [1992] *Acta Juridica* 131. 21
Malan, FR, (1995) *TSAR* 782 25
Malan, FR, Pretorius, JT, (1996) 8 *SA Mercantile LJ* 399 25
Matson, J, "Subrogation Claims Against Auditors: What is 'The Purest Equity'?" (1979) 6 Ohio NULR 313 38
Matthews, P, "Stopped Cheques and Restitution: Another View" [1982] JBL 281. 16
Millett, Sir P, "Tracing the Proceeds of Fraud" (1991) LQR 71 . . . 141, 162, 181, 183
Millett, Sir P, "Recovering the Proceeds of Fraud," *Ferrier Hodgson's House Magazine,* May-August 1993 135
Millett, Sir P, "Equity's Place in the Law of Commerce" (Chancery Bar Association 1997). 107
Mitchell, C, "Defences to an Insurer's Subrogated Action" [1996] LMCLQ 343 . . . . 38, 40
Mitchell, C, "The Civil Liability (Contributions) Act 1978". 157

Moss, G, Toube, F, "Cross-Border Enforcement of Security" (1997) 16 IBFL 1 . . 89
Nagel, CJ, Roestoff, M, "Verrykingsaanspraak van bankier na Betaling van Afgelaste Tjek" (1993) 56 THRHR 486. 22
Nicholson, KG, "Recovery of Money Paid Under a Mistake of Fact" (1986) 60 ALJ 459 16
Nolan, R, "The Triumph of Technicality" [1996] CLJ 436. 117
O'Dell, E, "Restitution, Coercion by a Third Party and the Proper Doctrine of Notice" [1997] CLJ 71 . . . . 45, 73, 82, 197
O'Malley, JD, "Subrogation Claims Against Banks on Forged Cheques" (1966) 51 Cornell LQ 441 38
Oakley, AJ, "Is Knowledge Still a Prerequisite to the Imposition of 'Accessory Liability' " (1996) 10 TLI 53 141
Oelofse, AN, "Die Toepassing van die Reël in *Price v Neal* in Suid-Africa" (1981) 3 MBL 120. 17
Ogilvie, MH, "Recovery of Money paid under Mistake of Fact: When the Bank Loses" (1986-1987) *Banking and Finance LR* 413 17
Oldham, M, "Neither a Borrower nor a Lender be: The life of *O'Brien*" [1995] 7 CFLQ 104 50
Pretorius, C-J, "Mistaken Payments by a Bank on a Countermanded or Dishonoured Cheque – The Condictio Sine Causa and Condictio Indebiti" (1994) *57* THRHR 332. 21
Pretorius, C-J, (1995) 58 THRHR 733. 25
Proksch, L, "Recission on Terms" [1996] RLR 71 66
Rafferty, N, "Forged Cheques: A Consideration of the Rights and Obligations of Banks and their Customers" (1979-80) 4 *Can Bus LJ* 208 6
Rickett, CEF, "Banks and the Recovery of Mistaken Payments" (1994) 16 NZULR 105 164
Rickett, CEF, "The Financier's Duty of Care" (1998) 114 LQR 17. 200
Sales, P, "The Tort of Conspiracy and Civil Secondary Liability" (1990) 49 CLJ 491 . . . . 28, 141, 155, 203
Scholtens, JE, "Elusive Payments and the Condictio Indebiti" (1959) 76 SALJ 119 18
Schroeder, GJ, "Handling the Complex Fidelity or Financial Institution Bond Claim: The Liability of the Insured's Officers and Directors and Their D & O Carrier" (1986) 21 Tort & Ins LJ 269. 38
Sinclair, JD, and Visser, C, "Recovery of Payment made under a Mistake of Fact" [1984] ASSAL. 21
Smith, LD, "Three Party Restitution: A Critique of Birk's Theory of Interceptive Subtraction" (1991) 11 OJLS 481 . . . . 2, 166
Sneddon, M, "Lender and Independent Solicitor's Certificates for Guarantors and Borrowers: Risk Minimisation or Loss Sharing?" (1996) 24 ABLR 5. 62
Sneddon, M, "Unfair Conduct in Taking Guarantees and the Role of Independent Advice" (1990) 13 UNSWLJ 302 62
Sparkes, P, "The Proprietary Effect of Undue Influence" [1995] Conv 250

Sonnekus, JC, "Ongeregverdigde Verryking en Ongeregverdigde Verarming vir Kondikering in Drie-Party Verhoudings" [1996] TSAR 1. 2
Stassen, JC, "Die Regsaard van die Verhouding tussen Bank en Kliënt" (1980) 2 MBL 77 3
Stassen, JC, Oelofse, AM, "Terugvordering van Foutiewe Wisselbetalings: Geen Verrykingsaanspreeklikheid sonder Verryking nie" (1983) 5 MBL 137 . . . 18
Stassen, JC, "Countermanded Cheques and Enrichment – Some Clarity, Some Confusion" (1985) 7 MBL 15. 21
Stevens, J, "Restitution or Property? Priority and Title to Shares in the Conflict of Laws" (1996) 59 MLR 741. 107
Swadling, W J, "A Claim in Restitution" [1996] LMCLQ 63 . . . . 107, 127
Thompson, M, "The Enforceability of Mortgages" [1994] Conv 140. 44
Tiplady, D, "The Limits of Undue Influence" (1985) 48 MLR 579 . . . . 42, 48
Underhill & Hayton, *The Law Relating to Trusts and Trustees*, 15th ed (1995) . . . 140
van der Merwe, D, "Judicial Institutions in the Civil Law: Towards a Theory for Common-Law Adjudication" [1993] TSAR 580 2
van Zyl, DH, "Unjustified Enrichment and Restitution: An awakening Giant creates Confusion" (1996) 21 TRW 1 3
Virgo, G, "Reconstructing the Law of Restitution" (1996) 10 TLI 20 . . 108, 109, 193
Visser, C, "Payment of a Stopped Cheque" (1993) 1 *Juta's Bus L,* 32–33 22
Visser, DP, "Daedalus in the Supreme Court: The Common Law Today" (1986) 49 THRHR 127. 2
Visser, DP, "Error of Law and Mistaken Payments: A Milestone" (1992) 109 SALJ 177. 19
Visser, DP, "Unjustified Enrichment" [1993] ASSAL 229 22
Waring, AE, "Where the Buck Stops" (1980) 43 *THRHR* 416. 22
Watts, P, "Restitution - a Property Principel and a Services Principle" [1995] RLR 49 208
West, RW, "Easy Come, Easy Go; UCC, s 30418 and the Restitutionary Rights of Banks: *National Savings and Trust Co v Park Group* " [1985] *Detroit College Law Review* 681 6
Whitty, NR, "Indirect Enrichment in Scot's Law" [1994] JR 200 and 239 2
Zimmerman, R, "Synthesis in South African Private Law: Civil Law, Common Law and *Usus Hodiernus Pandectarum*" (1986) 103 SALJ 259. 2

Index